D1061656

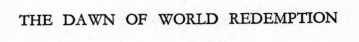

THE DAWN OF WORLD REDEMPTION

The Dawn of World Redemption

A SURVEY OF HISTORICAL REVELATION IN THE OLD TESTAMENT

By

ERICH SAUER

Translated by

G. H. LANG

With a Foreword by F. F. BRUCE, M.A.

WM. B. EERDMANS PUBLISHING COMPANY
GRAND RAPIDS   1952   MICHIGAN

TABLE OF CONTENTS

5

CONTENTS

FOREWORD

By F. F. Bruce, M.A.

THE DAWN OF WORLD REDEMPTION is the first of two volumes in which my friend Erich Sauer, Director of the Bible School, Wiedenest, Germany, has covered the whole range of Biblical theology. Together with its companion volume, *The Triumph of the Crucified*, it reviews the whole process of divine revelation which culminates in Christ, in such a way as to present clearly to the reader the historical unfolding of God's saving activity.

The twofold work in its German dress is highly esteemed in Germany and the other German-speaking areas of Europe; it has been greeted with unstinted praise by many well-known Christian leaders, including Dr. von Bodelschwingh, of Bethel-bei-Bielefeld, and Professor Köberle. It has been translated into Dutch, Swedish, and Norwegian, the Norwegian translation being warmly commended to the people of Norway by Professor Hallesby. Translations into French and Spanish are also in preparation.

Our gratitude is due to those who are responsible for the appearance of this English translation. We have nothing quite so good, as far as I know, by way of a handbook of evangelical theology based, not on the logical sequence of most credal statements and dogmatic treatises, but on the historical order exhibited by the Bible itself. The thoroughly Biblical character of the whole work, in form as well as in substance, is a sheer delight.

It is assured of an appreciative reception here for its own intrinsic worth. Mr. Sauer has a profound knowledge of the Biblical text and an unusual theological insight, coupled with gifts of original thought and vigorous expression. Good wine needs no bush; but as one who realized the value of these volumes when I first read them in German several years ago, I am specially pleased to see them made available to a still wider circle of readers in their English dress, and I cordially commend them to all English-speaking students of the Christian faith.

F. F. Bruce

Head of the Department of Biblical History
and Literature, University of Sheffield.

7

TRANSLATOR'S PREFACE

THIS excellent work, and its equally excellent companion *The Triumph of the Crucified*, were written as one book. My esteemed friend, the Author, gave me the privilege of reading the original manuscript. I know no English books that correspond to these and I felt that they ought to be made available to English readers. To this Herr Sauer gladly consented. The war greatly retarded the work, but at length, by the help of God, and the hearty co-operation of several friends, the books are now offered to all who search into the words and ways of God.

Of the friends mentioned my special thanks are due to Mr. R. C. Thomson, late Senior Translator at the Foreign Office, for carefully scrutinizing the translations of both books, and making many valuable suggestions.

But I am especially happy that Herr Sauer and his wife were able to go through both translations with me in minute detail. Their competent knowledge of English has assured a degree of exactness in representing his meaning scarcely otherwise to have been attained.

I have added a few notes, marked [Trans.], and the matter in square brackets is mine.

Quotations from Scripture are given in the English Revised Version or the American Standard Version, but frequently, where the writer's thought follows some particular turn of the German, a more literal rendering in English is given.

These works have had a quite remarkable circulation in German, before, during, and since the war. They have been translated into Swedish and Norwegian, and one into Dutch. Also a Spanish translation is being prepared. May the illumination of the Spirit of truth attend them in English.

G. H. LANG

AUTHOR'S NOTE

IT is with gratitude to the Lord that I see my two books, *The Dawn of World Redemption* and *The Triumph of the Crucified*, being published in English. I have read and approved this translation and have used the opportunity at the same time to make some improvements and changes from the German text. I am very much indebted to the translator of both books, Mr. G. H. Lang, for his very careful and most reliable work.

The text contains many Scripture references (in *Dawn of World Redemption* about 2,200, in *Triumph of the Crucified* about 3,700). They are intended, not only to prove from the Word of God itself the statements given in the books, but also to help those readers who will use what is here offered for their private Bible study or in preparation for preaching the Word. Not seldom they are at the same time an expansion of the line of thought.

In the German editions I have given theological literary references. But as these are not of great profit to the English reader, I have omitted them in the English edition. German-speaking English readers may find them in the German editions. Quotations are set everywhere in inverted commas.

It is my prayer that God will use this English edition to the blessing of readers and to the glory of His name.

Wiedenest.   ERICH SAUER

9

AUTHOR'S PREFACE

THE history of salvation stands or falls—nay, it *stands* with the authority of the Lord Jesus. It is an undeniable fact that Christ distinctly acknowledged those portions of the Old Testament which are most challenged, as, for example, the literal historicity of Adam and Eve (Matt. 19: 8), the actual occurrence of the Flood (Matt. 24: 37, 38), and the miraculous experience of the prophet Jonah (Matt. 12: 39, 40). Most striking is His acknowledgment of the book of Daniel; for from this very book, today so much attacked by unbelief, He took the chief designation of His own Person ("Son of man", Dan. 7: 13, 14; Matt. 26: 64). Indeed, it was with this book that He linked Himself by the only oath He ever took (Matt. 26: 63, 64; and comp. Matt. 24: 15). And as regards the future, He expected His own personal return in glory (Matt. 24: 27–31) and the literal establishment of the kingdom of Messiah as foretold by the prophets (Matt. 19: 28; 25: 31 ff.; Acts 1: 67). It was the same with His apostles. His attitude to the Old Testament was theirs.

According to Dr. Evans, in this Bible of the Lord Jesus (John 5: 39), the Old Testament, the phrase "thus saith the Lord" occurs 3,500 times. For Christ, the personal living "Word" (John 1: 14; Rev. 19: 13), *a mere tittle or jot of the written Word was of more value than all star worlds and sun systems of the entire universe.* "Verily I say unto you, Till heaven and earth pass away, one jot or one tittle shall in no wise pass away from the law, till all things be accomplished" (Matt. 5: 18; comp. 24: 35; John 10: 35). And Paul, His greatest apostle, confesses: "I believe *all* things which stand written in the law and the prophets" (Acts 24: 14).

Faith in the Holy Scripture as a Divine revelation, and in its indestructible authority, is therefore no mechanical idolization of the letter and no small-minded unchristian bondage thereto, but has on its side the greatest spiritual personalities of salvation's history, including even Christ Himself, the Son of God. "The revelation stands, nay, it continues for us in the Scripture; it is continuing—there is no avoiding it—in the *Bible texts, in the words and sentences,* in that which the prophets and apostles wished to say, and have said, as their testimony."

Thus we explain the history of salvation by reference to the *King* of that history. The whole revelation is a circle, and

Jesus Christ is the centre of this circle.   He is the sun, and from
Him the whole circle is illuminated.

But if anyone, through unbelief or half belief, takes up a
lame attitude to the Scripture, and particularly in reference to
> the opening chapters of the Bible,
> the prophecies of Daniel,
> the meaning of the Cross,
> the bodily resurrection and
> the personal return of Christ,

to him will the *beginning, the middle, and the end* of the Divine plan
of redemption be unintelligible, and the wonderful divine temple
of the history of salvation will remain to him a closed building.

The Bible, as the record of salvation, is one complete whole,
an organism throbbing with life, and a system of prophecy
wrought out in history according to plan.   It is "a marvellous
structure, of which the ground plan was prepared in advance", a
harmonious, graduated whole, with perfect proportion and accord
in all its parts, and having Christ as its goal.   And the theme
of the kingdom of God, with the rhythm of its progressively
developing epochs and periods, is the leading basic melody of this
whole majestic divine symphony.[1]

But we have to "bow down, observant and attentive, if we
would catch the harmony of things acknowledged and existing".
Thus can we interpret the Scripture as a record of God's plan of
salvation.   Only thereby is justice done to the essential and true
nature of the Bible.   It is to be read "age-wise", that is, according
to the dispensations, economies, gradations, and groupings.
Here the human spirit stands on the very highest possible prophetic watch-tower.   Worlds and ages come within its expanded
field of vision.   Here it looks beyond the narrow circle of its
own personality, beyond the frontiers of nationality and civilization, yea, beyond all the bounds of the present and of time itself.
Here it embraces past, present, and future at once, surveying at
the one time that which is and that which is coming into being,
indeed its enlightened vision penetrates right into the heart of
the All-Highest, even into the depths of the Godhead itself.

It is in this spirit that we would now enter upon our task, even
the attempt to give an outline *of the "pilgrimage" through the
millenniums of the Divine unfolding of salvation, from the creation of
the world onward to Christ, the Redeemer of the world.*

No attempt is made to be exhaustive.   Nor is it intended to
give a comparison between the Biblical and the modern philosophical conceptions of the world, or to set over against each other

---

[1] In the Protestant Church this was chiefly emphasized by men such as Cocceius,
Bengel, and Franz Delitzsch.   Especially the nineteenth century, the century of
historical research, was, in the sphere of theology, that of special studies of the
historical development of the Divine revelation.

the positive and the liberal-critical attitudes to the Bible in general. The book is not a defence of the faith, but a history of salvation. Too wide an extension of its task would have exceeded the space available. But, taking for granted that the Bible is right, the book does deal in all seriousness with the historical unity of the Bible, and seeks to review the Biblical plan of history and the development of mankind as they are therein represented from God's point of view in their harmonious variety, their cosmic universality, and their progressive ordering.

As regards the outward features of the present work, an attempt has been made to achieve general comprehensibility. For easier reading the whole has been divided into many small sections.

I am very conscious of the great imperfections and incompleteness of what is here set forth, yet I commend the whole work to the Lord and His grace. My prayer to Him is that He may use it to the service of His saints. Now to Himself, the "King of the ages, the incorruptible, invisible, only God, be honour and glory from eternity to eternity. Amen." (I Tim. 1: 17).

ERICH SAUER

Wiedenest, Rhineland, Germany.

INTRODUCTION

*"Blessed are the inquirers who inquire not concerning
the Eternal but for the Eternal."*

THE creation, the redemption, and the consummation of the
world—like three outstanding sublime hieroglyphs, these
three problems stand forth in the spiritual history of mankind. Never yet has any people passed them heedlessly by.
Rather have the greatest minds of all ages striven to interpret
them.

The answers have been varied, contradictory, often completely incomprehensible. System after system has been devised,
one cosmogony after another has been followed. On the ruins
of the one another builds *his* thought-structure, and still today
man wrestles about them with all the energy of his mind.

Yet all the time the answer is there! God Himself has given
it plainly. His eternal thoughts are in no wise mere "ideas"
floating far above the course of all earthly affairs, but are creative
deeds, which at one and the same time directly incorporate themselves within all history, interweave themselves closely and
deeply with it, and manifest themselves effectively "in, with,
and beneath" it all. "The history of the ages is the history
of mankind, and the history of mankind is the history—of
God".

But the answer which God gives is—Himself; His own
being in the person of His Son. As the eternal "Word" the
Son is the centre and sun of all Divine revelation in the entire
universe.

All things proceed from God: here the primeval basis of the
past unveils itself, the nature of world-*creation* (Col. 1: 16; John
1: 3).

All things are completed by God: this explains the question
of the present, the process of world-*redemption* (Rom. 11: 36).

All things move back to God: here the goal of all the future
reveals itself, the essential character of all world-*consummation*
(I Cor. 15: 28).

Thus is God the Lord, revealed in Christ, the Rock of all the
ages, the personal, living, primal basis of all existence.

But the eternal Word revealed itself through the spoken
Word, and the spoken Word became the written Word, and the

written Word became the Bible. Hence the Bible is the key to world events, the Book of mankind, *the* Book of history.

Therefore all depends upon understanding *it*. Without it we are but creatures who grope and fumble in a dungeon completely without light. But upon whom the Bible rises the sun rises, and with it heaven and all its radiance. His path is illuminated, his life becomes light, time is transfigured, the divine conquers, and more and more he understands that great word,

"NOW IS ETERNITY".

PART I

THE FOUNDATIONS OF THE BIBLICAL HISTORICAL REVELATION

CHAPTER I

THE PRE-CREATION ETERNITY

" The sense which one can fathom is not the sense."

Gᴏᴅ is the one, eternal, absolute Spirit (John 4: 24). Spirituality, unity, and eternity are of the very essence of His being, and He Himself is the sum of all highest, most perfect life. But as such He is at the same time the most real of all realities, self-determining *Ego*, conscious Personality, indeed, eternal super-personality, and all finite attempts by the human intellect to explain His infinite being are eternally vain.

Therefore "proofs" of the existence of God cannot be given. The Scripture itself never once attempts it. For the idea of God transcends all human means of thought, and the mere attempt of a dust-begotten creature even to wish to "demonstrate" God (!!) is nothing else than a childish over-estimate of self, yea, the boundless presumption of small-mindedness and morbid delusion. God as God is the eternal and infinite, and as such can never be the thought-problem of human mole-like speculation.

Nevertheless the so-called "proofs" of God have a value not to be underestimated. Even for Kant the teleological and the moral evidence had significance. They prove that faith in God is consonant with reason, and make the visible world a witness and symbol of the eternal. They compel the thoughtful mind to a final unavoidable alternative: *Either* our thinking rests on an unescapable chimera, *or* God exists, and then our thought is the expression of an unconditioned all-embracing reality.

God must exist: this is the testimony of universal Nature:

as the Cause of all, the primal basis of the world: this belief is required when we look into the past, and inquire as to the origin, the "whence" of all existence. This is the "cosmological" proof of God (Aristotle, Cicero, Leibnitz, Schleiermacher).

as the world's Master-Builder, of consummate artistic skill and beauty: this belief is required when we look into the present and recognize the order, the "how" of all existence (Rom. 1:

20; Psa. 104: 24; 94: 9). This is the "physico-theological" proof of God (Socrates, Aristotle, Leibnitz, Wolff).

as the One Whose plans give purpose and goal to the world: this belief is required when we look into the future and inquire as to the meaning, the "whither" of all existence. This is the "teleological" proof of God (Socrates, Plato, Philo, the Scholastics). *telos* (Greek) = goal.

And further:

God must exist: this is the testimony of the human soul:

as the highest conception of the understanding—for how indeed could the highest of thoughts be unreal? This is the "ontological" proof of God (Anselm).

as the supreme Lawgiver to the will (or conscience)—for how can the moral law have come into being without a legislator? This is the "moral" proof (Kant).

as the only Giver of full happiness to the emotions—for why does the soul find no rest till it rests in God? This is the "psychological" proof (Tertullian, Augustine, Schleiermacher).

Thus all things on earth witness to His existence: the world without and the world within us, the outer and the inner man. Without Him the world is only an "all-devouring grave" an "eternal cud-chewing monster," a giant organism, which down to the smallest and minutest details is, indeed, regulated with exactness and with a purpose, but in its vastness and totality has as its very motto that it is without goal and without purpose. Without Him all value in the world is only unreal fancy, and the basis of all that is full of meaning is for ever that which is without meaning. No; in view of the existence of unsearchable wisdom in the entire universe the unbelief that denies God is only a phrase devoid of thought, a brainless, dull-minded stupidity. Only "the fools say in their heart: There is no God" (Psa. 14: 1).

God is love (I John 4: 16). Love is the deepest element of His life, the innermost fount out of which His nature eternally flows forth, the creative centre that begets all His working and ruling.

But love is a trinity. Augustine has said: "If God is love, then there must be in Him a Lover, a Beloved, and a Spirit of love; for no love is conceivable without a Lover and a Beloved." Now in men there may be a love-bond in which a *duality* of persons —and in that duality precisely—finds its satisfaction; but nevertheless the conception of love itself always involves a trinity: because

it always proceeds *from* the Lover:

it always moves *toward* the Beloved:

it always intertwines the two together through the common Spirit of *union*;

"Where love is there is trinity" (*Ubi amor, ibi trinitas*: Augustine).

Thus far human thought can grope its way. But the fact that three persons of the Godhead actually correspond to these three fundamental conceptions of the idea of God, this only the revelation of the eternal God Himself can make known. "The Father is the One *out of* Himself existing, the Son is the One *to* Himself attaining, and the Spirit the One *in* Himself moving God." The Father is the Lover, the Son the Beloved, the Holy Spirit is the Spirit of Love.

Three divine Persons and yet *one* God: the Son, by nature equal with the Father and yet voluntarily subordinate to Him (I Cor. 15: 28), Cause of all causes and yet Himself uncaused—truly here are mysteries upon mysteries. Here the finite spirit stands for ever before the riddle of the infinite. Even in endless eternity finite thought, conditioned by space and time, never can attain to the sphere of God beyond space and time. For like can be discerned only by like and thus God only by God.

This divine mystery is one revealed by stages in the sacred history. First God revealed His *unity,* and this in express contrast to the polytheistic environment and polytheistic inclinations of the Old Testament covenant people (e.g. Ex. 20: 1, 2; Isa. 45: 5, 6). Only after the lapse of centuries, when faith in the unity of God could no more be uprooted in Israel (which came to pass six centuries B.C. through the captivity in Babylon, after which polytheism was no more a temptation to Israel) God revealed in the new covenant the *plurality* in the unity. For is Jesus of Nazareth more than a prophet, is He in His nature God, then here a Divine *duality* reveals itself; and is the Spirit of God not merely a force but a Divine Person, then here the Divine *tri-unity* reveals itself.

In the New Testament this tri-unity stands forth for the first time at the baptism of Jesus (Matt. 3: 16, 17), and then especially in the Great Commission and the command to baptize (Matt. 28: 19). Hence also the many "trinitarian" passages in the New Testament (e.g. II Cor. 13: 13; I Pet. 1: 2; II Thess. 2: 13, 14; Eph. 2: 18–22; Heb. 9: 14). The *word* "trinity" (tri-unity is better than trinity) is indeed not in the Scripture, but the *fact* is, as is shown in the foregoing. All philosophical speculations concerning the content of "the trinitarian problem" are, however, to no purpose and mostly from an evil source. (Consider the Trinitarian controversies of the fourth to sixth centuries. Arius).

What did God do before the foundation of the world?
This question has received very different answers. Some have simply declared it to be unjustified (Luther); others have attempted to explain it philosophically (Origen). The Bible takes a middle course, in that it at the same time conceals and

reveals, and with divine condescension clothes its information as to the eternal and super-temporal matters in the form of thoughts from the realm of creation and space (e.g. Isa. 43: 10).

For God Himself as the eternal there is no limit of time, no sequence of "before" and "after." He surveys all times at once, and therefore to Him the world in all its extensions is already eternally present. His creative word did indeed give to it its temporal, historical beginning, but in His thought it was already present from eternity, without a beginning and timeless. But of this organic connexion of eternity and time, as generally of God's whole thinking, no creature is able to form any conception.

In this sense the Bible gives a sevenfold answer to the question as to what God did prior to the foundation of the world.

i.   Before the foundation of the whole universe God had been in eternal loving intercourse with His Son. Already "before His works of old" He possessed the eternal "Wisdom" (Prov. 8: 22, 23), the "Word" which later appeared in Christ (John 1: 14). Thus, "in the beginning," this Word was already "with God," present eternally with Him in the intercourse of a mutually responsive fellowship[1] (John 1: 2). And the Father loved the Son, who afterwards testified on earth, "Thou lovedst me before the foundation[2] of the world" (John 17: 24). "And now glorify thou me, Father, with thyself, with the glory which I possessed with thee before the world was" (John 17: 5). So then the Son was with the Father

the eternal Word (John 1: 1, 2),
the eternal Wisdom (Prov. 8: 22, 23),
the eternally Beloved (John 17: 24),
the eternally Glorious (John 17: 5).

ii.   Before the foundation of the earth-world God had created the angels and the stars. Therefore He says to insig-

---

[1] Schon damals "im Anfang" war dieses Wort "zu Gott bin," stand ewig mit ihm in hinstrebendem Gemeinschaftsverkehr (John 1: 1). English, usually equal to any demand, cannot here give the full force by any literal translation. The German "zu Gott bin" and "hinstrebendem" gives the force of the Greek accusative with pros (pros ton Theon) in this passage, that is, motion towards an object: the Father and the Son, in the whole mental and moral being of thought and affection, ever moving towards each other in the activity of Deity. Westcott's note is valuable. Of the pros in verse 1 he says: "The idea conveyed is of being (in some sense) directed towards and regulated by that with which the relation is fixed (John 5: 19). The personal being of the Word was realized in active intercourse with and in perfect communion with God. . . . This life . . . was realized in the intercommunion of the divine Persons when time was not." English expresses the same idea of moral motion in such a phrase as "I was drawn to him." [Trans.]

[2] Thoroughly false is the translation "downfall" sometimes offered of the Greek word katabolee, used here and in ten other places. The word in question never has this meaning in the Greek language. The proper meaning is "The laying down of the foundations, founding, establishing" (comp. II Macc. 2: 29; Heb. 6: 1; Josephus, Porphyry, Polybius, Plutarch). The sense of the word has nothing to do with the happenings in Gen. 1: 2.

nificant man: "Where wast thou when I founded the earth? . . . Who has laid its corner stone, when the morning stars shouted for joy all together and all God's sons exulted?" (Job 38: 4, 7; comp. 1: 6; 2: 1).

iii. Before the foundation of the world God settled the counsel of salvation for the individual. Therefore before the beginning of the world He already wrote their names in the Lamb's book of life (Rev. 13: 8; 17: 8); indeed, prior to all creation He had appointed them in love unto sonship and holiness (Eph. 1: 4, 5). But therewith "*before* all time" He also promised them life (Tit. 1: 2), and therefore, from the standpoint of God as above time, His grace is thus given to us "*before* the times of the ages" (II Tim. 1: 9).

iv. Before the foundation of the world God conceived the counsel of salvation for the church. Already from eternity that amazing structure the "body" was determined by the Redeemer. Therefore "from before the ages" the Christ-mystery was already hidden in God "that those of the nations should be fellow-heirs and fellow-members of the body and fellow-partakers in Christ Jesus of His promise through the gospel" (Eph. 3: 9, 6).

v. From the foundation of the world God had prepared the kingdom for His own. Therefore will the King say one day to those on His right hand, "Inherit the kingdom which is prepared for you from the foundation of the world" (Matt. 25: 34), and therefore is the hidden wisdom of the mystery already "before the ages" appointed to our glory (I Cor. 2: 7).

vi. Before the foundation of the world God had appointed His Son to be the Mediator of the pre-determined counsel of salvation. The Son is the Lamb, without blemish or fault, before-known, prior to the foundation of the world being laid (I Pet. 1: 20).

Christ is the Mediator of world-*creation*: "for in him has everything been created which is in the heaven and on the earth" (Col. 1: 16; Rev. 3: 14; John 1: 3).

Christ is the Mediator of world *preservation* : for "He upholds the all through his almighty Word." (Heb. 1: 3; Col. 1: 17).

Christ is the Mediator of world-*redemption*: for "it was the good pleasure of the whole fulness to dwell in him and through him to reconcile all things unto himself." (Col. 1: 19, 20; Eph. 3: 11; 1: 4; Heb. 1: 2; I Pet. 1: 20).

Christ is the Lord of world-*judgment*: for "the Father has committed all judgment unto the Son" (John 5: 22).

vii. But from eternity the Son was willing to carry out the work of redemption. Therefore His later death on the cross was an offering of Himself to God "through the eternal Spirit" (Heb. 9: 14), that is, through His eternal Spirit through which

Christ performed all His other works also, and in which finally He presented Himself to the Father, in obedience unto death, which death, although carried out in time, is nevertheless an act above time.

So behind all the course of time, there stand eternal realities. Endlessness flows into time, even as time shall at last flow again into eternity. Thus, according to the eternal plan, the Father chose the Son in advance as the Redeemer, and determined to "send" Him into the world which was to be saved as the highest, inexpressible "gift" (John 3: 16; II Cor. 9: 15); and at the same time, and according to the same eternal plan, He appointed to Him, as the Mediator of the salvation, the host of the redeemed as His "inheritance" (Psa. 2: 8).

Thus the Son became the gift of the Father to the world, and the world, so far as it is redeemed, became the pre-temporal gift of the Father to the Son (John 17: 6, 9, 24). Therefore, also, could the Son, in His high priestly prayer, designate those who, at the time He was on earth, had not yet been born again, but who should later come to believe, as those whom the Father *had* then already given to Him (John 17: 24; comp. 20), and Paul could say, "Whom He justified them he also glorified" (Rom. 8: 30).

The historical unfolding of this eternal decree of redemption, thus conceived in God, becomes in time the covenants and testaments of God with mankind; of which the goal is the "eternal covenant" which the blood of God's Son has dedicated (Heb. 13: 20). "Father, I will that they whom thou hast given me may be with me where I am." (John 17: 24.)

But all these mighty words stand in the Scripture not for the satisfaction of curious inquisitiveness, nor even only for the intellectual completion of our picture of the history of the world's salvation, but in order to show us the *greatness of the Divine love*. Even before all the ages of time the Highest concerned Himself with your glory and with mine. Before the sea raged and swelled, before the earth was built or its foundations were sunk, yea, before those morning stars exulted and those sons of God shouted for joy, God, the Almighty, even then had thoughts on me. On *me*, the worm of the earth, who have given Him so much trouble and labour with all my sins; on *me*, He Who is God, the Ancient of days. Truly these are depths not to be fathomed, and which the heart of every man despairs of being able to describe in words. Here we can only bow and worship, and lay our life at the feet of Him, the All-loving.

THE CREATION OF THE UNIVERSE

"IN the beginning God created heaven and earth." By the Word of His power He called forth systems of suns and stars. "He spake: it came into being; He commanded: there it stood" (Psa. 33: 9; comp. ver. 6).

i. *The Origin of the Creation.*

The general question *why* God created a world at all no one is able to answer. As the absolute One, the "blessed God" (I Tim. 1: 11) He exists on His own account, eternally suffices for Himself, and needs no other who should exist for His sake. He is indeed love, and love by the necessity of its nature needs a beloved, another ego, to which it can lovingly reach forth. But the Ego was already eternally present in God. In the *Son* the Divine love enjoyed, without beginning and without end, full unfolding and unceasing satisfaction: "Thou hast loved me before the foundation of the world" (John 17: 24). Therefore the only thing that can here be said is: God has created the world because He willed to create it. Certainly indeed His will and His freedom are not uncontrolled arbitrariness; so that the decision to create must have been formed on eternal grounds within the Deity, but what these are God has not revealed to us, and with this we must rest content (Rom. 11: 33, 34).[1]

ii. *The Purpose of the Creation.*

The question *whereto* God created the world is answered more plainly in the Scripture.

(1) *The revealing of the glory of God.* Everything that God does has Himself eternally as its goal; it comes to pass "for *his* name's sake" (Psa. 23: 3). for *Himself* throughout (Eph. 5: 27), "to the praise of *his* glory" (Eph. 1: 6, 12, 14), so that "*God* may be all in all" (I Cor. 15: 28). For since God, by virtue of His perfection, must always wish the highest, and since He Himself, by virtue of His Deity, *is* the highest, He must always have that which is within His own nature as the goal of His will. Therefore must His work be so ordered that it may lead to *Him* and have its end in *Him*. Thus the purpose of the creation of the world must consist in the unfolding, setting forth, and displaying of the glory of God. Himself is its beginning, middle, and

---

[1] Heb. 1: 2 declares that God appointed the Son to be heir of all things. The next clause reads: "though whom *also* he made the worlds." This "also" shows that the appointment as heir was made before creation, which suggests that the creation exists by the will of the Father for the glory of the Son. See also John 3: 35. [Trans.]

ultimate objective, the first and the last, the Alpha and the Omega. (Rom. 11: 36; Col. 1: 16; Heb. 1: 2).

(2) *The revealing of the love of God.* But this self-displaying plan of God must be perfect, and therefore unfold itself in a double manner. Not only His omnipotence, omnipresence, and omniscience, but also His righteousness, love, and truthfulness must be manifested.

The former can indeed be effected in the realm of space and matter, that is, in the mineral, vegetable, and animal kingdoms; but the latter demands the creation of morally free personalities, and therefore a *spiritual* kingdom within created beings. But just because holiness is the essential nature of God, therefore in His world plan the higher purpose of the material must lie in the moral realm, and the chief ground for the very creation of a world must be the magnifying of the moral qualities of God as the Holy, Blessed, and Wise, by the creation of morally free personalities. Only in them, namely, in the angels and in mankind, can God perfectly display His glory in creation.

But the essence of such spiritual life, and the essence of all true morality in general, is not only an outward, objective carrying out of law and a merely legal freedom from sin and guilt, *but a personal, organic* participation in the moral life of the Deity itself. For God, as the supreme lawgiver, has appointed the moral ordering of the world according to His nature, and He is *love,* the most perfect love (I John 4: 16). Therefore the moral appointment of free creatures must also be an appointment to *love,* and the supreme final purpose of world creation must consist in the self-unfolding and self-displaying of God as the Perfect, Holy, and Loving One, in the establishment of a fellowship of life and love between the Creator and the creature. But this means that God has called the world into existence so as to be able to love it, and that it should love Him in return. His goal evermore is to lead it to an eternal share in the enjoyment of His holiness and love, and thereby to blessedness and glory (comp. Rom. 8: 17).

The determined purpose of world creation being so high, it is no wonder that the stamp of divinity lies also in especial manner on the Biblical account of the creation. The six "days" clearly divide into two triplets, the members of which correspond exactly to one another.

The first triplet contains the works of division (of the light from the darkness, the upper waters from the lower, the dry land from the sea). The second triplet contains the works of quickening and adorning, (sun, moon, and stars; fishes and birds; land animals and man).

On the first day God created light; on the fourth day the light-bearing stars: on the second day the air and the sea; on the fifth the birds in the air and the fish in the sea: on the third the land and the plants, that is, the lowest grade of earthly life; on the sixth day the animals and man, that is, the highest grade of earthly life.

Thus the work of the six days bears unmistakably the stamp of the number three, which so often in the Divine revelation is the symbol of the Godhead. After it has, by three self-ascending creative impulses, attained a certain height and resting point, it pauses, and then, returning to the starting point, resumes, as it were beginning afresh, so as again by a threefold ascent to reach its summit. The creating of light is the first beginning: the creating of the light-bearers the second beginning. Thus this double tri-unity becomes a deep symbolic prophecy in numbers concerning the origin, character, and goal of the earth-system in general. All is from Him, through Him, and unto Him. In all He will magnify Himself.

iii. *The Greatness of Creation.*

1. *The Host of Stars.* The horizon of the Bible is immeasurable and universal. God's Word speaks not only of the earth and of time, but above all of heaven and eternity, and it describes the world above as a multiplicity of heavenly spheres. "The heaven and the heaven of heavens cannot contain thee" (I Kings 8: 27)[1]. Far from seeing in this small earth "*the* world," constituting the mathematical centre and chief point of the entire creation, to the Bible the nations are but as a "drop in a bucket," as a "grain of sand" which remains in the scales (Isa. 40: 15); and to it the islands are as "small dust," and the whole of mankind as "grasshoppers" (Isa. 40: 22). Indeed, the whole globe is to the Bible only a "footstool" to the heavenly throne (Matt. 5: 35; Acts 7: 49). "The heaven is my throne, and the earth the footstool of my feet" (Isa. 66: 1). But no one would be so foolish as to imagine that the footstool to a throne is the central point of a palace, or surpasses the throne in size or importance. No, "all nations are as *nothing* before him" (Isa. 40: 17). "When I consider the heaven, the work of thy fingers, the moon and the stars which thou hast prepared, what is man, that thou thinkest upon him, and the son of the earth that thou regardest him?" (Psa. 8: 3, 4).

The size of our own earth surpasses indeed all thought. All that man has built on the whole world, ships, cities, and villages, taken together, would not occupy 300 cubic miles; Professor Bettex, indeed, reckons only 98 cubic miles. But the earth contains more than 260,000 *millions* of such cubic miles! And

[1] The Hebrew word for heaven stands always in the plural (ha-schamayim), where the ending "*im*" is the masculine plural, as also in cherub*im* and seraph*im*. So also in Eph. 4: 10 "all the heavens", and II Cor. 12: 2 "third heaven."

yet it is itself but an astronomical atom among the whirling con-
stellations, only a tiny speck of dust among the ocean of suns of
the universe.   In the glowing ball of the giant sun alone there
is room for over one and a quarter million (more exactly 1,297,000)
such earths; and an express, non-stop train, driven furiously,
would need more than 169 years to reach the sun, the distance
being some 93 millions of miles.

But the sun itself is only one star among a mighty spherical
shaped group of 400 stars; for since the arrangement of the nearer
stars visible to the naked eye "stands in no perceptible relationship to the Milky Way, all these stars must form a great, nearly
spherical group of stars, to which our sun belongs" (Prof. Klein),
and which, according to Professor Riem, consists of about
400 suns.

And here the distances are still more immeasurable.   Light,
that in a single second travels seven times round the entire
equator, requires fully four years and three months to reach our
nearest neighbour among the suns, the fixed star Alpha Centauri
(in the southern sky).   For light travels at about 187,000 miles
a second, and the equator of the earth is between 24,000 and
25,000 miles in length.   And to star 61 in The Swan, our third
nearest neighbour among the fixed stars, the swiftest express
train of the world would have to travel 60 millions of years,
that is, 9.7 light years (Prof. Klein).   And yet in comparison with
the starless abyss of space itself the stars in such a system of suns
stand *extraordinarily near together*.

Proof of this to the unastronomical night observer are the
thickly-crowded, diamond-like twinkling points of light in the
constellation called the Pleiades, not far from Orion, which forms
a similar star-system to "ours."   "The splendid spectacle which
the Pleiades present in a telescope is heightened when one knows
that these luminous stars, sparkling like diamonds against the
dark background of heaven, form a great star-system among
themselves.   This is proved by the fact that all the stars of this
system move forward through space *together*, while at the same
time all the individual members move together around a centre
of gravity common to them all."   So that the Pleiades not only
seem to be a star-group, but are actually such a locally inter-
related group of fixed stars.   How star upon star sparkles here!
The photographic plate, indeed, shows here 1,681 stars upon an
area of the heaven not larger than the disk of the moon, and in
the further vicinity about 5,000 more (Klein).   And the distances
between these individual stars which to our sight are contracted
indeed to nothing, are actually thousands of millions upon
thousands of millions of miles.   Yet this is only the *beginning*
of universal space!

What, then, must be these distances which lie behind and

between such groups of star-islands, till we arrive finally at the actual chief ring of the spiral Milky Way, which ravishes with its hundred-millionfold "star-dust" the eye of the inhabitant of the earth! And then follow, in further immeasurable distances, yet other Milky Way systems, such as the Andromeda universe with its innumerable suns, or even the unfathomable spiral nebula H 156 in the constellation of the Great Lion, whose distance is estimated at over 500,000 light years (G. Wolf).

Taken together all this shows that the stars are as thinly scattered in the universe as if one should happen on earth on a single pinhead every 20 or 60 miles (Prof. Schwarzschild), or as if one should sprinkle *one* quart of water over the whole surface of the earth, that is, over some 196,000,000 square miles (Prof. Riem). Nor with all this must we forget, that these "water-drops" and "pinheads," of less than one twenty-fourth part of an inch in diameter, are those glowing and fiery worlds with surfaces of millions upon millions of square miles and a capacity which exceeds hundreds of thousands of millions of millions of cubic miles by ten thousands of millions of millions.[1]

Upon the question how, in view of such vast proportions, our tiny earth, though not as to matter or space, yet morally and in respect of salvation, can be the centre of the universe, we remark: "As a place Sedan is of no significance, but because of the decisive battle of William I against Napoleon III, it has become world-famed and a chief turning point in European history. Thus it has attained a *historical* significance which stands in no proportion to its geographical importance." World history often shows that places in which the most mighty battles, of century-long significance, were decided, were in themselves, as to situation and size, small and insignificant. See further pp. 91, 92.

But the totality of such vastness, *embracing the entire creation*, is the universal framework of the *history of salvation*. "The Lord has established his throne in the heavens, and his kingdom rules over all" (Psa. 103: 19). It is only in connexion with the starry world that we become conscious of the extent of the Divine counsel of salvation, and therefore let us set salvation's record as found in the Bible against the flaming golden background of its cosmic super-history. Only then will its centre and focus, the cross of Golgotha, be rightly esteemed; then the whole universe arches itself over the cross: "The foot of the cross remains on earth, but its head reaches into the distances of the starry world with their cosmic history," and overwhelmed we hearken to the promise of the Lord: "Fear not, thou *little* flock:

---

[1] Thus, for example, the diameter of the sun is 868,750 miles, its superficial area over 2,334,000 millions of square miles, and its capacity over 351 billions of cubic miles.

for it is your Father's good pleasure to give to *you* the kingdom" (Luke 12: 32). "Lift up your eyes to the height and see: who has created these? He who leads out their host by number, who calls them all by names . . . Jehovah, the Lord of hosts is his name" (Isa. 40: 26; 51: 15).

2. *The Host of the Angels.* Now to what end do these worlds exist in the etherial space? Has God any pleasure in dead matter? Is He not the God of the living? Can inanimate matter praise Him, the Lord of all life? (Psa. 30: 9). Or is not rather the starry world of God everywhere filled with personal life?

In fact, if only our small earth, this speck of dust amidst the whirling suns of the universe, carries organic life, "then in meaningless contrast to it there stands millions of dead star-colossi. Then were the immense universe a limitless extinct waste, in which only on this tiny earth, as a marvellous exception, the solitary flower of life blooms."[1] Then the fiery splendour of the millions of suns, which yet illuminate nothing, were only "a vast meaningless and purposeless firework in the dead universe," and all the stars and heavenly bodies were only burning or burnt-out craters!

Quite otherwise speak the prophets and apostles of the Divine revelation. The Word of God knows of thrones and lordships, of principalities and authorities (Col. 1: 16), of sons of God and morning stars (Job 38: 7), of the host of the high in the height (Isa. 24: 21), of cherubim and seraphim (Rev. 4: 6–8; Isa. 6: 2, 3), of archangels and angels (Jude 9: Rev. 5: 11; 12: 7). And all these it describes by the same term, "host of heaven", *as it uses for the stars.*[2]

From this viewing and naming of the two together we perceive a reference of a more profound nature. For otherwise how could the "morning stars" *sing* together, and at the same time *shout for joy* with the "sons of God"? (Job 38: 7). How could the starry world of God *worship* the Creator? Will the dust praise Him? Will it proclaim His truth? But "Thou art the existing one, Jehovah alone! Thou hast made the heavens, the heaven of heavens, and all their host, the earth and all that is thereon . . . and *thou makest these all living, and the host* of the heaven worships thee" (Neh. 9: 6). And how else could the psalmist, similarly, in connexion with the angels, call upon the stars also to praise God?

---

[1] And yet there are on the earth over 200,000 species of plants, with 300,000 species of fungi; and further, 80,000 species of beetles (Bettex), 200,000 species of butterflies (Prof. Dennert), and the total number of all species of life is over two millions.

[2] Thus in Deut. 4: 19; Isa. 34: 4; Jer. 8: 2 the term describes the material stars; in I Kings 22: 19, Luke 2: 13; Rev. 19: 4, the angels. In other places it means both at once (for example, Psa. 148: 1–6; Isa. 24: 21–23; 40: 26; Job 38: 7).

Praise Jehovah from the heavens,
    Praise Him in the heights!
    Praise Him all His *angels*,
    Praise Him all His hosts!
    Praise Him *sun* and *moon*,
    Praise Him all ye *stars* of light! (Psa. 148: 1–3).

No, all this is more than mere poetic rhapsody. It proves that between angels and stars there is not merely a figurative comparison, but an actual and real connexion, although one whose details are still obscure to us.

Nevertheless this one thing we already perceive: that the angels, in unnumbered hosts, sometimes individually (Acts 5: 19), sometimes in organized bodies (Rev. 12: 7; Col. 1: 16), take part in the history of human salvation. In this respect they are

(i).   Observers of our walk (1 Cor. 4: 9; Eph. 3: 10),

(ii).   Messengers[1] of our King (Luke 1: 11; Matt. 1: 20; Dan. 9: 22; Rev. 1: 1; 22: 6, 16; Heb. 2: 2).

(iii). Helpers in our distresses (Heb. 1: 14; Acts 12: 7; Dan. 3: 25, 28; 6: 22; II Kings 6: 17; Luke 22: 43).

(iv).   Fighters for our final victory (Dan. 12: 1; Rev. 12: 7–9; 19: 11–14; Dan. 10: 13, 20).

(v).   Guardians of the Divine world-order (Dan. 4: 13, 17, 23; I Cor. 11: 10).

(vi).   Executors of the Divine judgments (Isa. 37: 36; Acts 12: 23; Matt. 13: 30, 41; Rev. 14: 19; 15: 1, 6, 7).

(vii). Worshippers because of the Divine acts of redemption (Luke 2: 13, 14; 15: 10; I Pet. 1: 12).

3. *The Throne of God.* And yet! All that is "visible is temporal", only "the invisible is eternal" (II Cor. 4: 18). But the stars are visible and therefore will pass away: "They all will wax old as doth a garment, and as a mantle wilt thou roll them together" (Psa. 102: 26). The eternal world of God must therefore be still higher, far *above* the stars, *in the invisible, beyond all things visible*.

There is the throne of God, there the dwelling place of the angels, there the heavenly Jerusalem, which is the mother of us all (Gal. 4: 26). Thither "above all the heavens" was Christ exalted (Eph. 4: 10), and is now at the right hand of the Father "become higher than the heavens" (Heb. 7: 26). There dwells the All-Highest as the fountain of light for all worlds, and from Him streams out all life throughout the creation (Acts 17: 25, 28).

The thought of such a supreme throne existing in the universe must readily be acceptable to the reflecting mind. The whole universe is ruled by the law of ascent. Truly God is present everywhere and interpenetrates with His life the whole creation (Col. 1: 17; Acts 17: 28). But this does not exclude that, *above*

[1] Whence the word "angel." in Greek *angelos*, from *angello*, I dispatch, I send.

all the fields of light, there is a special pinnacle of light where His glory most perfectly displays itself. In even a stone there flashes a reflection of the Divine thought; yet finer in a rose; still more arrestingly in the song of the nightingale; more spiritual still in the human eye; and among mankind what different stages there are between the humblest and neediest up to the finest of the sons of men, in Whom dwells the fulness of the Godhead.

Thus also on earth there are wastes and deserts with no inhabitants; inhospitable regions with but few; fruitful places with many; regions of beauty and yet greater beauty with the greatest fulness of earthly life. So it is also in the heavenly places; there are small and great stars, cold and hot, dark and radiant; there are led and leading stars, planets, and suns, abysses of space and families of suns: and so there is also above them all *a central point of the universe, a place of the most immediate presence of God, a dwelling of the most concentrated glory-light, even the throne of God.*[1]

But the light in which He dwells is superior to all things visible; it is something other than the radiance of all suns and stars. It is not to be beheld by earthly eyes; it is "unapproachable" (I Tim. 6: 16), far removed from all things this side (II Cor. 12: 4). Only the angels in heaven can behold it (Matt. 18: 10); only the spirits of the perfected in the eternal light (Matt. 5: 8; I John 3: 2; Rev. 22: 4); only the pure and holy, even as He Himself is pure (I John 3: 2, 3; [Heb. 12: 14]).

Therefore down here only figurative language can be used of things heavenly. Even the term "above" as used of the Eternal is not to be understood in a purely local sense (Psa. 139). It is the perceptible representation of the "beyondness" of the Divine. It is the symbolical setting forth in terms of space of the sublimity of the super-spatial. This is why the Bible figuratively represents this "super" by "above," the spiritually superior through the spatial term to be "higher," the "super" temporal and the "super" spatial by the figurative "above" space. And because God, the Lord of the heaven, is at once the most perfect and the All-highest, therefore the Bible seizes as its symbols the most precious things of earth and speaks in a language of precious stones of the throne of light of His glory.

The blue sapphire speaks of the heavenly nature (Ex. 24: 10; Ezek. 1: 26).

The crystal jasper of holiness and light (Rev. 4: 3; comp. 21: 11; 22: 1).

The green rainbow of emerald speaks of covenant faithfulness and renewal of life[2] (Rev. 4: 3; Ezek. 1: 28).

---

[1] Otherwise the ascension of Christ were only a becoming invisible, but not ascent to heaven.

[2] In very ancient times green was the emblem of life, as in Ur in Chaldea 2000 B.C.

But we bow down and worship Him, and say, in the concluding words of the *World Harmony* of Copernicus (1618):—

> Great is our God and great His power,
> And of His wisdom there is no end.
> Praise Him sun, moon, and planets,
> In whose speech may a song of praise for ever
>   resound:
> Praise Him, ye heavenly harmonies,
> And also ye, the witnesses and confirmers of His
>   revealed truths;
> And thou, my soul, sing the honour of the Lord
>   throughout thy life.   Amen.

CHAPTER III

THE ORIGIN OF EVIL

And yet! Into this universe, which was appointed to the highest, which the Creator had called that it should become a vessel to reveal His glory, there has entered a breach. The united harmony of the spheres is destroyed by a harsh discord. Sin has appeared, and criminally set itself against the holy, loving plans of God to reveal Himself. Through the sin of mankind this lower earth is devastated (Gen. 3: 17, 18; Rom. 8: 20), and, in the heavenly world above, as the history of temptation in the Bible premises, a fall had taken place among the angels prior to the fall of Adam and Eve (Gen. 3: 1–7; 2: 15).

Yet how this was possible, and why God permitted it, no one can say. The origin of evil remains for ever a mystery. Even the few hints that the Scripture gives are no more than suggestive.

1. *Satan before the Fall.* God's universal kingdom of creation is divided, as it appears, into a number of provinces, the material and spiritual organization of each of which is entrusted to a definite angel prince as, so to speak, viceroy of God. Thus there are angels for children (Matt. 18: 10), for adults (Acts 12: 15), for whole lands and nations, as Persia (Dan. 10: 13), Greece (Dan. 10: 20), Israel (Dan. 10: 21; 12: 1).[1] This assumes that in the world of light as also in the world of darkness there are angel *organizations,* which wield power in certain regions and hold ranks differing according to the size of the respective areas. Thus the Scripture speaks, for example, of the archangel Michael and his angels, as well as of the Dragon and his angels (Rev. 12: 7). In fact Paul speaks of "thrones, governments, princedoms, and authorities" not only in the visible but also in the invisible world (Col. 1: 16; Eph. 1: 21).

Satan must have been such a special Prince before his fall. From the position of authority which in the present time he still holds it is to be inferred that, at least before his fall, a mighty region was legally committed to his rule; and the fact that it is on the earth that he is operating suggests that this region was the earth and the surrounding atmosphere.

This finds its definite confirmation in the Word of God. The Lord Jesus Himself designates Satan as the "prince of

[1] In this lies the kernel of truth of national polytheism, the venerating of many gods.

32

the world;" see John 12: 31; 14: 30; 16: 11. Paul terms him the "prince over the powers of the air" (Eph. 2: 2). When at the time of the temptation Satan offered to the Lord all the kingdoms of the earth, and said, "I will give to thee this whole power and its glory; for to me it is granted (or delivered—*paradedotai*), and I can give it to whom I will" (Luke 4: 6), the Lord so far acknowledged this authority that He did not contest the present power of the devil to dispose of the kingdoms of the world and their glory (Matt. 4: 8–10).

And when in the Revelation, regarding the end-time of the present economy, it is said that "The authority over the world is come to our Lord and his anointed, and he shall rule as king in all eternity" (Rev. 11: 15; comp. 19: 6), there likewise lies in these words the testimony that down to that moment the kingdom of this world stands under the domination of another, even the "prince of the world." Now we understand also why the archangel Michael, when contending with the Devil concerning the body of Moses, dared not bring against him a railing judgment, but said only, "The Lord rebuke thee" (Jude 9).

Indeed, even after Golgotha and Pentecost the governmental position of Satan over his world-region continued, for in the period of the church the apostle John testifies that "the whole world lies in the evil one" (I John 5: 19), and Paul speaks repeatedly of the "authority" of Satan (Acts 26: 18; Col. 1: 13; Eph. 2: 2). He uses the same word whereby in the letter to the Romans he designates human officials (Gk. *exousia,* Rom. 13: 1, 2), and thus intimates that the rulership of Satan is equivalent to a "kingdom" (comp. Matt. 12: 26).

ii. *The Fall of Satan.* There must therefore have arrived in the prehistoric eternity a moment when this world-prince of God renounced his allegiance to the Most High, and thereby changed from a "Lucifer," a "Lightbearer" of the Divine glory,[1] into an "Adversary" of God[2] and a "slanderer" of His saints.[3]

From that time on a mighty breach runs through the cosmos, and an organized opposing kingdom of evil confronts the universal kingdom of God (Matt. 12: 26). Satan as a ruler has in turn princes and authorities under himself (Dan. 10: 13, 20; Eph. 6: 12), and the opposition between him and the kingdom of God is henceforth the theme and the essential subject of the universal super-history outlined in Holy Scripture.

[1] Lucifer in Latin equals "light-bearer." The name Lucifer originates in Isa. 14: 12 [R.V. "day star"] and is first a figurative term for the God-resisting king of Babylon; but who, however, in his turn, in the view of the prophet, as it would seem, is a type of his demonic overlord, Satan.

[2] Heb. Satan, *shatan,* i.e. enemy, adversary, quite generally: I Kings 11: 14, 23, 25; before a court Psa. 109: 6; in Num. 22: 22 even of the "angel of Jehovah."

[3] Gk. *diabolos,* i.e. devil; from *dia-ballo,* to cast through, to criticize; in an antagonistic sense, to accuse, either falsely (2 Macc. 4: 1) or by saying the truth (Dan. 3: 8): comp. Luke 16 : 1 with Rev. 12: 10.

The description by Isaiah of the overthrown king of Babylon appears, as the Rabbis already supposed, to include in its view the fall of this powerful prince of light: "Oh, how art thou fallen from heaven, thou brilliant star, son of the dawn! . . . thou thoughtest in thy mind: 'I will ascend into the heaven, high above the stars will I erect my throne, will make myself like to the Highest.' But now art thou thrust down into the world of the dead, to the deepest corner of the underworld" (Isa. 14: 12–15). Ezekiel also, as it appears, borrows from that prehistoric event his illustrations for the description of the fall of Tyre: "Thou sealest up the sum, full of wisdom and full of beauty, thou wast an anointed cherub that coveredst . . . thou wast blameless in all thy doings from the day of thy creation until guilt was found in thee. Thy mind was lifted up because of thy beauty. Thou hadst thoughtlessly forsaken thy wisdom on account of thy brightness" (Ezek. 28: 12–15, 17).

Yet in general the Holy Scripture says scarcely anything concerning this fall of Satan, directly, indeed, nothing. As the record of salvation it purports to show to man by means of prophecy and history the way to redemption, but it will not give him a systematic view of the world or eternity in a philosophic form; for should it do so no man would understand it. For this reason it speaks of the origin of evil only as a background and indirectly, only in incidental figurative hints, but never in direct doctrine, and nowhere in continuous unveiled form: "The secret things are Jehovah's" (Deut. 29: 29).[1]

But in any case the belief in the existence of a personal devil is the belief of Jesus and His apostles (Matt. 4: 1–10; 12: 27; Luke 10: 18; Rom. 16: 20; II Cor. 11: 14, 15; Rev. 12: 7–9; 20: 2, 10). It is impossible for one who does not share this primitive Christian belief to understand Christ and His apostles. Nevertheless almost always the modern man rejects from the outset the idea of a devil because he thinks nearly always of the popular, repulsive, foolish, grotesque representation of the devil of the Middle Ages. But in truth Satan is gifted with the highest intelligence, fallen indeed, but none the less an exceedingly powerful spirit being, whose existence is in no way assailable philosophically.

iii. *The First Sin and the Condition of the World.* But with the fall of Satan there must have been associated the ruin of the region over which he ruled, as is evidenced by the organic connexion between spirit and nature, and by the later and resembling fall of man, though this last to a smaller extent (Gen. 3: 18). World and earth catastrophes occurred as counter-

[1] I Tim. 3: 7 and Luke 10: 18 are almost the only fairly clear passages which speak of the fall of Satan, and even in these it is not quite certain. II Pet. 2: 4 and Jude 6 refer in our view to Gen. 6: 1–4.

workings of the righteousness of God against this cosmic revolt. The creation was subjected to vanity (Rom. 8: 20, 21).

All details are hidden from our knowledge. Only this is certain, that death and destruction in the world of plants and animals raged on the earth for unthinkable periods long before the race of man. This is proved very clearly by the geological strata and the stages of the development of the prehistoric animal world. The strata of the earth beneath us are simply "a huge cemetery that is enclosed in its stony field." Indeed many rapacious beasts of the prehistoric time were terrible monsters with the most voracious and deadly power of destruction.[1]

With this corresponds also the testimony of the Old Testament. For the commission of man, recorded therein, not only to dress but also to guard the garden of Paradise, as also the fact of his temptation by a hostile, deceitful power, opposed to God, show already in the Old Testament that evil did not originate primarily in man, but that it had existed before him in another creature, so that prior to the time of man, before his fall and the cursing of the ground connected therewith, there had already existed a breach and a disharmony in creation.

In both old and more recent times there have been God-enlightened men who in this connexion have expressed the conjecture that the work of the six days of Gen. 1 was properly a work of *restoration*, but not the original creation of the earth, and that originally man had the task, as a servant of the Lord and as ruler of the creation, in moral opposition to Satan, to recover for God the outwardly renewed earth, through the spreading abroad of his race and his lordship over the earth.

Thus Prof. Bettex says that man should originally, "as the vice-regent of God, gradually have *reconquered* the whole earth." Also Prof. v. Heune, who likewise upholds the restitution theory, says, "that the great operation of *bringing back* the whole creation to God, starts with man. In man, matter and spirit, God's Spirit, meet. The man Christ Jesus, God's Son, has carried to victory the decisive conflict with Satan and the consequences of this must work themselves out. Therefore the cross stands at the centre of universal history."

The geological periods must therefore have been either *before* the work of the six days, and the "days" themselves be conceived as literal days of twenty-four hours, or the "days" of Gen. 1 must be taken to signify periods, and be considered as the geological ages of development in the history of the earth.

In this way it might be possible to find a reconciliation between the Biblical account of the world's origin and that of

---

[1] In this manner also the Tübingen palæontologist Freiherr von Heune connects the fact of death in the pre-Adamic creation with the fall of Satan as the God-appointed "prince of this world."

modern natural philosophy.   Traces of such an explanation of
the record of creation are found in ancient Christian literature as
early as the time of the church father Augustine (about A.D. 400).
In the seventh century it was maintained by the Anglo-Saxon poet
Cædmon.   About A.D. 1000 King Edgar of England espoused
it.   In the seventeenth century it was specially emphasized by
the mystic Jacob Boehme.   In the year 1814 it was developed by
the Scottish scholar Dr. Chalmers, and in 1833 further by the
English professor of mineralogy William Buckland.

There are also very many German upholders of this teaching,
as for instance, the professor of geology Freiherr von Huene
(Tübingen); and well-known are the English scholar G. H.
Pember, and also the Scofield "Reference Bible", so widely
circulated in all English-speaking lands.   From the Catholic
side there are Cardinal Wiseman and the philosopher Friedrich
von Schlegel.

Naturally in numerous details these show substantial devia-
tions from one another, especially on the question whether the
following six "days" were of four-and-twenty hours or long
periods.

Others again believe that the whole development is one
uniform continued sequence, *without* a special intervening entire
destruction and "restoration" of the earth; one single colossal
process, distributed over immense creative periods.   In this—
whatever the method may have been (into which science may
search) under Divine guidance, and, as it appears, since the fall
of Lucifer, also not without Satanic cross-workings—there came
a gradual ascent in the forms of life.   Finally man, *without* connexion by descent with the animal world, was placed on the stage
of world events, in order to set out on his earthly course from
the garden of Paradise expressly prepared for him.

However, in no case can there be here absolutely certain
knowledge.   For this primary event, evil entering the world
and bringing into disorder the originally pure and good creation
of God, is precisely that prehistoric occurrence which devastates
all things, which confuses our own being, in which we are all
involved, and which helps to condition our whole present
existence in all its manifestations, including its thinking!   Therefore neither as to time nor fact can we form an adequate conception of it, but have merely the duty to recognize the weighty
facts of this mystery and, in view of them, to act according to
conscience and responsibility.

For the rest, it behoves us to forego all further questions
and to have the courage to confess openly our ignorance and also
the humility to perceive that earthly thought never can comprehend universal super-history; and that our intellect often

views eternal things as contradictory only because, fallen into sin and bondage as it is, it is itself in opposition to the laws of the other world.   There is nothing really so irrational as rationalism.   Whoever wishes to peer into God's secrets must be adorned with the threefold ornament of humility, reverence, and faith; and where these are found the soul can restfully commit to the Most High all matters not revealed (Rom. 11: 33-35; Job 38: 4-7).   Only in eternity will all questions be cleared up. Only when the Lord comes will all veils disappear (I Cor. 13: 9-12).   Till then we are men that wait in hope.

PART II

THE ORIGINAL REVELATION

CHAPTER I

THE APPOINTED VOCATION OF MAN IN PARADISE

GOD set mankind on the earth. In Eden He planted that wonderful Garden that should be its possessors' delight and pleasure, for "Eden" means "pleasure land, loveliness." Paradise was the beginning of the ways of God with man here on earth.

Christ and the New Testament guarantee the historicity and literality of the opening chapters of the Bible. Everywhere the Lord and His apostles treat them as accounts of actual events; indeed they even draw from them dogmatic conclusions. Matt. 19: 4–9; Rom. 5: 12–21; I Cor. 15: 21, 22; I Tim. 2: 13, 14; Jas. 3: 9; I John 3: 12; Rev. 20: 2; "If therefore the New Testament is truth, then Gen. 1–3 is history." Whoever rejects or explains away this history of the first beginnings is thereby in opposition to the absolute authority of the Lord Jesus and His apostles. For details see the Appendix "The Trustworthiness of ancient Biblical History."

Paradise was

    i. The Home of an Indescribable Bliss,
    ii. The Starting-point of a Wonderful Task,
    iii. The Arena of a Mighty Conflict,
    iv. The Scene of a Tragic Collapse: and thenceforth it is
    v. The Longed-for Goal of a waiting Mankind.

I. THE HOME OF AN INDESCRIBABLE BLISS

Majestically the lord of the earthly creation ruled the Garden, and all the work of his hands prospered. The flowers bloomed with such beauty as the human eye has never again seen, and the trees bore the most glorious fruit. In the vegetable and animal world a wondrous breath of heavenly peace prevailed; and, above all, God Himself, the Creator of the universe, held ungrieved intercourse with men and granted them the enjoyment of His blessed presence (Gen. 3: 8).

Where the earthly Paradise was situate cannot be stated with certainty. Some have suggested Armenia or the Syrian-Arabian desert. In any case the Phrat (Gen. 2: 14) is the Euphrates and

Hiddekel the Tigris (comp. Dan. 10: 4, the Aramaic *Diglat*).
That the district of Eden must have lain high is proved by the
circumstance that it was the birth-place of great rivers (Gen. 2:
10). The Garden is not Eden itself, but "in" Eden (Gen. 2:
8, 10). That later the name of the district passed to the Garden
itself (e.g. Ezek. 28: 13) is a common occurrence easily to be
understood. The rivers Pison and Gihon cannot with certainty
be identified. It appears that substantial changes in those
regions were effected by the Flood.

The word "paradise" is derived from the Persian and means
in the first place simply a park or forest which surrounded the
royal stronghold. Thus Nehemiah 2: 8 speaks of a certain
Asaph, the keeper of the royal forest (Heb. *pardes*). Similarly,
Solomon in the sentence "I made me gardens and parks" uses
for parks the same word "paradises" (Eccles. 2: 5; comp. Song
of Songs 4: 12). The Septuagint translates by "paradise"
whenever in the Hebrew the word "Garden," Eden, is found.
In the New Testament the word occurs only three times (Luke
23: 43; II Cor. 12: 4; Rev. 2: 7).

But God had placed man in Paradise not for enjoyment only:
he was also to be active and produce fruit; and thus the garden
became for him

II. THE STARTING-POINT OF A WONDERFUL TASK

(1) MAN AS A PERSON

From the point of view of salvation's history God, world,
and man are the three essential realities of all that exists. To
recognize them is the task of our understanding. A threefold
consciousness has therefore been granted to man; a consciousness of God, of the world, and of himself; and in correspondence
with this the Creator has given to him the organs which capacitate
him for this threefold consciousness.

The world man perceives through the senses (feeling, smelling,
taste, hearing, sight) which are exercised by the bodily organs
(nerves, nose, palate, ears, eyes). It is through the body that
we attain to *world* or *sense* consciousness.

The *Ego* we perceive through the soul. For man is far more
than a sensitive member of external nature; he is a self with
volition and individual personality. This is revealed to him
directly through his own inner being, and thus through the soul
he attains to *self*—or *Ego*—consciousness.

And so that he might finally rise to the Creator, God gave
him the spirit. Through it he attains to *God* consciousness.

Thus man is a trinity in unity, and his invisible inner being
consists of two substances to be clearly distinguished; for the
Word of God is able to pierce "to the *dividing* of soul and spirit"

(Heb. 4: 12), and the apostle further testifies: "But he, the God of peace, sanctify you through and through, and your whole *spirit,* together with *soul* and *body,* must be preserved blameless unto the coming of our Lord Jesus Christ" (I Thess. 5: 23). "Spirit and soul are one as to their nature (the right *dichotomy*), but different substances (the right *trichotomy*)" (Delitzsch).

Thus "spirit" is that part of our personality which, as the higher consciousness, is directed toward the Divine and supersensual; whereas "soul" is the lower component of our inner man which has cognizance of the earthly and creaturely.[1] The soul attains merely to self consciousness, but the spirit attains to God-consciousness.

The soul attains merely to self consciousness, and even this only with the help of the spirit, but the spirit attains to God consciousness.

The soul is the connecting link between spirit and body. Only through its mediation can the spirit act on the body; for the spirit is to the soul the "substance interwoven from within and above" even as the body is the same "from outward and beneath." Hence the soul is the bond between both these; it is, as it were, a "body" for the spirit, even as it is itself enclosed by the body as its own material frame (see Tertullian).

According to the Scripture, the body should be

a temple of the Holy Spirit (I Cor. 6: 19),
a sacrifice for true service to God (Rom. 12: 1),
an instrument of righteousness (Rom. 6: 13),
a means to the glorifying of God (I Cor. 6: 20),
a seed-corn for the glorified spiritual body (I Cor. 15: 43–47).

Without redemption, the body is

a door of attack for the enemy (Gen. 3: 6; Matt. 5: 28–30),
the body of sin (Rom. 6: 6),
a body of humiliation (Phil. 3: 21),
a decaying earthly tent-dwelling (II Cor. 5: 1–4),
a seed-corn of a Satanically ruined resurrection body (Dan. 12: 2; John 5: 29).

Of this triunity of the human personality the Mosaic tabernacle is an image. "In the same figure a Christian is portrayed: his spirit is *sanctum sanctorum,* the All-holiest, the dwelling of God, in the darkness of faith without light, for he believes what he neither sees, nor feels, nor grasps. The soul is a *sanctum,* the holy place; here are seven lamps, that is, all kinds of understanding, discrimination, knowledge, and perception of corporeal

---

[1] One sees this specially in the use of the adjectives "soulish" and "spiritual". "Psychical" (soulish) occurs six times in the New Testament and always in inferior contrast to "spiritual", I Cor. 15: 44 (twice), 46; 2: 14; Jude 19; Jas. 3: 15 ("natural", R. V. sensual).

visible things. The body is the portico, the *atrium* (forecourt) which is manifest to every man, so that one can see what he does and how he lives" (Luther).

Thus in the nature of man there correspond
world consciousness, self consciousness, God consciousness,
body, soul, and spirit,
atrium, (forecourt), holy place, All-holiest.

It is from the All-holiest, from the spirit, that God rules over soul and body. Here lies, preserved in the conscience, even as in the ark of the covenant, the unchangeable Divine Law. Here is the actual place of revelation of the Most High in us, even as in the tabernacle God dwelt over the cherubim. And as then the cloud of glory, the Shekinah, floated above the throne of grace, so does this indwelling of the Divine Spirit in our spirit bring to us [as regenerate believers] the consciousness of peace and joy (Rom. 8: 16). For the throne of God in us is no judgment seat, but a throne of grace, and the sceptre of His sovereignty is salvation. Thus are we permitted, like that tabernacle, as a pilgrim-tent of God to go through the world-wilderness, till at length we reach the goal, eternity, the heavenly Canaan (comp. II Cor. 5: 1–4).

With such a vocation for man we now comprehend also why it is in precisely the account of his creation, as the crown of the creation, that for the first time the Word of God rises to a poetical song of joy. The form of Hebrew poetry is that of thought-rhyme, parallelism of members and verses, not of sounds. Now therefore the Holy Scripture celebrates the creation of the *tri*-unity, man, this wonderful act of the *tri*une God, in poetic strain, through a *three*fold rhyme, a threefold "God created:"

And God *created* man after his own image;
After the image of God *created* he him;
As man and wife *created* he them. (Gen. 1: 27).

(2) MAN AS THE IMAGE OF GOD

But the true God-resemblance of man does not really consist in that he, as consisting of spirit, soul, and body, is a triunity in unity and thus reflects the triune being of his Creator;

nor in that his body is already in advance formed after the likeness of the glorified resurrection body of the Son of God, which, by virtue of the super-temporality of God, had already been eternally existent as the prototype in the mind of the Creator (Phil. 3: 21);

but it consists in this, that he, as a spiritual and moral being, gives expression in a creaturely manner to the *inward* characteristics of God.

Two sides are to be observed of the Bible teaching as to the

God-resemblance of man: a resemblance that can be lost, and one that cannot be lost. For, on the one hand, this God-resemblance is indicated as something that was lost through the fall and can only be regained through the redemption (Col. 3: 10; Eph. 4: 24; Rom. 8: 29; I Cor. 15: 49; II Cor. 3: 18), and, on the other hand, there is still recognized an image of God even in fallen man (Gen. 9: 6; I Cor. 11: 7; Acts 17: 28; Jas. 3: 9). First, man is an image of God in the wider sense in so far that he is in general appointed to be for eternity a moral, indestructible personality, with self consciousness, understanding, reason, a power of moral judgment, conscience, and freedom of will; to which is added his vocation to rule, through which he, as ruler of the earth, is to be an image of the Lord as Ruler of the universe (Gen. 1: 26–28). This is the image of God as a *plan,* as the essential feature of human nature in itself, without which man would simply cease to be man.

But actually and inwardly this comes to pass only if a man does truly reflect the spiritual and moral nature of God by his practical condition of holiness and love: this is the image of God in the narrower sense of condition and possession. The image of God in the first formal sense did not perish through the fall of man; yet as an inward and material possession it is lost. "The wheels of the mechanism indeed remain; but its running is disturbed. The flower and its calyx are still there; but its tinted enamel and its scent are gone." Hence the necessity of the redemption.

(*a*) *The Endowment.* God Himself is the prototype. Spirituality, liberty, and blessedness form the three fundamental characteristics of His holy, loving nature. He would now in man, as in a copy, be glorified. Therefore God endowed him with the three powers of his spiritual and soulish inward being. He gave him will, intellect, and feeling. That he might partake of the freedom of holy love He granted to him, *will*; that he should in true knowledge mirror the divine spirituality, *intellect*; that he should rejoice in the divine blessedness, *feelings*.

(*b*) *The Sanctification.* For this reason the goal of all sanctification is described in the New Testament in corresponding manner. As regards the spiritual power of *thought* it says that we have put on the new man which "is being renewed unto full *knowledge* after the 'image' of him who has created it" (Col. 3: 10). In reference to the moral condition of the *will* it is said that the new man "after the 'image' of God is created in true righteousness and purity" (Eph. 4: 24). And finally, as concerns the joyful experience of the glory of God, which with the whole personality—its thinking and willing—includes at the same time the joy of the *feelings*—we read, "But we all, with unveiled face beholding the glory of the Lord, become transfigured, according to the same 'image,' from glory to glory, as through the Lord, the Spirit" (II Cor. 3: 18).

(*c*) *The Mediator*.   But all these three rays unite in one, in the image of Jesus Christ, the Son of God, our Lord: "for those whom he has foreknown them he also afore-appointed to this, to become like to the image of his Son.   He should be the firstborn among many brethren" (Rom. 8: 29).   The image of the Father is none other than the only begotten Son (Col. 1: 15; Heb. 1: 3).   In *this* image God created man according to *His* image.   Therefore in us the image of the Father reaches its exhibition in the image of the Son.   In the Son we are appointed to be sons.   Therein consists our resemblance to God (I John 3: 2).   Christ, the historical centre of salvation, is, at the same time, the prototype of the ultimate perfection of the universe.

Yet not in a moral sense only is conformity to Christ the final purpose of redemption, but also as regards the future spiritual body.   Therefore has Christ entered into the glory with a glorified human body (John 20: 14–29; Acts 1: 11), and therefore also we expect Him back from heaven as Saviour, as the One Who will "conform the body of our humiliation to the body of his glory" (Phil. 3: 21).   For "the first man is of the earth, from dust, the second man is from heaven.   And as the heavenly so are also the heavenly ones.   And as we have borne the image which is of dust, so shall we also bear the image of the heavenly" (I Cor. 15: 47–49).

(*d*) *The Goal*.   Consequently, when this spiritual body comes (Rom. 8: 23) the goal of all salvation will be completely attained. As truth, righteousness, and peace, the inner nature of the kingdom of God will unfold itself (Rom. 14: 17), and glory will be in all those who then awake in the image of their God.   In the holiness of their will, the wisdom of their knowledge, and the happiness of their feelings, the freedom and spirituality and bliss of the Creator will be perfectly displayed, and the three powers of their soul will become for all eternity a glorifying in the tri-unity of a creature of the triune self-determination of the eternal God.

But to all this there is added something special.   By the creation of man God had manifestly not only the thought that he, like the angels of heaven, as a pure and happy being, should glorify Him, but, inasmuch as He entrusted to him the earth as his sphere of rule, He also gave to him a special task which extended over this his dwelling place.

(3) MAN AS RULER OF THE EARTH

"Be fruitful and increase yourselves, people the earth and subjugate and rule it" (Gen. 1: 28).   In these words the royal appointment of the human race is plainly declared.   The capacity for this is the human spirit, which reveals itself above all in speech.

(*a*) *The Beginning.* What is a word? A sound, a note, a tone which goes out of the mouth! Yet much more! A conveyor of a motion of the spirit, an instrument for manifesting the intelligence, a sign, a sound-symbol of an activity of the soul. Only through the gift of the spirit and speech man becomes really man. Only thus is it that he receives the capacity of inward development.

By speech Adam began in Paradise the exercise of his royal authority. At the very beginning, even before the creation of the woman, God Himself brought to him the creatures of the air and the earth, so that he, discerning their natures, should give them suitable names (Gen. 2: 20): and thus was their "king" at the very beginning crowned by the Creator, and speech became, spiritually speaking, the "sceptre of mankind."

Thus speech is not, as unbelieving philosophers assert, an invention which man first made little by little within human society for the purpose of mutual intercourse. For God "spoke" to Adam even before He had given him Eve as helper, and in like manner Adam, before the creation of the woman, made use of speech in the naming of the animals. Rather therefore is speech an "instinctive emanation of the spirit" which, "passing out through the mouth, is a perceptible revelation of the intelligence" (Plato), "audible spirit" (Bettex). As an aptitude inherent in creation the gift of speech was present in man from the beginning; but it needed to be freed and released, and this God effected by giving to man the task of naming the animals.

What was the original language in Paradise cannot now be determined.

(*b*) *The Purport* of the command. But the earth—at least exterior to Paradise—in spite of its creation and government by the Most High, was a region that had not yet entirely reached its goal. Indeed, it appears that the condition of disharmony that with the fall of Satan had invaded this earthly realm (Rom. 8: 20, 21) was still existing everywhere in the earth outside Paradise at the time man was created. At any rate, the earliest Bible history indicates that the earth itself, in spite of the divine new beginning which set in with the creation of man, was not yet absolutely withdrawn from the operation of demonic powers.

This is proved by the command of God to man, not only to cultivate the garden of Paradise, but to "guard" it; as also by the fact that his temptation came through a hostile power opposed to God, appearing *on the earth* and making use of an animal of the earth. Furthermore, had the whole earth been everywhere a place of life and highest perfection, there would have been no need at all for a Paradise! But evidently the first created man, in ability and appointment, stood much superior to the earth, and therefore for him a special region must be prepared, so that he should have a residence corresponding to his rank and to the dignity of his calling.   So the planting of the garden of Paradise, regarded from the standpoint of the Bible, is a witness to the yet imperfect character of the earth outside of Paradise.

With this agrees the witness of geology.   For scientifically it is clearly to be recognized that many present forms of vegetable and animal life have an extraordinary resemblance, indeed, some of them, almost exact likeness, to the corresponding forms of life of the Tertiary Age, and even sometimes to the Chalk and Limestone Ages, thus standing evidently in organic connexion with them.   Now if one would teach that at the time of the first man the earth beyond Paradise was freed from all death and all disharmony—which the Bible does not expressly teach—then one must draw the inevitable yet most highly improbable conclusion that the animal species of the Tertiary Age which are like (!) those of the present day—we think here especially of the flesh-eating animals—were first destroyed, or as regards their instincts, their forms of feeding, and consequently their whole bodily structure, were transformed anatomically and physiologically, and then, after the fall of man, were once more created anew or changed back into a condition which essentially corresponded to their Tertiary condition.   But to accept this is a much greater difficulty than to regard as accurate the connexion of the present forms of animal and plant life with the fossils.

Therefore it is easier to believe that during the time of Paradise the species of animals outside of Paradise remained in their former partly wild state, and that if man had exercised and constantly extended his function as ruler in accordance with God's plan, the animal world would have attained at last to a final liberation from the bands of savagery and death.

Thus the extending of man's rule on the earth, provided he remained subject to God, signified a drawing of all things earthly into the sphere of the moral world-purposes, an increasing resumption of the earth for God and therewith a progressive leading forward of the creation to redemption and perfection. Paradise was thus the fixed point from which the uplifting of Nature into the sphere of the spirit should take its beginning. It was appointed by God to that purpose, "so that from here the whole earth should develop into a Paradise.   The garden is the Holy of holies, Eden the holy place, the whole surrounding earth the vestibule and court.   The climax is, that the whole shall be transformed into the glorified likeness of that Holiest."

In this regard Adam himself counted not only as an individual, but at the same time as the primary ancestor and organic representative of the whole of his descendants, then already seen in principle "in" him (I Cor. 15: 22; Rom. 5: 12–21).   Therefore is it said first "Be fruitful and multiply and people the earth", and only afterward, "and subdue it to yourselves and rule it" (Gen. 1: 28).   So then the Paradise garden is beginning and end, start and goal, basis, programme, and type of the whole task of man on earth.

But this could be attained only by the man being placed in a moral conflict with the possibility of yielding to evil.   Only in a conflict could he "conquer;" only so could he obtain the crown of the "overcomer."   On the other hand Satan, the adversary of God, would not allow the work of his enemy, this man created pure and good, to go unattacked.   Thus, at the very beginning, there forthwith opened a highly significant struggle, and Paradise became

III.   THE ARENA OF A MIGHTY CONFLICT

With this its mysterious background it entered into the cosmic frame of universal super-history.   Behind Paradise stands the star world of God and the greatest revolt that has ever taken place, the conflict between Satan and God.

According to the principle of development the object of the temptation was adapted to the childlike intelligence of young mankind.   Therefore the command not to eat of the fruit of the tree.

Foolish indeed is the objection that to eat of a forbidden fruit was no more than nibbling a dainty on the sly and so a *small* sin; for to the first pair it was not simply to test the flavour of the fruit, but they wished, behind the back of the Creator, by a forbidden way, to rise to equal exaltation with Him (Gen. 3: 5). The prohibition as to eating from the tree was thus essentially spiritual, inasmuch as it established the absolute authority of God over men, and this as the true good.

Through not eating the fruit of the tree, that is, through victory in the temptation, Adam's moral consciousness, through the exercise of his freedom of choice, should attain to freedom of authority, and at the same time his service to the earth as its ruler should therewith become effective.   Each victory over temptation would have ripened and deepened his inner life.   More and more would he have recognized the good and seen through the evil, and would have grown out of the condition of childlike *innocence* into one of adult ripeness, of victorious *holiness,* with an attainment of a perception of good and evil like to that of God. "This tree of the knowledge of good and evil was become Adam's altar and pulpit, from which he was to render due obedience to God, recognize God's word and will and give Him thanks; and had Adam not fallen this tree would have been like a temple and cathedral" (Luther).   Thus, then, the tree was a sign of the rule of God over man and the subjection of man to

God. Even in the prohibition God wished far more to give than to withhold. The tree of knowledge had consequently in a double manner a divine purpose; it was a means in the hand of God for the education of man and by this for the transfiguration of the earth.

But then came the sin. In Eden man lost his Eden, and Paradise, this dwelling of delight and loveliness, became

IV. The Place of a Tragic Collapse

The serpent had promised man the knowledge of good and evil, and in a distorted form he has kept his word. But "instead of perceiving the evil from the free height of the good he perceived the good from the deep abyss of the evil." According to God's plan man through victory in temptation should have perceived what good is and what evil would be; but through sin he subsequently perceived what evil is and what good would have been. And because at the tree of knowledge he had wantonly sinned, he must now also be cut off from the tree of life (Gen. 3: 22, 23). Death entered the human race, and in Paradise began man's hell.

Yet man could never forget his native place. All peoples have sung of "Paradise Lost" and hoping and waiting have watched for its return. Therefore Paradise is

V. The Longed-for Goal of a Waiting Humanity

And in fact their hopes will not be disappointed. The final history will return to the opening history, and as at the beginning of the ancient earth there existed an earthly paradise, so at last on the new earth there will be a heavenly paradise (Rev. 22: 1–5). Moreover, after the Fall the Lord permitted the high calling of man to continue. Even now the glorifying of the earth and the perfecting of mankind still remain eternally connected.

Therefore the Scripture intimates repeatedly a deep connexion in the history of salvation between the earth and mankind. "Thus Paradise corresponded to the man in innocence, the land under curse to him as the fallen man. So to Israel, as the typical people of God, corresponded the Promised Land as the type of the future Paradise. Similarly, to each religious and moral decline of that people there corresponded a darkening and desolating of its land (Deut. 28: 15ff.; Joel 2; Zeph. 1: 14ff.), even as to each period of spiritual reviving, there corresponded an uplifting of nature (Deut. 28: 8ff.; Psa. 72: 16, 17). Likewise at the death of Christ the sun became darkened, and the renewing of the earth announced itself at His death by the earthquake."

Similarly with the increase of sin in the time of Antichrist there will come an increased distress over nature (Rev. 16: 1ff.); but in the Millennial kingdom nature will be blessed with the whole of mankind (Isa. 11: etc.). Finally, with the close of human history the old universe perishes as to its form (II Pet. 3: 10; Rev. 21), in order that, with the glorifying of redeemed humanity, there may come a glorified "new earth" (Rev. 21: 1).

Therefore "the earnest expectation of the creation awaits the manifestation of the sons of God" (Rom. 8: 19), and therefore can it be brought "to the sharing of the liberty" only when "the children of God are in the state of glory" (Rom. 8: 19–22).

In Christ at last will mankind attain its blessed goal. He appeared on earth and completed His work. He humbled Himself, went to the cross and bore there the sins of mankind. Thereupon He ascended to heaven and now sits at the right hand of the Father, until at length He shall usher in the day on which He will present to Himself and to the Father His own people glorified (Eph. 5: 27).

Yet as the Son of Man He has perfected here the work which the Father gave Him to do. As man He bore here the crown of thorns which the unredeemed land, standing under the curse, offered Him; and therefore as man will He some day, as Head of His church, reign over the same earth, though then redeemed and freed from the curse (Eph. 1: 22). The *Divine* Redeemer became man and as such redeemed the *human* ruler of the earth, united him then to Himself in eternal, inseparable oneness, and at the same time effected the redemption of the earth. This is the way which grace found. Thus, then, the old vocation of man remains, and yet is it filled with wholly new content. In Christ as its head mankind attains the purpose of its appointment. As the last Adam (I Cor. 15: 45, 21, 22; Rom. 5: 12–21) He is for it centre, crown, and star. The whole human race is "a circle, and in the course of the outworking of salvation Jesus Christ is more and more wrought out as the Centre of this circle."

But it is one of the deepest secrets of the counsel of the grace of God that, in order to reach His great world-embracing objective, He did not set man aside when the latter, through his sin and fall, proved unworthy of his high vocation. "The gifts by grace and the calling of God are irrevocable" (Rom. 11: 29). As with Israel in the smaller sphere so here in the great, this note sounds alike, through sin and misery, destruction and salvation. In spite of all, the perfecting of creation is to be bound up with man. Though its development may proceed along other ways than it would have done had man not fallen by sin, yet the final purpose remains. And because it remains the way and the goal of God that man shall be the channel of blessing for the creation, therefore can the devil be cast into the lake of fire, and there be a new heaven and a new earth, only *after* the great white throne, that is, after the conclusion of the revealed history of the redemption of mankind (Rev. 20: 21; comp. 20: 11–15).

SIN AND GRACE

Man was great in his fall, but God was still greater in His mercy (Rom. 5: 20). Even as a sinner man remained an object of the Divine love (John 3: 16).

Nevertheless the fall of man brought with it a change of all world conditions. New principles were demanded which henceforth governed the whole history of mankind.

I. The Principle of Redemption

Without a fall human progress would have been a gradual ascent. It might well have been a history of ever increasing blessing but not a history of redemption. All would have been an uninterrupted upward development. But now in place of the capacity for the developing of man there entered the possibility and necessity of his redemption. Henceforth it was no more a matter of the *evolution* of his slumbering powers but of the *revolution* of the spirit by acts of divine love and a new creation. Thus the significance of the fall lies in the change of the determining foundation principles of all human development.

In fact, man was not fallen beyond hope. He remained redeemable, and God became to him Redeemer. This possibility is founded upon two facts. Man had not himself invented sin. His fall had not consisted in that he had acted from within, out of himself, purely by reason of inspiration completely his own, but in virtue of a temptation from without. Otherwise he would, of course, have become a self-originator of sin and thereby a devil. And even as he had not produced the evil either before or in his fall, so also he did not after his fall identify himself with it. At once he felt sin to be something foreign to him and made a distinction between himself and the evil. This is shown by his immediate feeling of shame and the covering of his nakedness with fig leaves (Gen. 3: 7, 10). This first attempt at overcoming the evil was indeed in vain; but it was an unmistakable sign that the man was not willing to succumb to shamelessness and baseness; that though he had acted against his conscience he did not add to this a deliberate killing thereof.

Those fig leaves thereby became a direct embodiment and symbol of his flight from the evil; and the sense of shame, through the feeling of guilt and impotence, became an as yet unconscious defence against the service of the flesh and thereby the first reaction against the might of sin, inasmuch as the man, though not able to overcome the evil, at least sought to flee from it.

II.   THE PRINCIPLE OF DIVINE SELF-JUSTIFICATION

But sin makes blind and man cannot perceive his corruption (Eph. 4: 18; Rev. 3: 17).   He believes in the good within himself and deifies his own nature (II Thess. 2: 3, 4): "Mankind is deity seen from below."   So long as he believes that, he will never lay hold of the redemption (Matt. 9: 12).

Therefore must opportunity be afforded to test his strength in all directions, so that he may attain at last to a recognition of his impotence.   Human collapse must become the method of divine reconstruction, which involves the many thousands of years in the plan of salvation and the manifold forms of the historical revelation in epochs and aeons.   At the same time, each period of the plan of salvation has necessarily the revealing of human failure as its goal, and the variegated distinctiveness and progressiveness of the whole have their educative purpose in this, that each of these dispensations shall set forth from a different angle the bankruptcy of the natural man.

Thus will all the moral powers of the individual and all social forms of the community be finally proved insufficient, and God's plan of salvation in Christ will be seen to be not merely the only plan, but as the essential, the only possible plan.   Thereby will God stand before His whole creation, in heaven and on earth, as justified, in that He ordained this way of salvation and no other.   The history of salvation will thus be an historical self-justification of God, an "historical Theodicy," and the course of revelation will constitute the proof of its own necessity; even as it is written; "so that thou [God] mayest be justified when thou passest sentence, and mayest stand forth as victor if one disputes with thee" (Rom. 3: 4).

III.   THE PRINCIPLE OF HUMAN COLLAPSE

In fact, man could not more completely make manifest his downfall than he has done and will yet do.
If God gives him self-determination,
    he falls into licentiousness;[1]
    in the epoch of the testing of freedom.
If God gives him authority,
    he proceeds to oppress;[2]
    in the epoch after Noah.

[1] Especially in Lamech (Gen. 4: 23, 24).

[2] As in Nimrod, the Hamite, the founder of the original Babylonian empire (Gen. 10: 6–12), whose race, according to Gen. 9: 5, was abandoned to unblessedness, and indeed in Canaan was to be "servants of all servants."

If God gives him promises;
    he sinks into unbelief;[1]
    in the epoch of the Patriarchs and the age following.
If God shows him his unrighteousness,[2]
    he exalts himself in self-righteousness;[3]
    in the epoch of the Law.
If God gives him Christ,
    then he chooses for himself Antichrist;[4]
    in the epoch of the gospel.
If God gives him the King,
    then he follows the Rebel;[5]
    in the epoch of the Millennium.

Thus is man in continual rebellion against God, and just as Israel was on a small scale so is mankind on a large scale a people "whose heart will always with determination go astray" (Psa. 95: 10). It is no wonder that all dispensations end with Divine judgment:

The period of Paradise—
    with the expulsion from the Garden;
The period of testing by freedom—
    with the Flood;
The period after Noah—
    with Babel and the setting aside of the nations;
The period of the Law—
    with the scattering of Israel;
The period of the church—
    with the tribulation under Antichrist;
The period of the kingdom of glory—
    with destruction and fiery ruin (Rev. 20: 9).

But then, when all conceivable possibilities are exhausted and the world-kingdom has used up all its forces, the kingdom of God will appear triumphantly (Rev. 11: 15), and in the new heaven and on the new earth will righteousness dwell eternally (II Pet. 3: 13).

IV. THE PRINCIPLE OF THE HOLY REMNANT

But if this goal is to be reached, then the catastrophic judgments during the interval must never be total. Otherwise the connexion between that which is past and that which is to come would be lost, and the new which should appear would be something independent and other, but not the continuation and advance of the former. That would have signified before all

[1] See especially Israel in the desert, ten times disobedient and murmuring, at the end of the patriarchal epoch of the promises of faith.
[2] The Law was a mirror of sin (Rom. 3: 20; 7: 7).
[3] See especially the Pharisees (Rom. 2: 17–21).
[4] John 5: 43; Rev. 13.
[5] See Gog and Magog (Rev. 20: 7–10).

the universe nothing else than an undisguised declaration of the bankruptcy of God, that all His former principles for the education of humanity had collapsed.

Therefore must there be always a remnant saved out of the judgments (Isa. 10: 21, 22; 11: 11; Ezek. 5: 1–4 (esp. ver. 3); I Kings 19: 18; Rom. 11: 1–10), so as to be the foundation of a further development. In the midst of the judgment of death there must constantly be established a new life ever superior to the evil. Only so could the unity of the whole be preserved, and the future be joined organically with the past and the present.

This is the significance of the godly in the world. In the judgment they are the agents of each fresh beginning and thereby of the entire unity of the plan of salvation. It is only through the "little flock" that the great salvation receives its firm coherency and its organic continuity. Only these, the insignificant of the world, are the human foundation for redemption becoming feasible. Without them every item of revelation would fall to pieces. Seemingly a superfluous factor in world affairs, actually they are "the great fellow-workers of God through whom the world, as to its continuance and its final organization, is determined. Their walk with God saves the world's future." Thereby they become the real carriers on of history in general, and, in the Scripture, of world chronology.

Genesis gives historical numerations in the genealogies in the *chosen* line only, especially Seth–Noah (ch. 5) and Shem–Abraham (ch. 11: 10, ff.; see also 25: 20; 37: 2). In the ancestral tables of the *non*-chosen lines there are no historical numbers. (Cain, Gen. 4: 17–26; the table of the peoples, ch. 10; Ishmael, 25: 12–16; Esau 36: 1–8). For God, the history of the little flock is the only "history."

So these two lines run through all ages; the ripening of the great "world" for the tempest of judgment and the preparing of the "little flock" for deliverance out of misery and distress.

This people stands forth among the peoples as a rock in the sea. Even the gates of the world of the dead will not overcome it (Matt. 16: 18); for with *its* stability stands or falls all hope for the world, and behind all hope stands for evermore the covenant faithfulness of the Redeemer.

Therefore though the oak of human civilization must again and again be felled by the axe of the judgment of God, nevertheless this "root-stem" continually survives, the "holy seed" out of which new life springs forth (Isa. 6: 13, and 11: 1), the "little flock" which receives the eternal kingdom (Luke 12: 32). So out of the night of judgment there continually flames forth the early blush of the new day, and in the tempest clouds of wrath appears the brilliant rainbow of the divine Redeemer (comp. Gen. 9: 13).

V. THE PRINCIPLE OF THE SECOND BEFORE THE FIRST

But for this purpose God always chooses the nothings (I Cor.
1: 26, 27).   Only thus is the self-praise of the sinner destroyed.
And for this very reason it is a pervading characteristic of the whole
course of redemption that God keeps on choosing the younger before the elder, sets the smaller in priority to the greater, and chooses
the second before the first:

not Cain, but Abel, and his substitute Seth;
not Japheth, but Shem;
not Ishmael, but Isaac;
not Esau, but Jacob;
not Manasseh, but Ephraim (Gen. 48: 14);
not Aaron, but Moses (Exod. 7: 7);
not Eliab, but David (1 Sam. 16: 6–13);
not the first king, but the second (i.e. not Saul, but David);
not the old covenant, but the new (Heb. 8: 13);
not Israel, but the church; and above all,
not the first Adam, but the last Adam (I Cor. 15: 45).

Thus God continually "takes away the first that he may establish the second" (Heb. 10: 9).   He chooses for Himself the weak
of the world, so as to put to shame the strong (I Cor. 1: 27).   He
calls the last and makes it first, and the first becomes the last
(Matt. 19: 30).   And all this comes to pass so that "no flesh shall
glory before him," but that "he who glories let him glory in the
Lord" (I Cor. 1: 29, 31).

VI. THE PRINCIPLE OF CONTINUOUS REFORMATION

And yet, what took place?   Out of the grace-endowed
beginning of life and strength there issued always a race full of
apostasy.   What the fathers won by faith was mostly lost by the
children as early as the third generation (Jud. 2: 7), and Jerusalem
become Babel must finally, exactly as the former "world," be
given up to the judgment of destruction.

But in order that, in spite of all this, the Divine plan should
not fail, within this shallow circle (meanwhile become great,
whose fathers were the standard-bearers of an *earlier* reformation),
there must of necessity now be called a new and smaller circle,
who should become the present transmitters of the revelation, so
that in them the reformation of the past should, as it were, be
requickened into a *new* reformation.   And because in the course
of time this is again and again accomplished, therefore the whole
process of redemption is governed by the principle of a continuous reformation, and the history of salvation is like a curve
with very marked zigzag movements in detail, but which nevertheless on the whole goes uninterruptedly upward.

VII. THE PRINCIPLE OF PROGRESSIVENESS IN THE HISTORY OF SALVATION

But a fresh Divine beginning is never merely a return to the old. In each reformation born out of collapse lay at the same time the seed of a life-programme for the future. Revelation and development are in no case opposites but belong together. In the sphere of the Bible, as elsewhere, there is an ascent from lower to higher, from twilight to clearness (Matt. 13: 16, 17; I Pet. 1: 10, 11; John 16: 12). In Abram God chose a single person; in Jacob this grew to a family; at Sinai this became a nation. In the present age God is gathering to Himself a super-national people *out of* all nations (Acts 15: 14); in the coming kingdom of God there will be a universal fellowship of peoples (Isa. 2: 2–4; 19: 25); and finally there will be a new heaven and a new earth (Rev. 21: 1).

But this is all God's work, not human "progress," no ascent of the creature out of the depths into the heights, but a condescension of the Creator out of the heights into the depths; no development of human powers until the unfolding of the highest, ideal humanity, but a leading on to divine, eternal goals through mighty acts of Divine intervention in love and power. Thus then, through Divine acting from above to beneath, will the earthly being be led from beneath to above, until finally God's glory is manifested in things created and everything earthly is transfigured in the heavenly (Matt. 27: 51; John 3, 13).

CHAPTER III

THE DAWN OF SALVATION

THE beginning of mankind has been compared to a sunny morning. Coming out of eternity, time, as it were, was holding happiness in its hands. In the blessedness of Paradise God had united heaven and earth. But then came sin. As a tempest black as night it broke in devastatingly and drove all this morning splendour out of the history of time. Thenceforth the earth stood under the shadow of death.

Severe were the consequences of the Divine judgment. By his disobedience man had denied the sovereignty of God and had thrust the Lord of all from the throne of his heart. Sin is mutiny against God, revolt against the Highest, rebellion of the individual will of the creature against the Divine universal order. The human "I" now stepped into the place of the dethroned God and became the king on the throne. According to God's plan man was to be, so to say, a spiritual Copernicus, like a point on the circumference, dependent upon God as his sun and centre. But instead of this, he had now fallen into the error of the Ptolemaic system, and set his own "*Ego*" in the centre of his life, around which everything else, God and the world, must rotate. "Therefore has God given him over to his *Ego*. Man is now wholly captive to his *Ego*. He expects his happiness, his redemption to come from his *Ego*. He justifies his *Ego*. He lauds his *Ego*, and all his thoughts circle around his *Ego*."

"And with this *Ego* there links itself the world which man in his delusion has preferred to God. With the *Ego* the world at the same time mounts the throne in him, and *God gives men over to the world also*. And because the *Ego* and the world cannot fill in man the empty place of God there sets in this raging hunger of the human soul, which torments itself, the hunger for self-assertion and for the world, for possessions and pleasure. This boundless insatiable hunger is a standing proof that at some time *God* had satisfied the human heart, that the human heart is intended for God."

i. *In detail also* God extends the judgment over the sinner.

The woman was included as to her highest calling, as mother and wife (Gen. 3: 16). Her smaller circle of family and house stood henceforth under the pressure of all kinds of cares.

The punishment struck the man in his masculine calling, in the wider circle of *his* work and his breadwinning (Gen. 3: 17–19). But in the man the calling of the human race *in itself* was simultaneously involved, for Adam, as head also of the woman, was

at the same time the representative of the whole race. Laborious
work, sickness, suffering, and death were from that time onward
the sorrowful lot of all men. At the moment of the sin spiritual
death entered (Gen. 2: 17), and with it also, under the Divine
judgment, freedom from bodily death was forfeited. The spirit
having severed itself from *its* centre, God, the life powers of
body and soul, in consequence of the judgment of God, tore
themselves loose from *their* centre, the spirit, and the end of this
separation of body, soul, and spirit is the death of the body
(Rom. 6: 23). Forthwith "life" is merely a gradual dying, and
birth is the beginning of death.

Before the Fall the human body, if not strictly immortal, was
at least only capable of mortality, but not mortal. To die was
no impossibility, but also no necessity. As Augustine put it,
man possessed both the possibility not to sin and not to die
(*posse non peccare et mori*), and also the possibility to sin and to
die (*posse peccare et mori*). Through victory in temptation he
was to ascend to the *im*possibility of sinning and dying (out of
the *posse non peccare et mori* into the *non posse peccare et mori*).
But after his overthrow he finds himself in the *im*possibility *not*
to sin and to die, that is, he *must* sin (he is in the *non posse non
peccare et non mori*).

But because Adam, as the ancestor of mankind, was at the
same time also its organic representative, death established itself
upon all his descendants as well. The fall was universal (Rom.
5: 12–21; I Cor. 15: 21).

Because of the propagation of mankind as spirit, soul, and
body there exists a mysterious organic connexion between each
individual and the whole human race, and by consequence with
Adam as the ancestor and original type of the whole. Each
individual is a part of his progenitors and a part of his progeny,
a point of transit of the blood stream of his parents and ancestors.
"The soul of all flesh is in the blood" (Lev. 17: 11, 14).

Hence the emphasis upon the genealogical trees in the
Scripture (e.g. Gen. 5; I Chron. 1–9), and the significance of the
laws of inheritance in family and people. Therefore also arise
the characteristic similarities and differences of nations and races,
and the corresponding and yet distinguishable inheritance of
thought and feeling from people to people, that is, from soul
to soul. Hence also the transmission of the imperfections and
failings in character of the ancestors, the advance of evil from
generation to generation, the radical, central, total corruption of
all, the root-sickness of the human soul, the lost state of each
individual, and the poisoned condition of the entire organism;
that is, original sin. "There is none who does good, not even
one" (Psa. 14: 3; comp. 51: 7; John 3: 6; Gen. 8: 21).

The sum total of all natural men forms an enormous racially

articulated organism, and each individual, through his mere birth, is inescapably a member thereof. He is "in" Adam (I Cor. 15: 22). Humanity is not simply a numerical total of many distinct individual persons, but one single colossal "body," which, according to its origin and nature, in a myriad manifold and differentiated branches, sets forth its first father, Adam. This involves the all-inclusiveness of the fall and the universality of sin (Rom. 5: 12; 3: 10–12, 23), with the necessity of the new birth of each individual (John 3: 3), and the incarnation of Christ as the Saviour and Redeemer (Rom. 5: 12–21).

ii. *Nature.* But inasmuch as Adam through his disobedience had denied the lordship of his Creator over himself, he had at the same time shattered his own lordship over the creation. It is true that his lordship in itself continued to exist (for man's vocation as ruler forms part of his unforfeitable likeness to God) (see pp. 41, 42, and p. 65); but the exercise and enhancement of this lordship plunges man thus severed from God into ever new difficulties. What should have been to him a blessing becomes his destruction. One has only to think of the effects of many new inventions. Thus the very height of his calling results in so much the deeper ruin.

And yet more. The earthly creation *in itself* had become involved. "Is the head with God, so are the members also. Does the crown of creation fall in the dust, so will the subjects also be thrown down in the crash." This is demanded by the organic connexion between spirit and Nature. From that there follows, with the entrance of the Fall, a "fixed association between spiritual and bodily distress, between inward and outward injury, between world-guilt and world-sorrow, between human sin and groaning creation."

With this corresponds also the diagnosis of modern medical science and psychotherapy; "Severe injury in the psychical [soulish] realm effects parallel conditions in the physical realm, as also psychical [soulish] relief can assist in releasing bodily restraints."

The material object of the temptation was taken from the vegetable kingdom, the instrument of the tempter from the animal kingdom. Therefore on account of man both of these realms, vegetable and animal, remain under the curse (Gen. 3: 17); and the creation, which through man should have advanced to redemption and perfection, remains until now subject to vanity.

Thus creation presents today that mysterious hybrid disharmonious condition, which in its conflict between happiness and unhappiness, wisdom and absurdity, purposeful adaptation and confusion, seems to render equally impossible both faith in God and denial of God.

"The world is so beautiful that for a time we can forget God and our guilt before Him, and the world is so terrible that we might on this account often despair of God."

"The world speaks to us as a revelation of God; it also stands rigidly before us as a riddle of God." Hence also the discord in the common human experience of nature, and man's wavering between glorifying nature and despising it, between happiness in nature and alienation from it, between worship of nature and treating it with contempt. The gospel first relaxes this tension by its message of the transfiguration of Nature, through the resolving of all the dissonances which now vibrate throughout Nature, by the bringing in of world-perfection and the coming of the spiritual body.

Jubilation and lamentation, kindness and cruelty, the joy of life, and the grief of death—this all now convulses the whole world-organism. At present Nature is like a sublime temple in a ruined condition, whose deeply significant inscriptions have been maliciously caricatured by a hostile hand. And man, the ruler of the earth, is doubly degenerate: "Either, in his beastliness, he becomes to the creature a Satan; or in servile fear, he kneels before the creature in worship. The deification of Nature begins where the knowledge of God disappears," and the "lord" becomes both slave and tyrant.

But throughout the creation there sounds a painful groaning, as it were a softly-spoken prayer. "With its melancholy inspired charm it is like a bride who, already completely adorned for the marriage hour, has seen her bridegroom die on the appointed day. There she now stands, with the fresh garland on her head, in bridal attire, but her eyes are full of tears" (Schelling, in his Lecture on the Philosophy of the Revelation).

And yet not without hope is she subjected to her groaning (Rom. 8: 20). Like a captive but expectant virgin, who stands on the seashore with uplifted head watching for her deliverer from a distant land, so does she yearn "in tense expectation" for redemption from her bondage to vanity.[1] "We know that the whole creation groans together and until now lies together in birth pangs" (Rom. 8: 22).

But what, then, shall she bring forth? The new heaven and the new earth!

Then all her longings will be stilled and her dumb prayer be answered. "In that day I will answer, saith Jehovah. I will *answer* the heaven, and this will *answer* the earth, and the earth will *answer* the corn and the new wine, and they, they will *answer* Jezreel" (Hos. 2: 21, 22).

[1] The Greek word *apokaradokia*, rendered [A.V. earnest expectation], by Luther "anxious waiting", signified literally an intense gaze with uplifted head (kara = head), the Greek prefix *apo* emphasizing the intensity. Paul compares the creation to a human form keeping watch with strained expectation—an ingenious basis for an artistic delineation of the hope.

But the very sorrow of the earth joins to serve the redemption of man. For just because it cannot offer him what he expects from it, it sets him free from his false hopes and fosters his yearning after the lost paradise. Thus shall the disappointments of the earthly help to liberate man for the longing after the heavenly, so that in the end he can confess: "See, to my health there came bitter grief" (Isa. 38: 17).

iii. *The Judgment upon the Serpent.* The dawn of salvation displays itself most clearly of all in the sentence upon the serpent (Gen. 3: 15). In this passage the first promise of the gospel shows how grace, streaming through the gloom of wrath, has turned the curse upon the serpent into the promise for man. At the moment when the sinner [Adam] stands before God, as the accused awaiting sentence of condemnation, no *direct* promise can, of course, be given. Nevertheless to him, listening and trembling, the sentence of destruction upon his destroyer must be a ray of hope for himself. Thus indeed was "the front aspect of the original gospel, judgment, but the reverse signified promise for mankind."

At first the meaning of the prophecy is still obscure; for if Satan is represented by the serpent, then the serpent's "seed" can be nothing else than the totality of all demonic and human beings who, as the God-resisting "brood of vipers" (Matt. 3: 7; 12: 34; 23: 33), would stand on the side of the Devil—thus not an individual but a plurality of beings. But then the harmony of the parallel and opposed clause demands that the seed of the woman also shall not be a single person but likewise a plurality of descendants, namely, the totality of all those who, believing, would stand on the ground of the promise given to the woman.

Only *indirectly* could the earliest of mankind gain the idea that the posterity of the woman would some day head up in a single individual. For the final sentence of the prophecy said that the *seed* of the woman would crush not only the *seeds* of the serpent but its very head, the serpent itself, which perhaps allowed it to be discerned that the woman's seed itself would also at some time culminate in a head, an individual.

Only today, looking backwards, and instructed through the interpretation of later prophecies and fulfilments (especially Isa. 7: 14; Matt. 1: 21–23; Mic. 5: 2; Gal. 4: 4), do we see that God here, for the first time—although not exclusively, yet inclusively, indeed chiefly—spake of Christ His Son (Rom. 16: 20; I John 3: 8). He, as the centre of humanity, is at the same time the centre of the woman's seed. Only from this do we understand why God did not speak of a man's seed but of a woman's seed (comp. Matt. 1: 18): and at the same time, by this prophetic word concerning the stinging of the heel and the crushing of the head, commenced that wonderful series of Divine utterances which declared beforehand "the sufferings appointed for Messiah (comp. the 'stinging of the heel') and His glories to follow thereupon" (comp. the "crushing of the head") (I Pet. 1: 11). Therefore there is already present here the double character of all later prophetic perspective—namely, the first and the second comings of Christ seen together in one picture (e.g. Isa. 61: 1–3, comp. with Luke 4: 17–20); and in this sense the original gospel is not only the original root but also the original type of all Messianic prophecy.

Thus the first word of promise is at once the most comprehensive and the deepest. In it is hidden the whole history and order of salvation. "General, indefinite, dark as the remote antiquity to which it belongs, like an awe-inspiring sphinx before the ruins of a temple full of mystery, so it lies, wonderful and sacred, at the threshold of the lost Paradise. Not till late in Israelitish prophecy does its solution begin to dawn.[1] But only the Son of Mary, the virgin, who endured for us all the stinging of the heel by the serpent, so as to crush for us all its head—He only has solved the riddle of this sphinx which was much too hard for saints and prophets (Matt. 13: 17; I Pet. 1: 10–12), in that He has *fulfilled it*." Only the culmination of the promise—Immanuel Himself—has set in the full light the scope of the promise. "It is only the New Testament which is the key to this hieroglyph of the Old Testament: it is only the gospel which is the exposition of the original gospel."

Immediately upon this first announcement of the redemption there followed

iv. *The Clothing of the Man and the Woman with the Skins of Animals*. For the first time the death of an innocent creature by bloodshed entered for the benefit of fallen man. The principle of sacrifice was established (Gen. 3: 21). And as the inadequate fig leaves were the expression and beginning of all human attempts at self-redemption, so now the first human beings, believing the Divine word and being thereupon clothed by God Himself, at the price of innocent shed blood, are the original type of all those who, through faith in the sacrifice of the Lamb of God (John 1: 29), have allowed themselves to be covered with the garments of salvation and the ornament of eternal purity and holiness (Isa. 61: 10; Matt. 22: 11, 12; Col. 3: 12; Gal. 3: 27).

Thus that clothing at the *outset* of human history became a prophecy in symbol of the *central* point of the history of salvation, of the cross of Golgotha, and at the same time a suggestion of the blessed *end* when God will at last have clothed His chosen

[1] First in the "Immanuel" prophecy (Isa. 7: 14, comp. Mic. 5: 2), and thus about 750 B.C., and therefore 3,500 years after the first announcement of the original gospel.

with the resurrection body and the wedding garment of glory (Phil. 3: 20, 21; II Cor. 5: 2–4; Rev. 19: 8).

v. *The Expulsion from Paradise.* Henceforth only outside of Paradise can man again find his paradise. For sin is separation from God. But God is the original source of all life. Thus sin is separation from life, which means death in spirit, soul, and body (Rom. 6: 23).

But if redemption is to be made possible, there must be expiation for sin; and, in order that it shall be righteous, this expiation must correspond to the guilt, and therefore consist likewise in separation from the Creator and from life, that is, it must consist in death (Heb. 9: 22). Only so can true life be restored. Redemption must consist in this, that death, the great enemy of man, must be made the means of his deliverance, and that which is the penalty of sin must at the same time become the way of escape from sin. Only through *death* can "*death*" be put to *death* (Num. 21: 6, 9; John 3: 14).

Thus did Christ "through his *death*" take away the might "of him who had the authority of death, the devil" (Heb. 2: 14); His death on the cross has slain the enmity (Eph. 2: 16).

To serve this end death must be possible to mankind in general, and hence also the necessity of expulsion from Paradise and the cutting off of sinful humanity from the tree of life (Gen. 3: 13, 24). To abide further in Paradise, with a continuous renewing of his outward life-power, would have meant nothing less for man than the eternal perpetuation of his sin, his condemnation to an irredeemable condition and so to a never-ending destruction. The sinner's bodily deathlessness would be eternal death to his soul and Paradise would have become Hell. Therefore however negative the expulsion from the Garden may appear, its purpose is nevertheless positive. In all His taking God was giving. He assigned the sinner to bodily death so as to save him from eternal death; and so the act of judgment is at the same time a gracious act of redeeming love.

Thus the door of Paradise had shut in a threefold sense; in the judgment on the man, the woman, and the creation; but also in a threefold sense the door of redemption had opened:

as the promise of salvation—in the first good news;

as a foreshadowing of salvation—in the reclothing of the first pair; and

as making salvation possible—in their expulsion from Paradise.

Threefold, too, is the inward possession which man after the Fall took with him on his earthly course:

Looking back on the past—the sorrowful *remembrance*, which still, thousands of years later, forms the historical background and remote framework of all folk-lore as to the lost Paradise;

Looking at the present—the confident *belief*, which gazes at
the rock and the star given in the promise of the original
gospel;[1]

Looking forward to the future—the hopeful *yearning*, a
daughter as it were born of remembrance and faith.   And
now this yearning floats before the wanderer as a heavenly
angel over the desert path.   It shows him oases in the
arid sands, quickens his strength, gives wings to his steps,
and joyfully directs his gaze to the goal:

"Blessed are they that yearn for home,
for to their home shall they come."

[1] From the first Adam believed in the original good news of the coming seed
of the woman (Gen. 3: 15).   This is proved by the name Eve (Heb. *Chavva*, Life),
which he gave to his wife (Isha, fem. of Ish, man, Gen. 2: 23), directly after the
original promise, and immediately before the expulsion from Paradise (Gen. 3: 20
and context).   "Sunken in death he nevertheless gave his wife so proud a name"
(Calvin), and thereby expressed his faith in the conquest of death by life.   So it was
"an act of faith that Adam named his wife Eve" (Franz Delitzsch), and from that
time the new name of his wife was for man the "reminder of the promise of God's
grace" (*mnemosymon gratiae Dei promissae*, Melancthon).   Or as Luther says of the
original good news: "On this Adam trusted and thereby was saved from his fall."
That Eve also in faith took her stand on the ground of the word of promise is
shown by her statement in Gen. 4: 1.

CHAPTER IV

TWO WAYS IN HUMAN HISTORY

THE new period bore a special stamp. Its chief purpose was to make plain what sin had actually effected in human nature. Therefore it was governed by three leading principles; it completed its course

(1) without special fundamental regulations from God (read Gen. 3: 14–19);

(2) with almost complete restriction of revelation to the witness of nature, conscience, and history;

(3) without fundamental earthly measures of supervision or of punishment for the sinner in the event of his disobedience.

On account of the second characteristic the period has been called "the age of human conscience." But inasmuch as conscience is not exclusively peculiar to this economy, but continues into later periods (comp. Rom. 2: 15; I Pet. 3: 16), while the absence of all particular ordinances and basic principles of supervision or punishment by God is the particular feature of this time, the name "period of freedom" appears essentially more correct. Nevertheless since "freedom" is much too ideal a conception, a still more suitable description is "the period of human self-determination." And because in that time God made Himself known to man not only through the witness of conscience, but through the threefold revelation in nature, conscience, and history, perhaps the best description of all would be "the period of general Divine revelation."

In the Paradise period there were prohibition and command (Gen. 2: 16, 17). The same was the case in all later economies. Here only, in the time between Adam and Noah, as the sole such period in the Divine plan of salvation, had mankind fundamental freedom to do or not to do what they would. No authority and no ruling power had been established by God to restrain the sinner in the self-revelation of his wickedness. Man was to have unrestricted opportunity to show what he could accomplish and to reveal what he would become when he "freely" evolves. Thus this second age of the plan of salvation became "the age of human self-determination," or, as Delitszch says, the time of "testing of freedom" of the human race. But the end is—the Flood.

Cain was the creator of the civilization before the Flood. At the same time he is the original and primary type of the entire human history springing out of him, so far as this developed in severance from God and without fellowship with the Most High.

I. THE SPIRITUAL AND RELIGIOUS NATURE OF CAIN

Cain was not a representative of religious indifference or open denial of God.   On the contrary, he brought to God an offering, and burned[1] with envy when he saw Abel's offering acknowledged and not his own gift.   But from lack of inward piety, despite his outward devotion, he became the first man who was "of [lit. out of, drew his nature from] the evil one" (I John 3: 12).

And from the false disposition of the offerer there resulted automatically a false element in his offering.   While Abel brought his *first* and *best* (Gen. 4: 4), Cain offered no firstling sacrifice, but the first thing that came to hand, something or other that he had just found.   And while Abel (surely in regard to the Divine institution of sacrifice on the clothing of the first pair with the skins of animals) offered up a sacrifice of blood, acknowledging thereby that his sin deserved death and could be covered before God solely through the substitutionary death of a guiltless sacrifice, Cain offered merely an expression of his dependence and thanksgiving, and this indeed a self-wrought production of his own strength.   Thereby he became the prototype of all who dare to approach the sanctuary of God without the shedding of blood (Heb. 9: 22), who indeed own themselves dependent creatures but not death-deserving sinners.

And from this point onward these two "ways" run through human history.

On the one hand the "way" of Cain (Jude 11); a religion of the flesh, a self-willed worship, the self-satisfied justification by works and the insubordinate *self*-redemption, which relies on itself and rejects substitution—this "idealizing" of one's own power, this theology of the first murderer, this "faith" of the serpent's seed (comp. Jas. 2: 19); but on the other hand, the "way" of Abel—the humble acknowledgment that sin demands death, the reliance of the guilty on the sacrifice appointed by God Himself, the enduring of persecution for the sake of the eternal goal, the expectation of the triumph of the *Divine* redemption through the *woman's* seed.

But the end will correspond to the beginning, only in reverse; the line of the murdered Abel will attain to eternal life (Heb. 11: 40, 4), but the way of Cain will perish.   The highest perfecting of "Abel" is Christ, and in Him the incarnation of the Holy God; but the highest development of "Cain" is the Antichrist, and in him the self-deification of the curse-laden sinner (II

---

[1] Gen. 4: 5: literally: "It burned in Cain;" "it became glowing in Cain."

Thess. 2: 4). Therefore the one way ends in the heavenly Jerusalem (Heb. 12: 22–24), but the other way in the lake of fire (Rev. 19: 20).

And as the first war in mankind was, as it were, a religious war (Gen. 4), so will also the last be, both before and after the earthly kingdom of God of the End-time (Rev. 16: 16; 19: 19; 20: 8, 9). But then the Divine patience will exalt itself to the exultant power of victory, and the faith of Abel will triumph over the religion of Cain.

II. Cain's Significance in Civilization

With his principle of self-redemption Cain became the beginner of all God-estranged human development. He who, according to the Divine sentence, was to be "wandering and fugitive" (Gen. 4: 12), in self-will resisted the curse, and, in defiant opposition to the Divine word, became the first of all men to build a fixed settlement, a "city" (Gen. 4: 17).

Thereby was given the basic tendency of all further human development, so far as it leads away from God; namely, overcoming the curse on the path of godless civilization, regaining Paradise without the experience of redemption, the combination of fleshly energy without the acknowledgment of God's sovereignty, and thus the self-redemption of mankind with the Deity excluded.

The name of this first human city is itself significant of this: "Enoch," "Inauguration," fresh start, overturning of all that preceded, the new beginning of a self-willed combined civilization in revolt against God (Gen. 4: 17).

Thereby this first city took its stand in opposition to the earliest gospel. Each is a fresh beginning after the collapse. But there it was a new beginning by God on the way of redemption; here it is a new beginning by mankind on the way of a God-excluding civilization.

The attainments of civilization are not in themselves contrary to God, but rather belong to the paradisaical nobility of man. Inventions and discoveries, science and art, refinement and improvement, in short, the advance of the human mind, these are entirely the will of God. They are the taking possession of the earth by the royal human race (Gen. 1: 28), the discharging of a duty to the Creator by God's ennobled servant, a God-appointed sovereignty and service for the blessing of this earth-realm. And only entire misconception of the most simple laws of revelation could charge the Holy Scripture with a retrograde mode of thought and hostility to culture. No; what the Bible rejects and what "Cain" is, is not civilization in itself, but the God-estrangement of millions of its representatives, the untrue "religious" make-believe, inconsiderate treatment of one's neighbours, the spirit of arrogance and rebellion, in brief, the revolt against the Most High.

And as unbrokenness and defiance characterized the "Cain" nature upwards and Godwards, so did oppression and violence mark its direction downwards and outwards to its fellow-men. In this way, Cain, the murderer of his brother, became the first agent of religious war and of warfare in general, the original type of all tyrants and sanguinary lords of the world, the father of the spirit of all mass-murder, of all brutality and barbarity. Therefore his city is the first foundation stone of all world empires that renounce God, so far as the spirit of the wild-beast rules in them (comp. Dan. 7: 2–8; 8: 3–7; Rev. 13: 1, 2); the start which in many ways gave much fateful direction to the otherwise so sublime and rich world-history, "through which the history of revelation winds its way as the water of Shiloah goes quietly (Isa. 8: 6). The one issues from tears of repentance; the other exalts itself over a brother's blood. There God's power unfolds the promised blessing; here human power struggles vainly against the Divine curse."

III. THE DOMINATING CHARACTERISTICS OF THE CAINITE CIVILIZATION

"As were the days of Noah, so shall be also the coming of the Son of Man" (Matt. 24: 37). As in the plan of salvation the divine principles, like a circle, turn back at the end to the beginning, so also in the history of civilization the final periods resemble the first. Therefore investigation of that ancient past is equally a message for later times, and especially is the Cainite civilization the germinal type for the world situation of the End-time.

It is this because of the following characteristics.[1]

(1) *Rapid advance of all mechanical arts*. The decisive bent of man's mind before the Flood was the attempt to compensate for the lost Paradise by one that was artificial. The "ascent" was quicker by the Cainites than by the Sethites; for "in their generation the children of the world are shrewder than the children of light" (Luke 16: 8). Through Cain came settled life and city building; through the roving[2] Jabal, nomad civilization. Tubalcain, "the hammerer", became the father of the smith's trade, and Jubal, the "undulating" (which his name means), was the creator of music. The last three were all sons of Lamech.

Thus the three chief occupations of human society had all arisen quickly, food, defence, and instruction, the tradesman,

[1] See G. H. Pember, *Earth's Earliest Ages*, ch. X.
[2] From the Heb. "jabal", originally to flow, stream, undulate.

the warrior, the intellectual; and thus were promoted
   feeding through Jabal—the material side of life;
   defence through Tubal-Cain—the harsh side of life;
   instruction through Jubal—the intellectual side of life.

As a worker in metals Tubal-cain became the founder of
"industry" and of all work in metals and iron in general; and
Jubal, who brought the tones of the lute to the "undulating",
became the creator of all soothing and inspiriting efforts in art
and music; while Lamech, his father, became the first representative of poetic art, as witness his song praising the sword
(Gen. 4: 23, 24).

The most significant testimony to the pre-Deluge civilization
is the Ark of Noah. Its measurements were gigantic. The *Ency.
Britt.* (vol. II, 364) gives "roughly 450 feet by 150 feet by 45
feet". This would give a capacity of more than 3,000,000
cubic feet. It is therefore comparable to our modern ocean
vessels. As other examples also show, it is the very buildings
of the greatest, indeed gigantic, measurements that belong likewise to immemorial antiquity, as the Pyramids and the Sphinx.
In 1609 the Dutch Mennonite Peter Jansen had a ship built at
Hoorn in Holland, to the same proportions but one-third of the
size, and it was found that such a ship certainly moved more
heavily, but as compensation for this it could carry *one-third
more cargo* than an ordinary ship of the same cubic space. And
it was for carrying, not specifically for sailing, that the Ark was
intended. Arca (Latin) = chest, box, case.

(2) *Great Increase of Population.* "Men began to multiply"
(Gen. 6: 1). Already in the time of Cain, apparently in his
advanced age, a city could be built (probably at first simply an
established colony), Gen. 4: 17. This is the less astonishing,
since the life-energy of the youthful race must at the beginning
have been very powerful. Also, with the long lives of the
parents, the number of the children must have been much greater
than later on; and, for the same reason, many generations must
have lived alongside of each other at the same time. With an
average of only six children per family, by the time Cain was only
400 years old he would have had far more than 100,000 descendants. Even at the present time the increase of the population
of the whole earth has been enormous. According to Prof.
Hennig, since the commencement of the nineteenth century the
mass of mankind has more than doubled (from about 900 millions
to some 2,000 millions).

The son "Enoch" that was born to Cain during the building
of the city (Gen. 4: 17), was apparently not his firstborn. Similarly, in the case of the Sethites it is not the firstborn who are
mentioned, but those who carried on the history, in this case
the ancestors of Noah. This is proved by the years of their

birth. For "even as Adam was not unmarried for 130 years, so neither was Seth for 105, nor Methuselah for 187, nor Noah for 500." See Gen. 5.

Cain's wife was one of the daughters (or female descendants) of Adam mentioned in Gen. 5: 4 (whom Cain "knew" in the land of Nod but did not first "take" there). Such alliances were at first necessary. Therefore to speak of the marriage of "brother and sister" is not correct, because in the very earliest period of mankind there were still no "families" at all, and therefore neither the particular love of "brother and sister;" for because all members of the same degree stood in equal "nearness" to one another they were also equally "distant." Therefore the reproach that these original unions were immoral is untenable.

(3) *Disregard of the Divine Law of Marriage.* Three women of the descendants of Cain are mentioned, but not even one in the genealogy of Seth. The names of these three Cainite women are Ada ("ornament," "morning," or "beauty"), Zilla ("the shady," possibly on account of the rich hair that veiled her), and Naama ("loveliness"). Their mention among the Cainites indicates that there the women took a more forward place than among the Sethites, and that outward beauty and sensual attractiveness were the chief features which were valued in them. But Lamech, the seventh from Cain, finally trespassed quite openly against the original marriage law (Matt. 19: 3–9) and became the first polygamist.

(4) *Rejection of the Call to Penitence and Faith.* Yet God sent witnesses to this apostate world with the warning cry to repent and return. But no one paid attention. No one gave heed,

> neither in the days of Enosh, when the pious joined together for united worship of Jehovah, the Lord, as the covenant God and Redeemer (Gen. 4: 26. See App. I, the Names of God);

> nor in the days of Enoch, to the warning by this prophet of the coming world judgment (Jude 14, 15; Gen. 5: 21–24; Heb. 11: 5, 6);

> nor also to Lamech, the Sethite, who waited for the promised "Comforter" and "Rest-bringer" (Heb., Noah), (Gen. 5: 29);

> and just as little to Noah, the "preacher of righteousness," one who testified against them for 120 years (Gen. 6: 3; II Pet. 2: 5).

On the contrary, gradually the Sethites also were overcome by the spirit of the age, and so at last there developed this general situation:

(5) *The Union of the Professing People of God with the World.*
In consequence, after Lamech the Cainites are no longer mentioned as a separate race, and when shortly the Flood came

they all perished together, the Sethites equally with the Cainites. Only Noah, the tenth from Adam, and his three sons, together with their four wives, were saved (I Pet. 3: 20).

And yet this whole world, although doomed to destruction, was full of self-praise.

(6) *Self glorification of Mankind.* While Sethite piety reached its height in Enoch, the seventh (Jude 14), it was Lamech, the seventh, who embodied the summit of Cainite rebellion. In him the line of the Cainites reached its full development, its self-glorifying goal, and therefore is he in the Biblical record the conclusion of the history of the Cainites. As has been said above, the attainments of civilization are not in themselves contrary to God, but here all things served to the benumbing of the conscience.

Lamech's song is a "hymn of victory upon the invention of the sword" (Gen. 4: 23, 24). "The history of the Cainites begins with a murder and ends with praise of murder. In its seventh member everything is forgotten; with music, social amenities, luxury, and display everything is benumbed. The curse of loneliness is changed into city life, the curse of being unsettled is turned into love of travel, the bad conscience into heroism, which makes the remembrance of the curse of God's ancestors only a support of one's own God-blaspheming self-consciousness. Thus all is pleasure and splendour, entwined and crowned with the flower of human wit and the soul's creative power, poetic art."

If by the "sons of God" (Gen. 6: 1, 2) fallen angels are meant (comp. Job 1: 6; 2: 1; 38: 7; Dan. 3: 25; II Pet. 2: 4; Jude 6, 7), then occultism and spiritism are likewise a distinct principle of the Cainite civilization. This explanation is upheld by the majority, e.g. Philo, Josephus, most of the Rabbis, the Septuagint, Kurtz, Delitzsch, Gunkel, König, Pember.[1] On the other side Augustine, Calvin, J. P. Lange apply the passage to the commingling of Sethites and Cainites. A fuller treatment is not possible here.

But at last the Most High gave His answer, and His answer was—the Judgment. After more than 1,500 years of Divine patience (See Gen. 5), in the tenth generation (ten is the number of completeness and of the conclusion of a completed development, even as, later, Abraham was the tenth from Noah—see Gen. 11: 10–26), the Flood destroyed the God-estranged sinful human race.

In the year 1925 Prof. Riem, speaking of the traditions of the Flood, referred to no fewer than 35 traces and gave 268 detailed accounts. "Among these 268 accounts the Flood appears 77

---

[1] [For a full examination, to the same effect, see the 15th edition of Pember's *Earth's Earliest Ages*, Appendix. Trans.]

times simply as the Flood, 80 times as an inundation, 3 times as a fall of snow, 58 times as rain. Among the last, once as a rain of hot pitch, once the earth is overflowed by a flood of tears, and 16 times the great conflagration appears. Twenty-one times the rainbow is seen, and almost always with express mention of its reconciling power."

CHAPTER V

THE COVENANT CONCERNING NATURE AND WORLD HISTORY (GOD'S COVENANT WITH NOAH)

THE Flood was past. The world of that time was gone (II Pet. 3: 6). A new period for mankind began.

Right from the start the governing principles for the future were given. The covenant of God with Noah formed the foundation for all future history of nature, mankind, and salvation.

i. *The Ordering of Nature.*

"So long as the earth stands, seedtime and harvest, cold and heat, summer and winter, day and night shall not cease" (Gen. 8: 21, 22; 9: 11, 15). The reason is remarkable: "*For* the invention and endeavour of the human heart is evil, from its youth on." Thus that which just before was the very ground for *destroying* him (Gen. 6: 5), becomes now the chief ground for *sparing* him. Here also is seen plainly the necessity for distinguishing the dispensations. Else one might perhaps believe in the existence of "discrepancies" which really do not exist. In truth there began now, after the Flood, the period of Divine patience (see Acts 14: 15–17; 17: 30), and "the passing over of the sins in the forbearance of God" (Rom. 3: 25); and with Noah, the "rest-bringer" (whose name comes from the verb *nuach*, to rest, see Exod. 20: 11; Deut. 5: 14), there set in a period of thousands of years of "rest" from Divine wrath.

At the same time man's kingly right over the earth was confirmed.

ii. *The Establishment of Human Authority.*

But now his attitude to Nature, especially in the animal world, is no longer that of the original harmony, but a relationship of force, oppression, and conflict. In Paradise the spiritual majesty of the earthly king had, in a certain sense, magically bound the animal world, but now it was a lordship with fear on the one side, and timidity, or indeed paralysing terror, on the other side. This is quite in keeping also with the right to kill animals and to use them—apart from their blood—for food, a right already, indeed, assumed earlier by man, but now first sanctioned by God (Gen. 9: 2–5).

It is to the covenant of God with Noah that the Rabbis connect their tradition of the doctrine of the seven Noachian commandments which are regarded as binding on all men (including non-Jews), the prohibition of blasphemy, *idolatry,* manslaughter, theft, *incest,* disobedience to authority, *eating of blood.* These, particularly the three italicized, lie at the base of the deliberations of the conference (the so-called "council") at Jerusalem and the brotherly advice given on that occasion to the Gentile Christians (Acts 15, especially vv. 20, 21).

iii.   *The Ordering of Civil Life.*

"He who sheds man's blood, by man, in return, shall his blood be shed" (Gen. 9: 6).   This introduced capital punishment for the murderer.   But this includes the supervision of the individual by the community and the appointing of public courts and legal penalties, and signifies nothing less than the introduction of governmental powers and therewith the foundation of all later creation of States (Rom. 13: 1–6; I Pet. 2: 13–17).   But since the death penalty upon the murderer is based upon the likeness to God of the murdered (Gen. 9: 6), this indicates that the exercise of justice must be practised on the principle of acknowledgment of man being in the image of God, and, by consequence, of the mental and spiritual nobility of man.   Therefore the Authority must depend not on brute force, but on the acknowledgment of the Divinely granted natural right in the human society.   Only so does it become the representative of justice and the "servant of God" to the benefit of its subjects (Rom. 13: 4).

This appointment of human authorities was at the same time a necessary addition to the sparing of mankind from a repetition of judgment by flood.   For if God, having regard to the inborn sinfulness of man, would not henceforth permit an exterminating judgment such as the Flood to come upon him, then He must, by the introduction of order and justice, set a barrier to sin taking the upper hand, and therewith lay the foundation for orderly civil and political development.   Thus natural, governmental, and civil order belong together.   Yet they must first become possible through the fourth, that is,

iv.   *The Order of Salvation.*

"Noah built Jehovah an altar and offered a burnt-offering upon the altar; and Jehovah said in his heart, No more henceforth will I curse the earth on man's account" (Gen. 8: 20, 21). The connexion between sacrifice and the covenant concerning Nature is here given unmistakably, and in such wise, indeed, that the sacrifice is the foundation of the covenant.

Three things are chiefly to be noticed: the name Jehovah, the altar, and the burnt-offering.   Jehovah is the covenant name of the Most High, the name of the God of salvation's history and of redemption (see Appendix I, "The Names of God").   To

Him must the hearts of the pious lift themselves. To heaven, to the "height" must their offerings and prayers ascend, if they are to reach His throne. So as to give this "upward" direction to the sacrifices, from now on there were erected on earth high places and altars from which they should "ascend" heavenwards in the fire.

The presence of God is indeed everywhere and is not restricted by the boundaries of an above and a beneath (Psa. 139); but in the language of worship the "other-sidedness" of God is illustrated symbolically by conceptions of space, the spiritually superior by the spatial "to lie higher," the "above" time and "above" space by the mental idea "over" space.

So, then, in this place, for the first time in the Bible, is an "altar" mentioned and the sacrifice termed "*olah*," that is the "ascending." The sacrifice of Abel is termed simply "*minchah*," i.e. a "gift" (Gen 4: 3, comp. the verb *manach,* to give, present).

But the clean animals offered, as all the sacrifices from the beginning of the world, themselves point to the sacrifice of Golgotha, the Lamb without blemish and without spot (I Pet. 1: 19, 20), Who is in truth the foundation of all preservation and salvation of the world.

But the connexion of the ordering of nature and the ordering of salvation shines out still more clearly in the sign of the covenant, the rainbow, which the Lord has set in the clouds to be the sign of His divine faithfulness.

From Gen. 9: 12–17 it appears that there had been no rainbow before the Flood. Apparently the conditions of the globe were greatly transformed by the Flood.

v.   *The Covenant Sign.*

The rainbow is "the coloured gleam of the sun breaking forth as the tempest clouds, dark as night, withdraw, the triumph of the sun over the Flood" (J. P. Lange). Like a heavenly bridge it joins the upper and lower worlds, and with its sevenfold radiance (with the green of the emerald as the colour of life: see Rev. 4: 3) it testifies to the covenant between Creator and creation. (Three is the number of God, four the number of the world; seven is the sum and union of both).

"Shining over the shadowed earth, so lately riven by lightnings, the rainbow illuminates the victory of divine love over dark and fiery wrath. Caused by the action of the sun on the dark clouds, it illustrates the willingness of the heavenly to interpenetrate the earthly; stretched between heaven and earth it proclaims peace between God and men; embracing the whole circle of vision it witnesses to the all-embracing universality of the covenant of grace."

In consequence it became the type of salvation and of redemption in general, and as such it appears at the throne of the Lord as Leader and Perfecter of salvation (Ezek. 1: 28; Rev. 4: 3). And as we here below see always only the *half* bow in the clouds—at once a type of the *im*perfectness of our present experience of redemption (I Cor. 13: 9–12; I John 3: 2)—so shall we sometime see "encircling the throne" the complete bow, and in perfection and glory praise the faithfulness of the covenant God. And thus will the rainbow become the Nature symbol of our eternal deliverance.

Thus everything connected with the rainbow is typical:

The time of arising—for it rises with the return of the sun (Ezek. 1: 28);

the manner of arising—for it shines as the transfiguring of the darkness by the light (Gen. 9: 14);

the sevenfold colours—for seven is the number of the covenant (e.g. Lev. 16: 14; and frequently);

the predominance of the green—for green is the colour of life (Rev. 4: 3);

the bow (i.e. bridge) shape—for it illustrates the union between Creator and creation (Gen. 9: 12–17);

the wide encompassing of the circle of vision—for it shows the all-embracing character of the covenant of grace (Gen. 9: 12, 15, "all flesh");

the eternal heavenly circle—for so it becomes a type of the Divine perfection (Ezek. 1: 28; Rev. 4: 3).

CHAPTER VI

THE PROGRAMME FOR THE RACES IN THE HISTORY OF SALVATION (THE BLESSING OF NOAH)

NOAH's blessing concerning Japheth and Shem, and his curse upon Canaan, the son of Ham, is the next significant event in the process of salvation. But while the covenant of God with Noah was the foundation of the succeeding history of nature, the world, and salvation, Noah's blessing and curse is its prophetical ground-plan, its programme for the races in that history.

i. *The accursed and unblessed condition of the Hamites.*

"Accursed be Canaan: let him be a servant of all servants under his brethren" (Gen. 9: 25). On account of the shameful sin of Ham (ver. 22–24) the family group of the Canaanites is here given over, in Canaan, Ham's son, as their ancestor, to be cursed, and the Hamite race generally to be unblessed.

In the most fateful manner the history of the world has corresponded to this prophecy. In Palestine, through the Semitic Jews, especially under Joshua (Josh. 9: 21–27; Jud. 1: 28–30, 33, 35) and Solomon (I Kings 9: 20, 21), the Canaanites were subjugated; and in Syria and North Africa, as Phoenicians and Carthaginians, they were conquered by the Japhetic Persians, Grecians, and Romans. But the other Hamites, who were not indeed cursed, but were assigned to a lack of blessedness—after a prosperous development in the beginning (especially under Nimrod, later by the Phoenicians and Egyptians)—have again and again had to groan under the yoke of oppression, especially the negro, the last particularly in America after the introduction of slavery. Not till after the North American civil war of 1861–1865 was slavery abolished in the United States. Even now it still prevails in great portions of central Africa, especially in the Mohammedan States.

ii. *The Semites as spiritual intermediary of redemption.*

It proved different with Shem. The most glorious blessing was apportioned to him "Blessed be Jehovah, the God of Shem" (Gen. 9 : 26). This form of praise, which expresses the blessing, not actually as "blessing," but as praise to the God who blesses, has its basis (as Luther long since remarked, "*propter excellentem benedictionem*") in the height and boundlessness of the promise to Shem.

Jehovah is the God of *Shem*; that is, the Semitic race is the bearer of His especial revelation. For *Japheth* God is Elohim, the creator, maintainer, and universal ruler (Gen. 9: 27); but for Shem He is Jehovah the covenant God and Redeemer (see the Appendix—"The Names of God"). Thereby Shem becomes the recipient and channel of His special redeeming grace, and henceforth the promise of spiritual salvation is concentrated in his descendants.

This salvation is brought to completion in Christ, for He, the Redeemer, as son of David descends through Abraham from Shem (Luke 3: 36); even as He Himself has said in the gospel of John (4: 22), "The salvation comes from the Jews"; and as His greatest apostle testifies, the "noble olive tree" of God's kingdom is "their" olive tree (Rom. 11: 24; comp. Eph. 2: 11–22; Rom. 15: 27; Gal. 3: 9, 14). So God's temple of His New Testament revelation rests upon the rock foundation of the Old Testament revelation given through God's prophets (Matt. 5: 17, 18; John 10: 35; Acts 24: 14; 26: 22), and in Christ the blessing of Shem has become the gospel for the world.

iii. *Great Extension of Political and Intellectual influence of the Japhethites.*

Japheth's blessing consists of three parts.

(1) "God give spreading out to the spreader out" (Gen.: 9: 27), or "God make it wide to the wide." The play on the words "He makes wide" (Heb. *japht*) and the name Japheth should be reproduced in the translation. Japheth was the father of the Medes (Heb. *Madai*, Gen. 10: 2), and the Greeks. In Hebrew the name is Javan, with which compare the Grecian description of themselves on the west coast of Asia Minor as Ionians. Consequently Japheth was the father of the Romans, Persians, and generally the Indo-Teutonic race. The Persians are kinsfolk of the Medes; the Romans are related to the Greeks. The Indians (Aryans) and the Germanic nations are connected with the Persians; with the Romans are connected the Romanic nations (Italians, French, Spaniards, etc.); with all, though more distantly, the Slavs and many others. Taken together they are all styled "Indo-Germanic" (Aryans).

But this means that, *according to the testimony of Old Testament prophecy, great extension of political and intellectual influence is the privilege of the Japhetic peoples.* The prophetic racial programme has so appointed. World history has brought about the fulfilment in overwhelming manner. In the first instance, indeed, the fulfilment took a reverse course, for sinful man is in perpetual rebellion against God.

In the ancient Orient not Japhethites but Hamites and Shemites were, for tens of centuries, the ruling civilized peoples.

In the Nile valley the Hamitic Egyptians ruled.[1] On the Euphrates and the Tigris (in Accad, Shinar, Babel and Nineveh), subsequent to an earlier civilization in Sumeria, Nimrod the Cushite, (thus a representative of the *Hamitic* race, which in Canaan and his descendants should become a "servant of all servants"), even became the first man in history to found a world empire (Gen. 10: 8–12). Thus in him the subservient race attained to supremacy.

According to the exact wording of the passage Nimrod was not the builder of the *city* of Babel (see Gen. 11) but the founder of the world empire of Babel, in that he, on the foundation of the already existing cities of Babel, Erech, Accad, and Calneh, from Shinar as the "beginning of his empire," extended his power to the north, that is Assyria (Gen. 10: 8–12). Also later, as the power of the Hamites waned and was apportioned among others, it was still not as yet Japhethites but, according to the testimony of history and Scripture, Semites who became the immediate heirs of the Hamitic world rule.

In the Nile Valley, the Hamitic Egyptians remained the rulers (Gen. 14: 1–4; 10: 22); in Mesopotamia it was the Semitic Elamites, and, since Hammurabi, the Babylonians (about 1900 B.C.). Then in Babylon the Kassites, and in Egypt (till Pharaoh Amasis, about 1600 B.C.) the Hyksos attained to power (about 1750 B.C.). In the Near East the Assyrians followed (about 1750–612 B.C.) and the New Babylonians, the latter under Nebuchadnezzar especially. But these all were Semites or Hamites, and already nearly two thousand years had passed since Noah had uttered his prophecies (about 2350 B.C.), and yet his predictions as to the peoples were still not completely fulfilled.

Then at last the decisive hour of the Japhethites struck. Under Cyrus the Persian the Japhetic race entered the arena with victorious strength. Semitic Babylon fell (538 B.C.), Belshazzar, the son and representative of Nabonidus, was slain, and the Japhethites became the lords of the Orient. Since then no Semitic or Hamitic race has succeeded in breaking the world supremacy of the Japhethites. The conquest of Babylon and the victory of Cyrus (the "shepherd" and "anointed" of the Lord, Isa. 45: 1; 44: 28) over Belshazzar the Semite, and also the simple words of Daniel 5: 30, "In that night was Belshazzar, the king of the Chaldeans, slain," embrace an event of mightiest significance in world history—*the decisive collapse of Hamitic-Semitic world sovereignty and the laying of the foundation of the Japhetic world rule.* Only a few years later Cambyses, the successor of

---

[1] The Egyptians (Heb. *Mizraim*) are Hamites, according to Gen. 10: 6, and see Psa. 78: 51; 105: 23, 27. They name themselves *Kemet*. The transition to the (Hamitic) negroes is the Nubian–Fula race, who are indeed very dark-skinned but in features are distinguished from the negro proper.

Cyrus, conquered Hamitic Egypt and established there likewise the Japhetic rule (525 B.C.). The Persian empire also was indeed not permanent; still, when the Greeks (333 B.C.) and the Romans (especially in the second century B.C.), the Teutons (A.D. 476), and the Latins took over the inheritance, it remained, through all individual changes, always in Japhetic hands.

Thenceforth the Japhetic race carried the palm of culture; and even as they ruled the earth geographically and politically, so also did they intellectually and culturally. While in its highest conception the blessing of Shem consisted in the concentration of all *spiritual* and *saving* powers, the blessing of Japheth included the widest *extension* of all *intellectual* and *worldly powers*. The blessing of the one was heavenly light, the blessing of the other was earthly success.

But for their vigour the Indo-European peoples were indebted to the idealism of their conceptions; the Greeks to their striving after beauty and truth, as in their art and philosophy respectively; the Romans to their reverence for order and justice, as in their State; and the Teutons to their adherence to liberty and fidelity. Through all these they became intellectually leaders of humanity and promoters and patrons of higher culture.

(2) But also *spiritually* Japheth was to attain to blessing. Therefore is it said: "Let him dwell in the tents of Shem" (Gen. 9: 27). For the very reason that Shem had been immediately before designated as the channel of revelation, dwelling in his tents can signify nothing else than partaking in his faith and the reception of the Japhethites into the fellowship of his spiritual salvation.[1] In fact the blessing promised to Shem has reached less to Hamitic and principally to Japhetic peoples (Gal. 3: 14).

The fundamental start for this was the dream-vision of Peter in Joppa (Acts 10: 9–17), which taught that the removal of the wall of division between Jews and heathen, which in *principle* had been completed already on the cross (Eph. 2: 14), was now *historically* carried out in the person of the Roman Cornelius; and thus, as regards the fulness of salvation, by this means a Japhethite, the first from among the nations, was allowed to enter the tents of Shem without joining the nation of Israel.

Then a further turning-point in the same direction was that other vision of Paul, when in Troas he saw a man of Macedonia, who called to him: "Come over, and help us" (Acts 16: 9, 10). Who knows what course the history of the world and the church might have taken if at that time the great apostle had been sent east, to India or China, instead of to the west! About the very time in which Paul made his missionary journeys a truth-seeking emperor of China, Ming-ti, sent an embassy to India, from which

[1] Thus already Jerome, Calvin, Luther, almost all the church fathers, and further, Lange, Keil, Delitzsch, and others.

occasion Buddhism entered China (A.D. 61–67). But it is the incomparable significance of that dream-vision in Troas that with it the hour had struck for the bringing of the message of salvation over to Europe, so that now Japhetic Europe was appointed to be the chief theatre for the wonders of the gospel and the citadel of the message of the kingdom of the heavens, and that night hour in Troas became the hour of spiritual sunrise for the western peoples.

(3) *"And let Canaan be his servant"* (Gen. 9: 27). The fulfilment of this prophecy has been attained only through gigantic conflicts.

The Phoenicians and Sidonians are among the descendants of Canaan; the fact that they and other Canaanites had Semitic language and culture does not contradict the testimony of Gen. 10: 15 as to their Hamitic origin. Relationship of language never absolutely proves race relationship, and vice versa; for in the first place, the confusion of tongues at Babel is an historical fact, and secondly, in the course of history, peoples, through migration and otherwise, have often changed their language, as for example, in the early Middle Ages, the Normans, the Lombards, and the Franks. The Phoenicians in particular, according to their own assertion, came from the Indian ocean (*Herod.* I, 1; VII, 89). Thus they must have passed through the central Semitic language area, and, on the way, in the course of time, evidently must have acquired the Semitic speech.

These Phoenician peoples belong to the descendants of Canaan. They are, as it were, the "Normans" (North men) of antiquity. Their strip of coastland in the north-east of Palestine, thickly peopled, was like a continuous city. Thus, as early as 1200 B.C., partly from love of adventure, partly from business interest, they began to found foreign colonies, especially in the western Mediterranean; and there quickly flourished in North Africa the aristocratic and capitalistic city of Carthage ("New City").

At the same time the Roman State was developing in Italy. Collision was unavoidable. It had to end in the destruction of one or the other rival. The first war led to the conquest of Sicily by the Romans (264–241 B.C.). The second was in the highest degree dramatic (218–201 B.C.). For when the Carthaginians, under the leadership of the heroic and gifted Hannibal, broke into Italy through the Alps and in brilliant victories at the Ticinus (218), at the Trebia (218), at the lake of Trasimeno (217), and above all at Cannes (216), had destroyed the Roman armies, and Hannibal was now expected at the gates of Rome, it looked indeed as if the old prophetic word, "Let Canaan be his servant," which had been so brilliantly fulfilled through Cyrus (538 B.C.), should now be put to shame, for a conquest of the Japhetic

Romans by the Phoenician Carthaginians would have signified nothing less than the establishment of a *Hamitic* world-empire.

But at length the decision fell.   At Zama, south of Carthage, the armies met (202 B.C.) and—Publius Cornelius Scipio, the Roman, was the victor.   Had Hannibal conquered, then probably no Roman empire would ever have arisen.   But in the antagonism between Hannibal and Scipio there was at the same time embodied the racial collision between Semitism and Hamitism with Japhetism.   For the language, religion, and culture of the Carthaginians was Semitic, while their race and blood were Hamitic.   By their defeat, the political racial rivalry was for ever decided.   Nothing in later centuries could alter this; neither the onslaughts of the Huns (A.D. 375–455), especially Attila (the battle on the fields of Catalan, near Troyes, 451); nor the Arabs' invasion (711–732; the victory of Charles Martel near Tours and Poitiers 732); nor that of the Mongols (the golden horde, under Jenghis Khan in the thirteenth century; the battle of Liegnitz, 1241); nor the Turkish wars, from the conquest of Constantinople (1453), the battle of Mohace in Hungary (1526), to the siege of Vienna (1683).

With Nimrod began, with Hannibal ended the drama of Hamitic world empire, and Scipio's brilliant victory sealed conclusively the work of Cyrus, the establishment of the world-rule of the Japhetic race.   "Let Canaan be his servant"—this it is which stands written, as with letters of fire, over the battlefield of Zama.

Thus in unique manner has world history justified the prophecy.   Its course follows exactly the determined plan.   All contrary activities of man collapsed and God had His way. Noah had been His prophet concerning the peoples.   The names of his sons had become symbols and tokens for the future. The descendants of Ham (= heat) inhabited the hot lands; the sons of Japheth (extension) spread themselves out over the earth, and the generations of Canaan (the subdued[1]) had to submit themselves to Japheth and Shem.   But in the line of Shem (The Name) the name and nature of the Redeemer were revealed, and in Jesus Christ, the Lord, who bears "the name which is above every name" (Phil. 2: 9), the name of the Father is now glorified for ever (John 12: 28; 17: 4; Phil. 2: 9–11).

---

[1] Comp. the cognate verb in Jud. 4: 23, to bow, to submit.

CHAPTER VII

THE JUDGMENT ON MANKIND AT BABEL

THE judgment of Babel is pressing upon mankind. Upon all spiritual and cultural history rests the mark of this shattering primal catastrophe. Vainly the world struggles against it, striving to conquer its curse by its own strength.

i. *The original scattering of mankind.*

According to the Scripture three motives led to the building of the tower of Babel; pride, a determination to hold together, and vainglory. Therefore the Divine judgment is also threefold. The pride that stormed upward was judged by the coming down of the Lord (Gen. 11: 4, 5); the determination to hold together, through the scattering and dividing; and the ambition for vainglory, through the name of shame. Henceforth the very city through which they intended to make a "name" (ver. 4), and precisely by its name, is a symbol of overthrow; and Babel, the "city of confusion," the city of "commingling"[1] is already, purely as a name of a place, a proof of the impotence of the sinner and the uselessness of all rebellion against God.[2]

ii. *The historical confounding of language a confusion of thought.*

The confounding of language is in the first instance something fourfold; a confounding of vocabulary, grammar, pronunciation, and phraseology, and in this sense there are today about a thousand languages and chief dialects. Yet is it something further.

Whatever the original language may have been, whether (as the rabbis and church fathers supposed) the Hebrew or the

[1] With Babel (*balbel*) comp. the Heb. *balal*, to confuse, to mingle. The proud cuneiform interpretation of the Babylonian *Bab-ilu*, that it means *Gate of God*, is mere popular etymology and unsound, because spellings such as *Bab-ili* and *Bab-ilam* are known, so that the name can have nothing to do with the Babylonian word *ilu* (Heb. *el*, Arabic *allah*), that is, God. Dr. Pinches, Assyriologist at the British Museum in London, believes that the word *Babel* is formed from the sound, like the English verb *to babble* (Ger. *babbeln, plappern*), with which comp. the French *balbutier*.

[2] Tower buildings were also later among the characteristic types of Near Eastern culture. For instance, king Hammurabi's code (about 1900 B.C.) says: "He made high the summit of the temple tower at An-na (Erech) . . .; he was the protection of his land, *who brought together again the scattered inhabitants of Isin.*" Within the temple area of each Babylonian city there stood a tower as its central point. Thus even today in Babylon there stands a giant ruined tower, the Birs Nimrod, concerning which, on occasions when the tower was renovated, it is often said in the ancient cuneiform inscriptions that *its top was to reach unto heaven.* Nebuchadnezzar heightened the summit of the step tower of Etemenanki "so that it *competed with the heaven.*"

Aramaic or (which is no doubt alone right) none of the old languages handed down to us, in any case the community of speech involved a vigorous uniformity of mental life. For because language is the phonetic manifestation of the mental, the mental part of all mankind must in special sense have been uniform so long as its expression, language, was uniform. The confusion of tongues was thus at the same time a *confusing of the basic mental conceptions of mankind,* since, through an act of God's power upon the human spirit, in place of the original oneness there set in a manifold cleavage in thought, feeling, and idea. Hence every language has its own special linguistic "spirit." Thus the confusion of tongues became at the same time a confusion of thought and conception.

"The original language in which Adam in Paradise had named all the animals (Gen. 2: 20) was, as it were, a great mirror in which the whole of nature was accurately reflected. But now God shattered this mirror, and each people retained only a fragment of it, the one a larger, the other a smaller piece, and now each people sees only a piece of the whole, but never the whole complete. Therefore also the conceptions of the nations in reference to religion and philosophy, art, science, and history vary so strongly from one another, and indeed often amount to a mutual contradiction."

Of necessity all this involved further consequences. With the deranging of *world*-consciousness there was conjoined a further deranging of *God*-consciousness.

iii. *Degeneration of Faith and Religion.*

At the commencement of human history there is present faith in the *one* God, Who revealed Himself in a threefold manner: in nature (Rom. 1: 19, 20), in conscience (Rom. 2: 2–15), and in history (Gen. chs. 1–11). The later heathendom is therefore a perversion of this threefold original: distortion of the remembrance of the original revelation, misinterpretation of the revelation in nature (Rom. 1: 23), and a confused conflict of soul with the revelation in conscience—these are the three fundamental elements in all heathen religion.

Nevertheless the Divine influence upon mankind through the *universal* revelation persisted. God held mankind like a very powerful magnet. "Indeed, He is not far from each one of us" (Acts 17: 27). God sought men so as to awaken in them a search after Himself, as a mother seeks the heart of her child so that it shall seek her in return: "that they should seek the Lord, if that they might feel after and find him" (Acts 17: 27). Therefore, by the working of God Himself, there came the strikingly great search and inquiry among the peoples, even among the heathen. But the tragedy is that Satan, the great deceiver, has turned aside this search of mankind on to a false track, so that man is seeking after God and at the same time fleeing from Him.   He will both have Him and thrust Him away from himself; he seeks God's blessing and avoids His presence; he will have nothing to do with Him, yet cannot get away from Him.

The original root in man of this religious discord and degeneration, according to the doctrine of the apostle Paul, is unthankfulness.   For "although they knew that there is a God they have not praised Him as a God, nor given Him thanks, but have become vain in their thoughts and their foolish heart is darkened." (Rom. 1: 21).   Viewed in detail, however, the following elements especially, through demonic misleading, brought about this transposition of values in the realm of religious life.

The conception of God and spirit *as such* is an inheritance from the original revelation, and so does not require to be first developed in the course of religious history.   The problem which must be searched out is how it came to be connected with the elements of nature.

First of all there was the observing of dreams, for in them there was a something that "moved" and "heard" and "saw" even though all the bodily members were inactive.   There "appeared" also the dead, likewise in action, and thereby "proving" their continued existence as "spirits."

Further, there was the observing of *death*.   For was it not here that this "soul," this invisible inward somewhat, while the dying man drew his last breath, forsook his body, as, so to speak, breath and air?   And then the dead man became so still! Is this not proof that there is no movement without the will of an inward "I," an indwelling, active, breathing soul?

But in *nature* without all is full of movement: in plants and beasts, in the courses of the stars, in the majestic tempest, in the raging of the rivers, in the mysterious magnet, in the sparks of fire from the stricken stone.   Is this not all a plain, irresistible witness of the existence and indwelling of mighty beings who are active in all these movements around us?—*So nature came to be regarded as animated by spirits, and thus animistic*[1] *philosophy arose.*

But because man knew no other "soul" than his own, the endowment of these nature spirits with the characteristics of the human soul was thoroughly logical; and furthermore, because these nature-spirits, corresponding to the overwhelming power of their elements, could be imagined only as beings of a higher and intensified form of life, these human characteristics had to be ascribed to them in a higher and intensified measure.   Thus there resulted of necessity a connexion between *demon* and *hero,* whereby the demonic ascended through the human into a

From Latin *anima,* i.e. "soul," the belief in nature being animated by souls.

personality, and the heroic through the demonic into the super-human.   This is the essence of the heathen conception of God.
Thus the heathen created his "god" according to *his* own image
(comp. conversely Gen. 1: 27).

Here enters the power of human language to form and develop
religious conceptions, for it is a peculiarity of the human mind
that, involuntarily and oft unconsciously, it sets the material
and the spiritual side by side and merges them both mutually
into one another.   Thus language humanizes things external to
man and speaks of a "smiling" sun, a "merry" brook, and conversely carries over the external into the human and speaks of a
"cold" loveliness, a "sunny" character, or a "radiant" joy.
With a yet richer fancy it speaks of the "arrows" of the sun (its
rays), the "stabbing" of the moon (Psa. 121: 6), the "windows
of the heavens" (Mal. 3: 10), the "eyelids" of the dawn (Job 3: 9).

So long as man held fast to the pictorial nature of these
figures of speech no danger arose, but rather, on the contrary,
an enrichment of his spirit.   But in the moment when darkened
through sin (Eph. 4: 18; Rom. 1: 21, 22), and led astray by demon
powers, he proceeded from this fanciful clothing of reality with
pictures to the belief in the reality of these pictures themselves,
there arose from this side also a new world of deifying conceptions, and speech ranged itself among the principal factors in
building up heathen religions.   To the further formation of the
conception of deity, and especially of the *history* of the gods
(mythology) and the heathen ideas of the other world, many other
driving forces co-operated; for example, the motives of fear and
of desire, the necessity of retribution, meditation as to world
origins, as also recollections of folklore and hero legends.

Grammatical gender is also significant in this connexion;
for in many cases this was the deciding factor whether one should
think of a divinity as masculine or feminine.

This all proves that there can be no question of any properly
national type of heathendom before the confusion of tongues.
Even if before the Babel judgment there may have been found
individual ideas of nature divinities, yet the proper national type
of heathendom had its beginning with the setting aside of the
human race as being one people and the splitting up of mankind
into separate nations (Deut. 4: 19; Rom. 1: 18–32).

But at the same time this all came to pass under *demonic
co-operation*.   For the deities of the heathen are no empty imagina-
tion.   According to the apostolic testimony of the New Testament Apollo, Diana, Aphrodite, and Ishtar, or whatever they
are all called, are no mere intellectual personifications of the
powers of nature, or mere ideal pictures of a wandering nature-
deifying fancy, but in their background they are somehow actually
existing demonic spirit powers, who, along the line of occult

inspiration, in national types of mythological dress—sometimes in luminous poetical clothing, sometimes in horrifying gloomy dress—revealed themselves to the various peoples.   Otherwise the great apostle to the Gentiles would not have been able, *by express appeal to the name of the Lord Jesus*, to drive out of that fortune-teller at Philippi a "Pythonic spirit," as the literal term is in Acts 16: 16.   Python was, among other things, a designation of the declarer of oracles at the shrine of Apollo.   In Delphi, the most important shrine and oracle of Apollo, there ruled as chief priestess the "Pythia" (a medium).   Compare also the medium of Endor (I Sam. 28: 7, 8, and Lev. 20: 27, "spirit").

Just as little could Paul have said of the non-Israelitish religions that "what the heathen offer they offer to *evil spirits*" (I Cor. 10: 20).   Thus there lies here a certain element of truth in national polytheism.   Consider the angel princes of Persia and Greece (Dan. 10: 13, 20).   Heathenism as a whole rests not only on error and deceit, but at the same time also on a spiritistic foundation.

Through all this the heathen, under demon influence, became the "creator of his gods."   To the manifoldness of national character and of other elements corresponded a manifoldness of religious maxims and basic moral ideals.

The Grecian says	:	Man, know thyself.
The Roman says	:	Man, rule thyself.
The Chinese says	:	Man, improve thyself.
The Buddhist says	:	Man, annihilate thyself.
The Brahman says	:	Man, merge thyself in the universal sum of all.
The Moslem says	:	Man, submit thyself.
But Christ says	:	"Without Me ye can do nothing," and in HIM
the Christian says	:	"I can do all things through Christ Who makes me mighty" (Phil. 4: 13).

"In his religion the heathen expresses his *godlessness*.   Religion is *the* sin, namely, the sin against the first command, the replacing of God by the gods;" "the most powerful expression of the opposition of man against God and contradiction within himself."

On the other hand even the conception of the gods (idols) has its basis in the idea of *God*.   With all its disfigurement, the false god is a caricature of the one true God.   Man in his religions is fleeing from God; but even in the flight he is held by God, cannot get free from the idea of God, and in his denial must bear witness of Him.   In heathenism truth and untruth, worth and worthlessness, lie, not only beside each other, but *in* each other.   "Therefore the relation of revelation to human religion is always a twofold unity; the gospel *breaks* the religions, is indeed their judgment, so far as they are lies and sins; the gospel *redeems* and *fulfils* the religions, bringing them to the original truth from which they derive and to which in their manner they witness."

Nevertheless, viewed as a whole, this is the false way of myriads of men. Throughout the centuries it has ruled mankind. "Whilst they held themselves to be wise, they have become fools" (Rom. 1: 22). Thereby the judgment of Babel became a judgment with most immense results. For the confusion of thought and intellectual intercourse involved in the dispersion of mankind and the setting aside of the oneness of the race, had as a consequence a *religious* confusion which far surpassed in significance the confusion of *speech*.

Also politically it had the most serious results.

iv.   *The Universal International Tension.*

From this time forward world history is a conflict between two forces; the centripetal force of the world empires, and the centrifugal force of the individual peoples. Representatives of the former are, for example, Nimrod, Nebuchadnezzar, Cyrus, Alexander the Great, and Napoleon. Representatives of the latter are, among others, the warriors of Marathon, Arminius, Gandhi, and, in general, all national risings and wars for freedom. The general aspect has been that the centripetal force of world conquerors has been repeatedly thwarted by the centrifugal force of individual nations. The most significant form of this mutual opposition is war, and therefore will wars and rumours of wars continue till the Lord shall come (Matt. 24: 6).

But in spite of all this, the Dispersion judgment has not been the cause of the origin and formation of nations *as such*, but of nations *separated* from one another in spirit, religion, language, and politics. The racial structure of mankind as such began immediately after the Flood (Shem, Ham, and Japheth), and so is no judgment at all. Also on the new earth there will still be nations (Rev. 21: 24; 22: 2). God strives after manifoldness in unity, that is, a *family* of peoples.

At the same time all this conflict of the forces that make history is overruled by the supreme Lord of history (Amos 9: 7; Isa. 45: 1–3), and thereby the history of the peoples becomes a *judgment* of the peoples. "Righteousness exalts a people; but sin is the reproach of the nations" (Prov. 14: 34). "All epochs in which faith ruled are brilliant and fruitful" (Goethe); but morally decayed civilizations go inevitably to ruin. The measure of the blessing of the peoples greatly depends upon the degree in which they observe the Divine orderings of creation and history. In this sense there are also conversions of whole nations to God, that is, national repentance, as seen in Jer. 18: 7, 8, and the city of Nineveh in the book of Jonah.

A nation is an *organism* (Hos. 11: 1), and therefore as a *unit* is called to account.   See the appeals of the prophets to the peoples, which always address the nations as units, for example, Amos 1: 2; Isa. chs. 13–23; Jer. chs. 46–51.   They live a uniform life through generations.   Therefore the descendants become sharers of the blessings or of the judgments for the deeds of their forbears (see Ezek. 35: 5, 6).   Only through all these things does the dramatic tension of the whole world explain itself, and the rise and fall of civilizations in the whirl of kingdoms and races.

Here also, of course, there still remain secrets of the Divine government upon which we cannot give light.   One has only to think of the Armenian people.

Divine ordinances in creation, history, and providence are:
Marriage and the family as the first germ of the whole.
Social status (I Pet. 2: 13, 14, 18; Eph. 6: 5–9; Col. 3: 22; 4: 1; I Cor. 7: 20).
Community of blood (Rom. 9: 3) and of history, of mentality and language, of education and custom.
Rulers (Rom. 13: 1–6; I Pet. 2: 13); since Noah (Gen. 9: 6).
Authority (I Pet. 2: 17; Rom. 13: 7) and obedience (Rom. 13: 5.)
Community life and administration of justice, the latter with the death penalty (Gen. 9: 6; Rom. 13: 4).
God-determined frontiers (Acts 17: 26).
Love of homeland and one's own people (Rom. 9: 3).
Respect for other nations.

v.   *The Redemption-goal of the History of Salvation.*

Nevertheless the confounding of the language did not signify that God was against *every* union of the human race.   On the contrary, the closest spiritual and most comprehensive fellowship of mankind is His very definite purpose (Mic. 4: 1–4).

But the unity which *He* wishes has *Himself* as its centre, it is "in Christ" His Son (Eph. 1: 10; John 10: 16; 17: 21, 22), Whom He has appointed as King (Psa. 2: 6; Zech. 14: 9).

But man desired a dethroning of the Creator, so as himself to take in hand the government; and this combination of fleshly energy stood like a bastion against the carrying through of redemption.   Therefore it had to collapse and "the scattering arm of God" shew itself.   Through the destruction of the demonic, fleshly unity was the true, divine, spiritual unity to be effected.   The abrogation of the universalism of the first revelation had therefore as its goal the more sure attainment of the final universalism, and therefore even the Babel judgment is also—grace.

vi.   *The Triumph of God at the Close of History.*

But mankind fights perseveringly against the Divine plan. The spirit of the defeated, rebellious Babel continues active in the subsequent centuries also; indeed, in the End Time it will even seem to have attained its goal and triumphed, and the Antichrist will complete the work of Nimrod (Rev. 13: 7, 8).

The history of the city of Babylon has

its pattern	— in the city of Cain (Gen. 4: 17);
its symbol	— in the tower of Babel (Gen. 11);
its chief commencement	— through Nebuchadnezzar (Dan. 2: 37. 18);
its progress	— in world history (Dan., chs. 2 and 7);
its completion	— under Antichrist (Rev. chs. 13 and 17);
its end	— by the triumph of Christ (Rev. chs. 18 and 19).

For after Antichrist will Christ appear and win the victory (Rev. 19: 11–21); and over the "harlot" (Rev. 14: 8; 17: 1–8), Babylon storming *upwards* against heaven, shall the "bride" triumph (Rev. 21: 9), the city of God which *descends* from heaven (v. 10), the new Jerusalem.

PART III

THE PREPARATORY REVELATION OF SALVATION

A—THE PROMISES AS THE BASIS OF THE GOSPEL

CHAPTER I

SALVATION AS CONTAINED IN THE OLD TESTAMENT

THE judgment at Babel had closed the original revelation. With Abraham began a completely new age. The ancestor of Israel, he is at the same time the "father of *all* believers" (Rom. 4: 11, 12). The blessing which those should receive who would be afterward won from the nations is indeed "Abraham's blessing" (Gal. 3: 14, with ver. 9). Also the church of the present age (Rom. 15: 27; Eph. 3: 6; 2: 11-19; Rom. 11: 24), and even the future kingdom of God itself (Luke 1: 72, 73), right on to the New Jerusalem (Rev. 21: 10; comp. Heb. 11: 16), rest on the basis of the promises to Abraham. Thus with Abraham begins the actual revelation of salvation and redemption. All that preceded was introductory and preparatory.

Abraham was not the first believer. Abel, Enoch, and Noah before him, and Melchizedek in his own time, had been men of faith (Heb. 11: 4-7; Gen. 14: 18). Therefore the special element in his faith does not lie in the fact of it but in its nature. The faith of all beforehand had been mostly limited to themselves or their immediate surroundings, and had thus resembled in the main a *point* or a *circle*. Abraham's faith, on the contrary, had effects going beyond himself. It was a faith with significance for the whole history of salvation, a faith for the future, more to be compared to a progressing *line*. Abraham embraced the promise not only for himself but also for his bodily and spiritual descendants. Thus he became, though at first the "one" (Mal. 2: 15; Ezek. 33: 24; Heb. 11: 12), nevertheless the ancestor of the "many" (Ezek. 33: 24), indeed, the "father of *all* believers" (Rom. 4: 11). Therefore he was the quarry, the rock, out of which the people of God are hewn (Isa. 51: 1, 2), the first recipient of the preparatory covenant and Old Testament revelation which in a special sense led directly to Christ, and which is the "holy root" that bears the noble olive tree of the kingdom of God (Rom. 11: 16-24).

i. *The Starting Point.*

In the rebellion at Babel mankind had attempted in united strength to withstand the Most High. Therefore a divine principle of separation and division had to be introduced to counteract their ungodly confederacy. They had tried to conquer heaven by their united sinful efforts, and had tried this in vain; but God purposed to use dispersion as His counteractive in order to open heaven, and it did this indeed. This came to pass in the call of Abraham. Thus in the history of salvation it is the contrast to the building of the tower, and, at the same time, its necessary consequence.

ii. *The Foundation.*

(1) *God's Freedom.* That God chose Abraham and not any other believer of his time—as Melchizedek (Gen. 14: 18–20)—was wholly an act of His free sovereignty. He is the Lord and Governor on the throne of the universe, and He distributes the figures on the chess-board of human history as He will (Rom. 9: 20). He does not, it is true, compel the believer to faith nor the unbeliever to unbelief, but leaves to each his freedom and self-determination (Matt. 23: 37; Rev. 22: 17). But *out of* the number of the wicked He chooses individual wicked men (for example, Pharoah of Egypt; Rom. 9: 17), so as to show in them a special example of His power to judge; and *out of* the number of believers He chooses individual believers so as to make them special agents for tasks in the outworking of salvation (I Cor. 12: 4–11, 29, 30). It was in this sense that even Abraham was called. He was, as it were, an *official* person, responsible to prepare for the mediating of salvation.

(2) *God's Grace.* It follows that the choice of Israel was not based on any special later superiority of this people. On the contrary God, who appointed Mary Magdalene, who had before been demon-possessed, to be the first announcer of the resurrection (Mark 16: 9; John 20: 11–18) and Matthew the taxgatherer to be the first witness of the New Testament (Matt. 9: 9), and Who always condescends to the lowly and insignificant (I Pet. 5: 5; Luke 1: 52), has indeed described the people of Israel as a thorn bush as regards its character (Exod. 3: 2, 3; Mic. 7: 4), and as regards its numbers has already said in the Old Testament, "not because you were more than all peoples has Jehovah inclined himself to you and chosen you, for you are the least among all peoples" (Deut. 7: 7). Thus the choosing of Israel conforms to the lowly outward appearance of the divine revelation. Nowhere in the Old Testament is there any approbation or racial exaltation of the unregenerate Jew. On the contrary, it is precisely the Old Testament that is full of direct,

glowing words of judgment denouncing the holy wrath of God against apostate Israel. In the sense of the Old Testament, "chosen people" (I Chron. 16: 13; Exod. 19: 5; Amos. 3: 2; Psa. 147: 19, 20) does not mean "selected, good people" (see Isa. 1: 4; Rom. 2: 24), or "before-appointed to be the politically-dominating people unto world subjection and spoliation," but simply to be "a separate people unto *service* in the course of salvation." And here it is that the Jew in the most fearful manner has failed (I Thess. 2: 15, 16). Not *Jew*-glorification is the purpose of the whole plan (Ezek. 36: 22, 23, 32), but the self-glorification of the grace and holiness of God as the God of Jews and non-Jews (Psa. 115: 1; Isa. 44: 23; Rom. 3: 29).

(3) *God's Honour*. And in the fact? The plain view of Holy Scripture is again and again distinctly this, that in spiritual susceptibility the Jew has quite often been surpassed by the non-Jew; in faith, by the centurion at Capernaum, a Roman (Matt. 8: 10); in love, by the compassionate Samaritan (Luke 10: 25–37; 17: 16); in sacrificial striving after true wisdom, by the Queen of Ethiopia (Matt. 12: 42); in repentance, by the people of Nineveh, that is Assyrians (Matt. 12: 41). "Many widows," said Christ, "were in Israel in the time of Elijah, but to none of them was Elijah sent, but only to Sarepta of the *Sidonians*, to a widow; and many lepers were in Israel in the time of the prophet Elisha, and none of them was cleansed, but only Naaman the *Syrian*" (Luke 4: 25–27). "Woe to thee, Chorazin, Woe to thee, Bethsaida, had such works come to pass in *Tyre* and *Sidon* as are come to pass in thee, they had long ago repented in sackcloth and ashes. . . . And thou, Capernaum . . . had such works come to pass in *Sodom* as are come to pass in thee, it had stood till this day" (Matt. 11: 21–24). And in Isaiah God said of Israel as His "slave," "Who is blind if not my slave, and so deaf as my messenger whom I send? who is so blind as my familiar friend, and so blind as the slave of the Lord?" (Isa. 42: 19). But if we inquire as to the ground why, in spite of it all, God made this precise choice, the answer runs, so that no flesh should glory before Him, but that "he that glorieth let him glory in the Lord" (Jer. 9: 23, 24; I Cor. 1: 27–31). The more primitive the material the greater—if the same high standard of art can be reached—the honour of the master; the smaller the army the mightier—if the same great victory can be won—the praise of the conqueror.

And thus out of all the suns and stars of the universe God has chosen this tiny earth, and on it the small land of Canaan, and in it the people of Israel, the "smallest" of all peoples (Deut. 7: 7); and in Israel the town of Bethlehem, that was too small to be reckoned among the thousands of Judah (Mic. 5: 2), and in Bethlehem itself—the manger. And from the manger it went on to the cross! Thus God chooses always the insignificant: to be the first witness in the New Testament, Matthew the tax gatherer; to be the first announcer of the resurrection, Mary of Magdala, once demon-possessed (Mark 16: 9; John 20: 11–18); to be the most prominent apostle, Paul the "chief" of all sinners (I Tim. 1: 15). But the whole results in the revelation of the Divine greatness. It is the "foolish" measure of His holy jealousy (I Cor. 1: 21, 25, 27). The very choice of the insignificant is the very method of the Divine honour.

(4) *God's Wisdom.* In addition to this there is a further Divine motive which originates from God's wisdom as to the instruction of the whole human race. In the history of Israel, as a "refractory" race (Acts 7: 51), shall all the peoples of the world be shown the fearfulness of sin, but also the glory of redemption, the seriousness of the crushing judgments, but also the depth of forgiving grace (Psa. 102: 14–16). Thereby Israel's history becomes an object-lesson on the stage of world affairs given that the nations of the earth should perceive what judgment is and what grace is (Isa. 52: 10; Ezek. 39: 23–27). But for this, on account of the dullness of mankind, that is, of all men toward God, a quite impressive and obvious example was demanded. This was a requirement of the Divine wisdom in the education of mankind, and this is also one reason for the choice of the people of Israel.

(5) *God's Righteousness.* But in all this God's dealings remain just. In no way did Israel receive a preference. For to its higher privileges (Rom. 9: 4, 5; 3: 1, 2) there was correspondingly greater responsibility. Rights and duties balanced each other. Standing brings obligation (Luke 12: 48; I Pet. 1: 17). And upon no people has sin been so visited as upon the Jews (see Deut. 28: 64–67). In Israel all things reach the climax; the privilege and the judgment, the blessing and the curse. And its very choice is the reason for quite special severity: "You alone have I chosen out of all the races of the earth. *Therefore* will I visit upon you all your iniquities" (Amos 3: 2). And when Israel in times of great judgment appeals to its standing in grace, and would, as it were, wheedle the rod of chastisement out of the hand of God, saying "My God! We know thee still, we Israel," then the brief Divine answer runs: "Israel has rejected the good. Let the enemy pursue him" (Hos. 8: 1–3).

iii. *The Accomplishment.*

But outwardly the new limitation of revelation did not signify that God had cut off every kind of connexion with the peoples that had been set aside. On the contrary, there remained also to the nations a fivefold Divine self-witness, even if more indirect.

(1) *The Symbolic language of Nature.* From the beginning in the works of creation the "eternal power and divinity" of God had been perceived by the spiritual eye (Rom. 1: 19–21).

(2) *The Conscience language of the Soul.* Even the heathen "who have no law" are themselves a law, "in that their consciences bear joint-witness and their thoughts one with another accuse or else excuse" (Rom. 2: 14, 15).

(3) *The Spiritual language of lofty Wisdom.* In the heathen world itself there is found so much lofty and profound thought that it can be explained only by an activity of the Divine wisdom, producing knowledge in the human mind in general, as with Socrates, Plato, Lao Tze, Zarathustra, and in general with so many poets and thinkers of the nations. Therefore the early church fathers spoke with right of the "seed-corns of the Word" in the heathen world (especially Justin of Sichem in the second century); and to this is to be added that, together with the natural moral qualities given to man by creation, certain general moral remembrances still survive among the peoples from the original revelation.

(4) *The Authoritative language of Human Government.* The human governing power is "God's servant" (Rom. 13: 4), an order instituted by God Himself, existing in history ever since the covenant with Noah (Gen. 9: 6). Without ruling authority human society would quickly become flooded with evil and sink into absolute devilry and religious, spiritual, and moral barbarism. But in rule God stretches forth His guardian hand. He stands behind the authority and works through it. The rulers of the earth are His tools. Therefore in the Word of God the eternal "Wisdom" speaks thus concerning itself: "Through *me* kings exercise the ruler's charge and regents publish righteous ordinances. Through *me* rule the rulers and princes, all authorities on earth" (Prov. 8: 14–16).

(5) *The Language of Events in World History.* Even *after* the choice of Abraham and Israel God's guidance in the history of the peoples continued unchanged. He turns the hearts of kings as water-brooks and leads them wherever He wills (Prov. 21: 1). He raises up Hadad of Edom (I Kings 11: 14), and Reson of Damascus (I Kings 11: 23), Tilgath-pilneser of Assyria (I Chron. 5: 26), and Cyrus the Persian (Ezra 1: 1), and already in the Old Testament He named the last His "anointed," before whom *He* led the way so as to cast down nations before him, on behalf of Israel His servant (Isa. 45: 1–7; Jer. 51: 11). And to Babylon He says: "Thou art *my* hammer, *my* weapons of war: and with thee will *I* break in pieces the nations; and with thee will *I* destroy kingdoms" (Jer. 51: 20). And finally, concerning the external ordering of Israel's history, He says: "O children of Israel, are you not to me as the Ethiopians? Have not I led

Israel out of Egypt, and the Philistines out of Caphtor, and the Syrians out of Kir?" (Amos 9: 7).   Thus the setting aside of the Gentile world was in no way an abandonment of their history by God.   Even as the God of Abraham and Israel He remains indeed the "God of the nations" (Rom. 3: 29).   The history of the human race entire was and remains "God's work" (Luther).

But this all came to pass that thereby "they might seek the Lord, if perhaps they might feel after him and find him" (Acts 17: 27).   From the viewpoint of the record of salvation the individual nations are "folds" (see John 10: 16), that is, Divinely ordered communities in preparation for the gospel,[1] which should assure the peaceful, protected proclamation of the message of salvation, the maintenance of the individual in decency and morals and " civil righteousness" (*justitia civilis*).   In a word, *World history is the scaffolding for the history of salvation*.   Not only has revelation a history but history is a revelation.   It is not only a "work" but a stimulating "word" of God.   It is a veiled self-unveiling of God, Who while revealing Himself, at the same time remains the "concealed" God, the "*deus absconditus*" [the hidden God] of Luther.   It is a sphere of the power, grace, and judgment of the Lord of the worlds as ruler of the nations.

Nevertheless, in respect of the revelation of *salvation*, the Gentiles were set aside, and this was the chief matter.   But here also their temporary, limited exclusion was only the way to their final re-acceptance and re-inclusion.

iv.   *The Goal.*

"In thee shall all the families of the earth be blessed" (Gen. 12: 3).   Here at the very start the final end is mentioned.   The singling out of Abraham was indeed necessarily to slow down the general advance of salvation, but so much the more would it, with fulness of wisdom, facilitate it and all the more surely lead it to its goal.   It was designed specially with a view to the universal aspect, the detail to the whole, the small to the great. The limiting of the revelation at first to Abraham was only the Divine method to serve the ultimate universality of the salvation.   The restriction was there, but its appointment had its own removal as its object.   God turned away His salvation from the nations so as to be able all the more certainly to give it back to them glorified.

Thus the phrase "History of Salvation," in the full conception of the terms, does not indicate a limited circle within universal history, but contemplates and interprets the whole history of mankind in its relation to God and from the watch-

---

[1] To this end also serve the Pauline figures of speech from the military, sporting, and judicial life of the heathen world.

tower of faith. "The march of the gospel through the world is the proper theme of world history." This is the one meaning of all history. Therefore the history of salvation in its full range is a "Theology of World History." God Himself, as the Lord of all history, stands at its centre. In the midst of universal history, that of the "world," He begins a particular history, that of revelation, in which He makes Himself personally present to man. In the former He works especially as the "hidden" God, in the latter especially as the God who "reveals" Himself. But both world history and the history of revelation have Himself as their common central unity. Viewed from this standpoint both belong to the history of salvation.

This is the meaning and the soul of the Old Testament. Therefore is it from end to end full of promises of salvation for the whole human race, especially throughout Isaiah. Of all books of the pre-Christian times the Old Testament is the most universal, embracing all peoples more than any other literature of that earlier world. It is the only writing of the ancient Orient which has the idea of the unity of the human race and the hope of a united movement of mankind to a common goal.

The opening chapters of the Old Testament at once show this, and especially the so-called Racial Table (Gen. 10). For this is not only the "letter of dismissal" of revelation to the now repudiated nations, but also a written guarantee that later they shall be received again. For in the very place where the sacred history begins to restrict itself to Israel, once again all the peoples of the world are enumerated, and thereby is granted to them an enduring place in the Divine revelation of the future, and they are thus assured that they are not forgotten in the loving counsel of God and shall never vanish without trace from the horizon of redemption. "An invisible green of hope winds itself through the withered branches of this catalogue of peoples." And thereby this list of seventy original nations enters into the viewpoint of the world-wide mission, and proclaims like a "Missionary Wall Map" the great truth that "God has *so* loved *the world*."

CHAPTER II

THE SURPASSING GLORY OF THE COVENANT WITH ABRAHAM

Abraham was called " Friend of God" (Isa. 41: 8; James 2: 23).

ABRAHAM is the "father of all believers" (Rom. 4: 11). As such he is not only the beginning but the pattern of all believing experience. There are, above all, four chief principles which in connexion with him are plainly introduced for the first time into the history of salvation:

i. The free character of salvation—in justifying and glorifying.
ii. The central basis of salvation —the resurrection power of God.
iii. The Mediator of salvation — the coming Seed.
iv. The goal of salvation — the heavenly city.

I. THE FREE CHARACTER OF SALVATION

The migration from Ur in Chaldea (Gen. 12) was not really the most significant event in Abraham's life, but rather that revelation on a starry night, almost ten years later, when God concluded with the Patriarch the covenant of faith (Gen. 15: 5, 18). That was the time when Abraham received the Divine declaration of justification, and it is there that in the annals of salvation the very first plain and express mention is made of the "justification" of a sinner (Gen. 15: 6; Rom. 4: 2–4).

(1) *The Justification.* But here it is definitely the time of its taking place which is the main and decisive point. For "*When was faith reckoned to Abraham unto righteousness*? before or after his circumcision?" (Rom. 4: 10). The answer runs: Not less than thirteen years before he was circumcised. Because the covenant of circumcision was first introduced when Abraham was already ninety-nine years old (Gen. 17: 1–14); but the covenant of faith and the justification took place before even the birth of Ishmael, and therefore before his eighty-sixth year (Gen. 16, esp. ver. 16; comp. 17: 1). Consequently Abraham had been justified already thirteen years before he was circumcised.

Upon this sequence Paul, in Rom. 4, builds his whole celebrated proof from Scripture that justification is through faith alone. As to Abraham himself, humanly speaking it might have been without significance whether the justification had been before or after the circumcision. God had, however, a prophetic end in view in this precise sequence. For through it Abraham was to become the "father of all such as without circumcision, but through faith alone, should become justified." But this was only possible if he himself received justification as one *un*circumcised. Therefore the sequence in his life of the two covenants is not a matter of indifference, but in relation to the development of salvation is prophetic. Through this very fact it became evident that circumcision cannot be a condition precedent to but only a "seal" of the righteousness by faith (Rom. 4: 11). But one sets a seal only to a completed document. Therefore the justification of Abraham must have been something completed and concluded in advance.

From this it follows that now, in later times, uncircumcised Gentiles do not need first to be circumcised to acquire justification, but on the contrary, the circumcised must have the faith of the still uncircumcised Abram. To attain to the temple of salvation the Gentile must not first pass through the ante-room of the Jews—that is, through the law—but the Jews must first pass through the ante-room of that faith which Abram already had while being, so to say, a "heathen."

Thus it is, set forth clearly that salvation is without human merit and that redemption is of grace, a free gift purely to faith, and proof is given that the gospel of the church age was foreshadowed in the covenant with Abraham. Thus the "new covenant" is the continuation and glorious perfection of the covenant with Abraham (Gal. 3: 9, 14; Rom. 4), and, consequently, according to its nature, is older than that "old" covenant which began with Moses (Heb. 8: 8, 9). "The patriarchial age is more evangelic than the law; as the age before the law is a prototype of the age after the law."

(2) *The Glorification*. But at the same time, with the justification, there was joined the assurance of the inheritance. "I am the Lord who caused thee to migrate out of Ur of the Chaldees, so as to give thee this land for an inheritance" (Gen. 15: 7). With the declaration of righteousness—this *beginning* of the new life—the patriarch thus received at the same time—and equally as a gift of God's free grace—the inheritance, the *goal*, of the new life (comp. Heb. 11: 8–10).

Upon this fact Paul, in Rom. 4: 13–17, places precisely the same value as on the first one. For it signified, as to its connexion with the historic-prophetic salvation, that just as justification was not connected with any kind of law (except the law of faith, Rom. 3: 27), so it would be with the inheritance, its completion and glorification. Therefore the law is neither the means of justification (see *Romans*) nor of sanctification (see *Galatians*), and nothing can set in doubt the title of the redeemed to the glorious inheritance. With the beginning of the new life its

G

title to the consummation is guaranteed. For all is a free gift
of divine grace (John 10: 28, 29; I Pet. 1: 4, 5; Rom. 8: 30).

(3) *The Sign of the covenant.* Thus it is of the highest significance for the understanding of the history of salvation to distinguish between the conclusion of *two* covenants in the life of
Abraham: the foundation covenant of faith in Gen. 15, and the
additional covenant of circumcision in Gen. 17. Both are
described as being a "covenant" (Gen. 15: 18 and 17: 9–11), and
between the two lie at least thirteen years. The first is the
eternally valid covenant of grace, given to the "heathen" Abram;
the other is a confirmatory covenant (Gen. 17: 7), appointed as a
"seal" to the already "justified" Abraham, not intended to last
eternally, but to be simply preliminary to, and to last only until,
Christ (Gal. 4: 2). But the first is the determining covenant;
grace is the beginning; and Gen. 15 is thus far the most basic
chapter of the Old Testament.

The covenant of promise included two promises, both of
double purport, and each with a covenant sign. The one is the
promise of *posterity* and develops into justification; its covenant
sign is the starry heavens (Gen. 15: 1–6). The other is the
assurance of the *land* and looks towards glorification; its sign is
the covenant sacrifice (ver. 7–21). Majestic and exalted is the
one; mysterious and dark is the other.

The offerings have been divided; the sun has gone down;
deep sleep falls on Abram. Terror, thick darkness, and anxiety
fill his soul. Birds of prey swoop down upon the offering, but
Abram scares them away. Finally the Lord passes between
the pieces of the offering, under the guise of a smoking furnace
and a flaming torch, and the covenant is concluded. From
the point of view of the history of salvation this is the most
significant covenant-making of the Old Testament (Gen. 15:
9–18).

But why so much gloom with a covenant of grace, this darkness and horror with the promise of light, why the birds of prey,
the smoking furnace, the flaming torch?

The sacrifices are Israel. What happened to them was a
type of the national destiny of this people. And this is gloomy,
full of terror and darkness (Deut. 28: 15–68). Therefore the
conclusion of the covenant itself takes place through a smoking
furnace and flaming torch. The birds of prey are the nations,
especially the Egyptians (Gen. 15: 13–16). But Abram scares
them away; for on account of the "holy root" Israel will be
granted preservation and maintenance (Rom. 11: 16, 24). "You
cannot bless us—for a curse lies on us: you cannot curse us, for
a blessing lies on us."

The passing between the pieces of the offering, which lay
over against each other in two rows, signified the filling up of

the " gap" between the two partners to the covenant, the smelting and forging together of their duality into unity and thus the perfecting of the covenant itself.   But that the Lord alone passed through (Gen. 15: 17, 18), and not Abram also after Him, signifies that the covenant is a pure gift of divine grace, that man neither works nor co-works therein, that God alone does all, and that man is simply the recipient (Rom. 3: 24; Phil. 2: 13).

II. The Central Basis of Salvation

Not only the sacrifice, but also the *victory* of the sacrifice is necessary for the completion of the redemption.   "Is Christ not raised, then is your faith vain" (I Cor. 15: 17).   Consequently the resurrection power of God is part of the determining ground of salvation.

Particularly in this is revealed again the spiritual connexion between the present age and the covenant with Abraham.   For both reach their acme in the faith that God is able to create life out of death.   There exists indeed an essential difference, in that Abraham's faith looked forward to something yet to be accomplished, while our faith looks backward to something already completed; and in that Abraham's faith expected a divine wonder in the realm of creation and in reference to an ordinary mortal man, while our faith confesses that such has already come to pass in the realm of redemption, and in reference to the Son of God Himself, our risen Saviour and Lord.

Twice, at the birth and at the sacrifice of Isaac, this came notably to the fore in the life of Abraham, and in such a manner that the second instance is the enhancing and glorifying of the first.

(1) *The Birth of Isaac.*   Abraham's faith was being steadily educated toward this high point.   Here lies the real reason why he must wait so long—till his hundredth year—for his heir (Gen. 17: 17).   "Death" (Rom. 4: 19) and "extinction" (Heb. 11: 12) must first have entered before the new life could be born. Upon this basis alone could Abraham's faith become "resurrection" faith.   Only so could he learn to believe on Him who "makes the dead to live and calls the non-existent as if it were already there" (Rom. 4: 17).   Hereto *must* he attain because he, as the "*father* of all believers" should also be the *prototype* of all believers, and because in all ages saving faith stands and falls with the resurrection of Jesus Christ (I Cor. 15: 17-19).

Thus there lies in the life-story of the Patriarch, as the Bible narrates it for us, something that is continuously and compulsorily prophetic—the waiting for the Seed was the chief matter in his life; and this *must* be so "for *our* sakes," we "who believe on him who has raised from the dead Jesus, our Lord" (Rom. 4: 17-25, esp. 24).

This faith stands out still more distinctly in the sacrifice of his son (Gen. 22).

(2) *The Sacrifice of Isaac.*   Faith is growth into God.   Therefore it requires a progressive education.   More and more must it be loosed from the earthly and attached to the heavenly.   In this sense there are in Abraham's life four ascending tests.   The highest was that on Moriah.

First there was the departure from Ur, the separating from his father's house and relations.   But, because the family of Abraham were idolaters (Josh. 24: 2) that meant separation from the *world* (Gen. 12).

Then came the separation from Lot, this indeed "righteous" (II Pet. 2: 7, 8) but nevertheless worldly-minded man (Gen. 13: 10–13; 19: 1ff.).   That meant release from all half-heartedness and lukewarmness, and thus separation from all *conformity to the world* (Gen. 13).

The third step was the dismissal of Ishmael, the son of his own human strength; and thus separation of soul and spirit (Heb. 4: 12), the parting from all thoughts and plans of pious *self-help* (Gen. 21).

The last was the sacrifice of Isaac, who was God's own gift to him as the promised seed.   Even the blessings which the Highest gave to him, faith gives back to the Giver; thus there is separation from even *divine gifts* (Gen. 22).   The worshipper takes the crown which he has received from the King, surrenders it to Him, laying it before His throne (Rev. 4: 10, 11); and says "To the Lamb be the blessings" (comp. Rev. 7: 12).

From this it becomes clear that the account of the sacrifice of Isaac, so much impugned, is not perhaps merely some chapter in the Old Testament which, in certain circumstances, could, as some think, be left out, but is the highest point in the life of the Patriarch himself; and, because he is the "root" of the revelation of redemption, it is to be viewed as prophetically symbolic, the culminating point of the promise which is the basis of the gospel in general.

In fact, the conception of sacrifice which is here taught is unique.   It cannot in any way be classed with the Canaanitish-Phoenician, Semitic, Indian, Aztec, or any other sacrifices of human beings: the sacrifice of Moriah is distinguished from them all by at least a threefold contrast.

(*a*) Firstly, by the *soul* of the sacrifice.   Not the form but the heart is the chief matter.   Abraham had "sacrificed" Isaac to God (Heb. 11: 17), and yet had not killed him.   The external completion of the act had been suddenly prevented by God Himself (Gen. 22: 12, 13).   Thereby was proclaimed the principle that it is not the external performance that makes the sacrifice to be a sacrifice, but the intention of the heart, not the presenting of the gift, but the devotion of the soul. This is a wholly inward and spiritual conception of sacrifice, which here for the very first time comes to the fore in the record of salvation. It was for this spiritualized conception of sacrifice that the later prophets of the Old Testament, in the battle against Jewish externalism, constantly strove with spiritual power (Isa. 1: 10–15; 66: 3; Jer. 6: 20; Hos. 6: 6; Amos 5: 21, 22; Mic. 6: 6–8; Psa. 40: 6–8).

(*b*) Secondly: by the *victory* of the sacrifice. Not death but life is the final goal of true sacrifice. Indeed the command to sacrifice the one and only person through whom the promise must be fulfilled must have seemed at first to the Patriarch to be full of contradiction. For how should the promises of God ever be possible of fulfilment, seeing that they were bound up with *none other* than this same Isaac, who, moreover, was at the time of the sacrifice without descendant (Gen. 17: 21; 21: 12)? Here appeared to be a conflict between the command of God and the faithfulness of God, which plainly was intolerable. Nevertheless, since God never can lie, there remained to reflecting faith a solution—either God would provide Himself a beast to be sacrificed in place of Isaac being offered (Gen. 22: 7, 8), or, in case it should really come to the death of the firstborn, He would raise him, as the bearer of the promise, again to life (Heb. 11: 19). He demanded a *burnt* offering (Gen. 22: 2, 3, 6–8); He required in Abraham's case, that Isaac, slaughtered with the knife (v. 10), should be burned to ashes. But, for the sake of His faithfulness and promises, this very Isaac, burned to ashes, He must bring again from death to life! And to this last supreme height it appeared that it would really come on Mount Moriah (Gen. 22: 9, 10).

This is Abraham's boldness of faith. So the Scripture testifies. In the very act of sacrificing his son he reckoned "that God was able even to raise him from the dead" (Heb. 11: 19). Therefore as he left his servants he had said to them "When we have worshipped, *we* (not "I") will come again to you" (Gen. 22: 5).

"Faith reconciles contradictions;"[1] and by this test Abraham's faith was ennobled unto becoming the type of the New Testament faith in resurrection. At the *birth* of Isaac it had first been a "faith in resurrection," in the sense of new quickening of impotent "dead" natural powers (Rom. 4: 17–20); but at the *sacrifice* of Isaac, it became, in the circumstances, a resurrection faith, ✳ in the sense of a literal resurrection of one literally dead. So the Patriarch gained "through the advancing activity of his faith the idea of resurrection, and, in the actual outcome of the narrative of the sacrifice—the sacrifice of the ram in place of Isaac—

[1] "*Fides conciliat contraria*" (Luther, who explains Gen. 22 as above).

he gained the idea of the true sacrifice, i.e. substitution" (J. P. Lange).   Therein he is a new type of our faith; for in the sacrifice of the Lord the resurrection belongs inseparably to the cross, and life triumphs over death (Rom. 8: 34; 5: 10; I Cor. 15: 17–19).

(*c*) Thirdly.   But the *goal* of Moriah is Golgotha.   Not the present but the future gave this sacrifice its highest value.   Therefore did it take place nowhere else than on "Moriah," the mount where "God is seen" (Gen. 22: 14), where later the Temple stood (II Chron. 3: 1), where upon the altar of burnt offering all the sacrifices which pointed to Christ would be brought, and where in the death hour on Golgotha the veil between the holy and the all-holy places would be rent (Mark 15: 38).   Thereby Isaac became a type of Christ and Abraham of God the Father, and the summit of the most decisive and fundamental covenant of the whole Old Testament became a symbolic prophecy as to the centre of *all* testaments and covenants of God, the cross of Golgotha.

Thus the sacrifice of Moriah announces three great salvation truths of the Biblical conception of sacrifice:

1.   The spiritual nature of sacrifice;
2.   The resurrection of the victim sacrificed;
3.   The personal fulfilment of the sacrifice in Christ.

And the last is the greatest of them all.

III.   The Mediator of the Salvation

(1)   *Abraham and Christ.*   Of Abraham's long life of 175 years (Gen. 25: 7) we know extraordinarily little.   Almost everything deals with the expected seed.   But it is this that is of the highest significance.   Before Abraham there had indeed been announcements of the coming Redeemer: of the Crusher of the serpent (Gen. 3: 15), of the Rest-bringer (Gen. 5: 29), of Jehovah, the God of Shem (Gen. 9: 26).   But all this came in very veiled form and extremely seldom—according to Biblical chronology only these three times in the course of almost twenty-five centuries!

But now, with Abraham, the expectation of the "seed" became the all-prevailing and chief thought (Gal. 3: 16), and, for the first time, stands in the foreground of all events in the sacred history.   So much is the "seed" the centre of the Patriarch's life that his history, as recorded in the Bible, occupies itself scarcely at all with his person, but almost exclusively, in nearly every chapter, with his expectation of the promised heir.   One has only to think of the first promise of the seed (Gen. 12), the conclusion of the covenant (ch. 15), the birth of Ishmael, the false seed (ch. 16), the circumcision covenant and the promise to the man of ninety-nine (ch. 17), the visit of the three men (ch. 18), the casting out of Ishmael (ch. 21), the sacrifice of Isaac (ch. 22), and the wooing of Rebecca for his son (ch. 24).

Thus the life-goal of the Patriarch lay not in himself but in the coming Mediator of salvation.   Abraham exists for the sake of Christ.

Christ lived *before* him (John 8: 58);

Christ lived *in* him (I Pet. 1: 11, comp. Gen. 20: 7).

Christ lived *after* him and moved before his vision (John 8: 56).

For this reason the sight of Messiah's day was the summit of his life.   Never in the Old Testament do we read that Abraham "rejoiced;" but in the New Testament the Lord Jesus speaks of it. And what was the ground of this exultant cry of joy of the Patriarch?   The Lord says: "Abraham, your father, rejoiced over this, that he should see *my day*; and he *has* also seen it and rejoiced over it" (John 8: 56).   Thus by the view of the coming Redeemer, Abraham's faith rose to exultation; and the like joy is imparted to all true sons of Abraham (I Pet. 1: 8).

But for Abraham himself the Redeemer is something manifold:

> the origin of his being (John 8: 58);
> the aim of his life (Gal. 3: 16);
> the secret purpose of his efforts (Gen. 15: 3);
> the strength of his service (I Pet. 1: 11, comp. Gen. 20: 7);
> the channel of his blessing (Gal. 3: 14);
> the goal of his hope (John 8: 56);
> the subject of his joy (John 8: 56).

(2) *The "Angel of the Lord."*   The spiritual significance of the covenant with Abraham is also the reason why *at this very moment* (Gen. 16: 7), for the first time in the history of redemption, the "Angel of the Lord" comes forward.   As the church fathers had already recognized,[1] this is no less a person than the Son of God Himself, the Word (John 1: 1; Rev. 19: 13; Prov. 8: 22, 23), who appeared later in Christ (John 1: 14).

Therefore He calls Himself plainly "*God*" (Exod. 3: 2, comp. 6), and is so named by the Bible historians (Gen. 1: 22, 11, comp. 1; Exod. 3: 2, comp. 4: 7; Jud. 13: 22, comp. 15).

Therefore *Divine characteristics* are ascribed to Him (Judges 13: 18, comp. Isa. 9: 6; John 12: 41, comp. Isa. 6: 1–4), and Divine *actions* (Gen. 16: 10; 18: 10, comp. vv. 13, 14; 48: 15, 16; Exod. 23: 20, 21; 14: 19, comp. 13: 21; Judges 2: 1; I Cor. 10: 4).

Therefore also is *Divine honour* rendered to Him (Gen. 16: 13, comp. 7; Judges 6: 22–24), which also He accepts (Josh. 5: 14, comp., on the contrary Rev. 19: 10; 22: 8, 9).

[1] Among later scholars we mention Calvin, Hengstenberg, Keil, Ebrard, Lange, and Stier.

And if this "Angel of the Lord" *before* He appeared to Abraham, had first appeared to Hagar (Gen. 16: 7), this is on the same principle that later the Risen One revealed Himself first to Mary Magdalene, not to His mother Mary or to John the disciple (John 20: 1–18; Mark 16: 9).   For He shows Himself first to the most afflicted and dejected.   He is the Saviour of the poor (Matt. 5: 3; 11: 5).

But that at exactly this point in the patriarchal age, He appears for the first time under this name and in this form of manifestation, rests on the fact that this patriarchal age is the very foundation of the revelation of salvation, the actual beginning of a more definite preparation of His own incarnation.

Therefore nothing can be more fitting than that just here the Son of God Himself, the true end of this incarnation, should appear for the first time, indicating at one and the same time His oneness with God and also a certain self-distinction from God.   To the father of the "seed" (Gal. 3: 16) appears the "Seed" Himself as the "Messenger,"[1] the "Angel of the Lord" (Gen. 22: 11, 15); and from now on throughout the whole Old Testament there runs an organic unfolding of this veiled self-revelation of the Son; from the "Angel of the Lord" (Gen. 16: 7), to the "Angel of the presence" (Isa. 63: 9; Exod. 33: 14; 23: 20, 21), on to the "Angel of the covenant" (Mal. 3: 1), unto, indeed, Jehovah Himself, Who will come suddenly to His temple (Mal. 3: 1).

IV.   The Goal of Salvation

In Christ faith arrives finally at its goal, heaven and the heavenly city.   Thus also Abraham.   He lived as a stranger in the promised land, and "dwelled in tents with Isaac and Jacob, co-heirs of the same promise; for he awaited the city which has the foundation walls, whose designer and master-builder is God" (Heb. 11: 9, 10).

Here below, an alien—there above, a citizen:
Here below, a tent (Gen. 12: 8; 13: 18)—there above, a city:
Here below, the altar (Gen. 12: 8; 21: 33)—there above, the face of God, the eating and drinking in His kingdom (Matt. 8: 11).

This is the heavenly calling of the Abrahamic covenant.

V.   The Epoch of the Patriarchs

The covenant with Abraham has developed in a remarkable manner, first in the life of the Patriarch himself, and then also in his bodily and spiritual descendants.

[1] In the New Testament also Christ is once named the "Messenger" (Apostle) of our confession (Heb. 3: 1).

(1) *The stages of development in the life of Abraham.* In the life of faith of Abraham five stages are plainly to be distinguished, whose beginnings are always signalized by Divine revelations of epoch-marking significance.

The first stage (Gen. 12 to 14) begins with the departure from Ur in Chaldea and the migration to the land of promise. This stage is connected especially with his *call.*

The second stage (Gen. 15 and 16) begins with the covenant of faith, when he was declared to be righteous, and with the sealing of that faith by the covenant sacrifice. The special significance of this stage is *justification.*

Then, after a waiting period of thirteen years (Gen. 16: 16, comp. 17: 1), which was the Divine answer to the precipitate action of Abraham over Hagar and Ishmael, there comes the third stage (Gen. 17 to 21). This begins with the changing of his name from Abram ("exalted father") to Abraham ("father of the multitude"), together with the introduction of the covenant of circumcision, and the dedication of the Patriarch to *devotion* and *holiness.*

The circumcision is indeed no *means* to justification (Rom. 4: 9–12) or sanctification (Gal. 5: 2–12), but it is nevertheless a *symbol,* or more exactly a *type,* of sanctification, and more especially of the principle of the surrender of the sinful self-nature unto death, the "cutting off" of the God-estranged life and all its impulses. Therefore the "circumcision not made with hands" is the "putting off of the body of the flesh," that is, being crucified and dead together with Christ (Col. 2: 11, comp. Rom. 6: 2–4).

Connected with this dedication is the fourth stage, the chief test and proof (Gen. 22) in the surrender of his son on Moriah; and thus finally, after this *supreme testing* of his faith, can the fifth stage arrive, the period of calm and repose from work, life's evening and *perfecting* (Gen. 23–25: 10).

(2) *The Transferences of the Covenant.* The covenant of God with Abraham continued as the foundation for the two following Patriarchs. For when it speaks afterwards of a covenant with Isaac and Jacob, this is not another, a new covenant, but simply a confirming, maintaining, and transferring of the same Abrahamic covenant to new participants (Gen. 26: 3; 28: 13–15; 35: 12). Therefore said God to Isaac: "I will maintain (establish, fulfil) the oath which I have sworn to thy father Abraham" (Gen. 26: 3); and to Jacob He revealed Himself in Bethel unreservedly as the "God of Abraham" and the "God of Isaac" (Gen. 28: 13). Moreover, He added to the promises no substantial and new covenant stipulations (Gen. 35: 12).

Such transferences of the covenant were necessary, because Isaac had Ishmael and the children of Keturah as brethren (Gen.

25: 1–4), as also Jacob had Esau as brother.   Therefore a special Divine promise was always needed to declare which one of all these should be the incumbent of the Abrahamic covenant. From Jacob onward, however, this was no longer necessary, since no one of his children was excluded from the blessing.   In consequence, transferences of the covenant cease from this point.

In all, Abraham had three kinds of posterity:

(a) purely *bodily*: Ishmael, the children of Keturah (especially Midian, Gen. 25: 1–4), and Esau (Edom);

(b) *bodily* and *spiritual*: Isaac, Jacob, and Israel, and

(c) purely *spiritual*: the believers from all nations (Rom. 4: 11, 12; Gal. 3: 14).

Thus there is threefold fulfilment of the promise given to him that his descendants should be as "the dust of the earth" (Gen. 13: 16), as the "sand by the sea" (Heb. 11: 12), and as "the stars of heaven" (Gen. 15: 5).   And Abraham became both "ancestor of a multitude of peoples" (Gen. 17: 5), which came to pass through his bodily and bodily-spiritual descendants; and also the channel of blessing for all families of the earth (Gen. 12: 3)—this is fulfilled in Christ and the spiritual blessing of redemption (Gal. 3: 14).

(3) *The Possessors of the Covenant*.   Abraham, Isaac, Jacob, and Joseph are the leading personalities in the period of the patriarchal promise of faith.   Faith is common to them all, and, as its foundation, the covenant promise.   Nevertheless this common possession shines in each case with a different brightness.

Abraham is the *seeking* and *finding* faith.   He looked first for the land, then for the heir, and finally for the heavenly city (Gen. 12: 1; 15: 3; Heb. 11: 10).

Isaac is the *enduring* and *resting* faith.   He endured on Mount Moriah (Gen. 22), renounced his wells so as to avoid conflict with his enemies (Gen. 26: 15–17, 20, 22), and made no such great journeys as Abraham, Jacob, and Joseph.

Jacob is the *serving* and *fruit-bearing* faith.   Although humanly less attractive than his brother Esau, he yet, on account of his faith in the promise, was preferred to his unbelieving brother (Mal. 1: 2; Rom. 9: 12, 13), and at last, after many years service, he attained to greater increase and fruitfulness (Gen. 29 and 30).

Finally, Joseph is the *suffering* and *triumphing* faith; in his humiliation, as also in his exaltation, a prophetic type of Christ.

But all four together, taken in this order, display the law of the growth of faith.   Faith begins with seeking and finding. It shall be glorified in its triumph.   But between lies the enduring and serving, and in the serving the fruit-bearing.

Thus the succession of the four Patriarchs is of the deepest significance.   We must begin with Abraham, and then pass through the experience of Isaac and Jacob so as to attain to the suffering and victory of Joseph. In this sense the history of the Patriarch's faith becomes the history of all experimental faith in general; and as the former reached its summit in Joseph as a *type* of Christ, so has the latter its perfection in Christ, the living One, Himself.

To carry forward the history of salvation directly to Him is the task of the next following period, that of the law.

CHAPTER III

ISRAEL'S CALL AND TASK

"IN Abraham—the gracious, creative rule of God, who calls the non-existing as if it were already there (Rom. 4: 17);
"In Isaac—life from the dead (Rom. 4: 19–24; Heb. 11: 19);
"In Jacob—undeserved, free grace and final glorious outcome; the man of God appears, who from being an intriguer becomes a hero for God[1]—this is Israel's origin."

Every thing in Israel's history is aiming at and bound up with its call and commission.

i. *Israel's Task.*

Israel has a double task. It was to be the *receiver* of the Divine revelation and the lodging-place for the World-Redeemer, and thus the birthplace for the Christian church (John 4: 22, comp. Rom. 11: 16–24). But it should also prepare the way among the nations of the world, and, as God's witness and missionary, be the *channel* to the nations of the revelation of salvation, so as to prepare for the evangelization of the world.

"At the first glance these two tasks contradict each other and appear irreconcilable; and yet in Israel they are completely reconciled. So as to be the homeland of the Messiah and the birthplace of Christianity Israel must be a self-contained people, *separated* from all the Gentiles, set indeed in sharp contrast to the Gentiles as the people of the revelation, who alone knew the living God, because to them He had made known His will in the law. On the other hand this people must be *spread abroad* among the Gentiles, dwell among them and have constant intercourse with them, so as to prepare the way for Christianity."

The recognition of this two-fold harmonious contrast of separation and world-wide contact, of concentration and expansion, of centripetal and centrifugal forces, is the only key for understanding the history of Israel. It may be otherwise expressed as the polarity between particularism and universalism, exclusivism and inclusivism. Without this key all remains obscure. This contrast shows itself most sharply in the culminating point of Israel's call, the promise of the Redeemer.

[1] Gen. 32: 28–30, Jacob means "heel-holder," outwitter; Israel signifies wrestler with God.

ii. Israel's Messianic Expectation.

Here is absolute *expansion*, a breaking through of all limitation and restriction: the Messiah is Saviour of the world (Mal. 1: 11; John 4: 42). Mankind is one family, with only one origin and one goal. Consider the genealogical tree of Gen. 10. The historian J. von Müller says rightly: "The whole universal history must begin from this chapter"; and Michael Baumgarten adds with equal right: "And with this chapter, as its final outcome, will it end." All peoples of the earth, with Israel, are sharers in the redemption. And as Israel in the history of revelation is God's "firstborn" son (Exod. 4: 22), so at last will they *all* become "sons" of God (Psa. 87: 4–6; Isa. 25: 6–8; 19: 25). With these thoughts Israelitic prophecy spanned the most world-embracing range that antiquity ever knew.

And yet at this very point there appears the most absolute *concentration*. For this Redeemer of the world is *one* man (I Tim. 2: 5), *one* descendant of David, *one* Saviour (Acts 4: 12). (See *Note* at end of this section). And the mightiest fact is that world history has spoken its "Yea" to this expectation! Jesus of Nazareth, the One, the Son of God, has been extolled by millions of men as Lord and Redeemer, and His spiritual wealth has been acknowledged by the leading peoples of human civilization as their guiding ideal for character and morality. But why is this expectation not found among the Romans and Greeks also, but only in the revelation to the "least" of the peoples? (Deut. 7: 7). Was it perhaps just a chance product of a high political instinct, or of a mere morbidly developed nationalism? Why, then, has He *as a fact* appeared precisely as the fulfilment of this prophecy, and, *in reality*, as the Saviour of the world, become "the banner of the peoples," [the standard, rallying point, leader]? (Isa. 11: 10; Rom. 15: 12). Perhaps by chance? Nay; here there is but one intelligent answer: the Bible is true. World history is its witness. The fulfilment is the confirmation of the prophecy. Unbelief must believe things yet more unbelievable than faith accepts. But we are not credulous enough to be incredulous.

To arrive at this double-centred condition of highest concentration and world-wide extension was the meaning of all Israel's history. Therefore all things connected with this people have been planned with regard to these two associated yet opposed requirements.

NOTE

That Jesus was an Aryan will, so long at any rate as historical science exists, be reckoned, even from a purely human standpoint, as simply fanciful. For

(i) Jesus' Israelitish descent is established unequivocally and unanimously in the historical records of the Bible (e.g. Luke 1: 32; Rom. 1: 3; II Tim. 2: 8; etc.), and historical knowledge must start with historical records.

(ii) Jesus' brother after the flesh, James, was one of the leading Christians in the church at Jerusalem which certainly consisted of *Jewish* Christians (Gal. 1: 19).

(iii) Jesus' Israelitish descent was never called in question by His Jewish enemies, and yet it was they who, in the most violent manner, sought to refute before the rulers and the people His Messiahship. But had they only the slightest ground to surmise that Jesus was only half-Jewish, or of wholly Gentile descent, this would have been for them the most illuminating evidence to produce in court before the eyes of all contemporaries to show that it was impossible for Him to be the predicted Messiah. That they *did* not do this proves that they *could not* do it. Also the later Jewish historians who, with the wildest hate in the most vulgar manner have abused Jesus, have at no time called in question His connexion by birth with the people of Israel; and thus the very enemies of the Lord become the most unchallengeable witnesses to His Israelitish descent.

But on the other hand Jesus was not purely Jewish, in the common sense of the term; for, although born "after the flesh," through Mary, "of the seed of David" (Rom. 1: 3; II Tim. 2: 8), yet through His supernatural birth He was infinitely more than the highest recapitulation and flower of the human possibilities of His earthly people. For precisely the activity and dynamic of *the man* which, in the racial life, is the real formative energy of people, State, and nation, was excluded in the birth of Christ (Matt. 1: 20). Thus He was indeed born *in* the Jewish people, but *without,* in the purely human meaning of the word, being a "Jew." As "God manifest in the flesh" (I Tim. 3: 16) He is super-racial, super-national, to *all* sinners alien by nature, and, at the same time, as Redeemer of the world, for *all* races the Saviour and Lord. Thus His virgin birth (Isa. 7: 14) has to do not only with His holiness (freedom from inherited sin), but also with His work as the Saviour (freedom from racial limitation). It is the indispensable presupposition for His Person and His work, the centre and the circumference of the circle for Him as both the Holy One and the Saviour.

iii. *Israel's Aptitude.*

No people is so capable as the Jew of keeping separate and yet being so widespread. No other is so national and yet at the same time so universal. "No other preserves so tenaciously its individuality and also remains in the midst of other peoples so self-contained and secluded. Yet again, no other so understands how to attach himself to all places and accommodate himself to all circumstances, as does the Jew. The Jew settles down in all places, is able to make room for himself everywhere, and yet everywhere remains a Jew!"

The land of Palestine also corresponds to this two-fold bridging of opposites, of world-separation and world-association.

iv. *Israel's Land.*

Palestine is a secluded land, situate like an island, like a garden, hedged around by mountains, deserts, and water (Isa. 5: 1, 2). Its coast is without [a natural] port; no river leads to its interior, and the sea which elsewhere so unites the peoples is to it a separating wall. Hostile neighbours surround it and isolate it on all sides, and the centres of world civilization are distant.

And yet it is the "centre of the earth" (Ezek. 38, 12), the bridge between the ruling nations of the ancient oriental world, placed where three continents most nearly touch, where the two national groups of ancient history, the Western and the Eastern, most nearly meet. From here roads lead in all directions and it is easy to reach the chief Gentile lands. It is therefore no wonder that the Babylonian-Assyrians and the Egyptians fought again and again for possession of this bridge. Before the children of Israel took possession of the land the following powers had owned it or exercised supremacy there:

before 2100 B.C. : the pre-Canaanitish original inhabitants;
before 2000   : the Hamitic Canaanites (Gen. 10: 15–20);
about 2000   : the Elamites (Gen. 14: 1–4);
about 1900   : the Babylonians (Hammurabi);
about 1500   : the Egyptians (the period of Moses and Amarna).

Compare in the third and second centuries before Christ the conflicts for Palestine between the Egyptian Ptolemies ("king of the south") and the Syrian Seleucids ("king of the north"); Dan. 11.

Above all, it was therefore no wonder that this situation was most favourable when the question arose of carrying the gospel out into all the world. "This is Jerusalem. I have set her in the midst of the peoples and lands round about her" (Ezek. 5: 5). Thus the land completely answered to the vocation of its inhabitants. The contrast between separation and universality shows itself in its case as geographical seclusion and central situation. Israel's position among the nations, according to Divine revelation for its history, was "*separate* from the peoples and yet *for* them."

NOTE

The name "Hebrew" is derived from the name "Eber" (the opposite, on the other side; Gen. 10: 21, 24; 11: 14, 15), and rests, apparently upon a family migration, unknown to us, of the forbears of Abraham from "beyond" the Jordan; and because Eber, as the seventh *before* Abraham, was the prime ancestor of *other* Semites also (e.g. Ophir and Havilah, Gen. 10: 25–30), the word "Hebrew" is at first the description of pre-Abrahamitic-Semitic family groups (see Gen. 14: 13; 39: 14, 17; 43: 32).   In the prophecy of Balaam (Num. 24: 24) Eber is named in the same sentence with Asshur.   Only later did the name become the *national* description of the Old Testament covenant people as a political and ethnic unit, in contrast to other though related peoples (Exod. 5: 3; I Sam. 4: 6; 13: 19; Jonah 1: 9).

The name Judah comes from the name of the fourth son of Jacob (Gen. 29: 35, *Judah,* Praise), and as the name of a people it refers first to the tribe of Judah only.   Not till after the division of the kingdoms (about 950 B.C.) does it indicate the whole southern kingdom of Benjamin-Judah (II Kings 16: 6; Jer. 32: 12); and finally, after the return from the Babylonian captivity (538 B.C.), the entire nation, the twelve tribes in general (e.g. Matt. 27: 29, 37).

The name "Israelite" is derived from Israel, the second name of the patriarch Jacob, given to him after his conflict with God at Peniel (Gen. 32: 28, "wrestler with God"), the properly *theocratic* name of the Patriarch.

ISRAEL'S DOWNFALL AND WANDERINGS

ISRAEL is the covenant people of God (Amos. 3: 2; Psa. 147: 19, 20), set apart for the purpose of spreading the message of salvation among the peoples of the world. This great, two-fold purpose of its vocation corresponds to all God's leading in its history.

I. ISRAEL'S EDUCATION

(1) *Divine training for separation* (1900–586 B.C.). "Get thee out from thy fatherland and thy kindred"—Israel's history begins with this command of God to Abram. "Thus it begins with separation, and, centuries long, all the ways of God with Israel tend to its separation, its *seclusion*, so as to strengthen its character as a people."

"The 'hedge' of the law (Eph. 2: 14; Psa. 147: 19, 20), Palestinian Judaism, the Hebrew Old Testament, the temple in Jerusalem, these are the four chief testimonies to this education of the people."

But after a millennium and a half, there is a change; and from then onwards, again through centuries, all is directed to the *scattering* of Israel among the nations. The turning point is the captivity in Babylon (606–536 B.C.).

(2) *Divine training for world-wide service.* From the Babylonian captivity (606 or 586), there entered

alongside of the Palestinian Judaism the Judaism of the Dispersion, the Diaspora (see Jas. 1: 1; Acts 2: 5–11):

alongside of the temple the synagogues, devoted rather to teaching than to sacrifice, but creating in all cities and lands new centres of Jewish life:

alongside of the Hebrew Old Testament the Greek translation, the Septuagint (LXX), destined to bring the law and the prophets and the melodious psalms of David not to the Jews of the Dispersion only, but also to the Gentiles.

Palestinian Judaism, with the temple and the Hebrew Old Testament, was in the highest degree a centralizing power; there also the innumerable communities of Jews living in the heathen world had their centre of gravity. On the other hand, the Diaspora, with the synagogue and the Septuagint, was a far-spreading power, ever striving after expansion. Through them Israel became a messenger of God, a missionary in the heathen world.

And yet—what happened?   In everything Israel opposed the plan of God.

ii. *Israel's Failure.*

(1) From the giving of the law until the Babylonian captivity (1500–586 B.C.) Israel's chief sin was idolatry (Exod. 32; Judges 2: 17; 10: 6; I Kings 11: 5; II Kings 16: 3, 4; Ezek. 8; etc.).   This means that in the very period in which all the Divine education aimed at *seclusion* and *separation* from the peoples of the world, Israel maintained idolatrous *intercourse* and *fellowship* with them, and also political union (Isa. 39; Hos. 7: 11).   Against Divine exclusion they set fleshly inclusion, against centripetal force centrifugal, against holy love faithless whoredom (Ezek. 16 and 23; Hos. 1–3; Isa. 1: 21).   And therefore, after centuries of patience, the sentence of God over guilty Jerusalem ran: "This city has been to me a cause of wrath and anger from the day that it was built until this day; wherefore I will cast it away from my presence" (Jer. 32: 31).

Nebuchadnezzar came.   Jerusalem was destroyed and the kingdom of Judah carried into captivity (586 B.C.).   But then came to pass the Jewish miracle.   *In* Babylon Israel was cured *of* Babylon.   Babylon itself, "the mother of all whoredom and idolatry" (Rev. 17: 5), became the place of cure for the whorish people.   Here, in the central city "of all the abominations on earth" (Rev. 17: 5), was the Jewish nation liberated from Babylonian idolatry, and with fresh tasks and aims the believing remnant of Israel returned from captivity (538).

(2) From the Babylonian captivity (538) onward all the ways of God with Israel were directed to preparing it for its *world-wide* mission among the nations.   But what did the people do now? It secluded itself and in proud self-exaltation despised the Gentiles as unclean "dogs."   Particularly under the leadership of the Pharisees, the "separated,"[1] this carnal emphasis upon their privileged standing reached its highest point.

So now Israel—precisely as contrary as before—against Divine universalism set a self-righteous nationalism, against world association a religious withdrawal from the world, against the mission to the peoples the centralizing of the People; and just as formerly, when God wished separation they practised association, so now when God wished association they culti- vated separation.   Thus at all times they were a people stiff- necked and resisting (Acts 7: 51), "people whose heart always prefers the wrong way" (Psa. 95: 10).

But Israel reached the highest point of its sin at the time of

---

[1] The word Pharisee is derived from the Hebrew *parash*, separated, secluded. It was in this spirit that the Pharisees carried on the work of making proselytes: Matt. 23: 15.

Christ.   By a triple gradation—by the rejection of the message of the kingdom of the heavens (Matt. 23: 37), by the murder of the Messiah on Golgotha (Acts 7: 52), and by the rejection of the testimony of the resurrection (Acts 4: 2, 3, 21; 7: 51, 58; 13: 46; 28: 25–28)—Israel committed the sin of *all* sins, the rejection of the Son of God.   And henceforth it stood under the Divine judgment.

Now the two "poles" of its character are in disharmony; and in fairly regular alternation Israel's history sways between avowed accommodation to the nations among whom it is dispersed, and decided emphasis upon its racial individuality.

In either case, such an attitude must lead to collapse.

III.   Israel's Downward Course

Israel's course was downward.   The downfall was completed in three great stages.   At first the people had

(1) *The direct rule of God:* from Moses to Samuel (1500–1100). Born as a nation at Sinai, Abraham's descendants had God Himself as "King:" "ye shall be to me a kingdom of priests and a holy nation" (Exod. 19: 5, 6; 15: 18).   "Moses has given us the law . . . so is he (God) king in Jeshurun" (the "upright" the "righteous," that is, Israel in its ideal vocation) (Deut. 33: 5, and see 32: 15).   Moses, Joshua, and the fourteen judges to Samuel inclusive were nothing else than mandatories for the time being of the Lord, for the performance of appointed individual tasks, longer or shorter.   Then they sometimes even returned again to private life (see Judges 8: 29–32).   There was no earthly kingdom. Gideon expressly declined it (Judges 8: 23), and the only one— his son Abimelech—who set one up did so in opposition to God and went miserably to ruin (Judges 9).

The earthly instruments of the heavenly King were the prophets (Deut. 18: 15), the priests (Deut. 33: 8–11), and the heroes ("judges," "saviours," "bringers of salvation," Judges 3: 9); and even the leadership of these men did not in the least rest upon any external legal title, such as birth (Judges 11: 1), vote, or position, but solely upon the inner call of God (Judges 2: 16; 3: 15; etc.).   There was no permanent external central *government*, but rather a central *altar*; for the unity of the people lay in its descent and its faith; and the tabernacle at Shiloh, as the common centre of the public worship of God, was the visible expression of this unity (Josh. 18: 1, 10; 19: 51; I Sam. 1: 3; 4: 3).

But this whole constitution was too "bad" because it was too good.   Only in a people devoted to God could it be fruitful. In the contrary case, it could not but operate to some extent as a "king*less*" time.   And exactly so it was with Israel (Judges 18: 1; 19: 1; 21: 25).   Therefore came at last the desire for a visible king (I Sam. 8).

Thence began the second period:

(2) *The indirect rule of God*: from Saul to Zedekiah (1000–586). Only with reluctance did God grant the request, for from the standpoint of the kingdom *of God* an earthly kingdom was a retrograde step, indeed, a rejection of Jehovah (I Sam. 8: 7). Nevertheless God held fast to His kingly rights. Centuries later He was still praised by the prophets and psalmists as the true king of Israel: "The Lord is our judge, the Lord is our lawgiver, the Lord is our King" (Isa. 33: 22, with 6: 5; 43: 15; Jer. 10: 10; Psa. 2: 6).

Out of this arose the peculiar position of the "king" of Israel. Because Jehovah is the actual King, the earthly kings are only *viceroys,* only a dynasty of hereditary governors with the title of king; wherefore also the choice was not a democratic election by the people, but rested entirely in the hand of God (Deut. 17: 15), Who announced it through the mouth of prophets (I Sam. 10: 1; 16: 1). The people possessed only the right of "installation", that is, of public recognition (I Sam. 11: 15; II Sam. 2: 4; 5: 1 ff.). The king was nothing more than "prince over the inheritance of *Jehovah*" (I Sam. 10: 1) and therefore king entirely by the "grace of God." And further, because in Israel the spiritual office stood nearer than the secular to the heavenly King, therefore, in the history of the kingdom of God, the prophets in Israel stood *above* the kings and were their counsellors, conscience, eyes, ears, guardians, and supervisors.

But even within this period, marked already by a much lower rule of God, Israel went downhill, and this again in three descending stages.

First they had

the *united* kingdom under Saul, David, and Solomon, (1050–950);
then after the division of the kingdom (975 or about 940)
the *double* kingdom, the divided Israel–Judah, until the Assyrian captivity (722 B.C.); and finally only
the *remnant* kingdom, "Judah" the two southern tribes (722–586).

With its last king, Zedekiah, the visible kingdom finally broke up completely; and thence forward Israel had only this last, namely:

(3) *The Suspended Rule of God*, i.e. the rule of God without formal legal arrangements. This exists from 586 B.C. until the establishment of the kingdom of Messiah. With Nebuchadnezzar began the "times of the Gentiles" (Luke 21–24). Since the destruction of Jerusalem Israel has stood under the rule of the nations of the world.[1] Not even the Maccabees' fight for

---

[1] For the present this has ceased by the setting up of the Jewish State in 1948. But they are to be dominated and oppressed by the last Gentile monarch, the Antichrist. Dan. 9: 27; Luke 21: 20–24; II Thess. 2: 4; Rev. 13. [Trans.]

freedom could alter this [168–141 B.C. (63)]. As in a game, Palestine passed like a ball from one hand to another; the Babylonians, the Persians, the Greeks (Macedonians), the Ptolemies (Egyptians), the Seleucids (Syrians), and then, after the Maccabees, the Romans, were lords of the land.

At last Israel was even exiled *out* of the land (especially after the rising under the false Messiah, Bar-Kochba—A.D. 132–135); since when, in consequence of the judgment of God, according to the testimony of the Old Testament itself, the people have been wandering as despised aliens among the nations. Nor are they only "a reproach and scorn, a byword and a curse in all places" (Jer. 24: 9; 25: 18; 26: 6; 29: 18; 42: 18), but Moses said specifically: "thou shalt find no ease among these nations, and thou shalt find no rest for the sole of thy foot, but *Jehovah* will give thee there an always trembling heart, and eyes languishing from longing, and an anguished soul . . .   At the morning thou wilt say, Oh, that it were already evening! and at even thou wilt wish, Oh, that it were already morning! because of the anxiety of thy heart which thou shalt feel, and because of the sight of the terrors which shall stand before thine eyes" (Deut. 28: 65, 67).

And Jehovah Himself, the God of the *Old* Testament, says: "As an enemy have *I* smitten thee with cruel chastisement on account of the greatness of thy guilt . . . on account of the multitude of thy sins have *I* inflicted on thee this great sorrow" (Jer. 30: 14, 15). And Jeremiah mourns: "Unsparingly has Jehovah wasted all the dwelling-places of Israel . . . Jehovah is become as an enemy. He has destroyed Israel" (Lam. 2: 1–5; comp. Isa. 63: 10). And thus *through the judgment-wrath of God Himself* the Jewish people is laden with lasting "reproach" and "shame" (Jer. 23: 39, 40), yea, to be a terrifying example of misery for all the peoples of the earth (Jer. 24: 9).

And yet "the grace-gifts and calling of God are unregretted" [on His side] (Rom. 11. 29). The "enemies" remain nevertheless, "beloved" (Rom. 11: 28). The "root" is holy (Rom. 11: 16), and, for the sake of Abraham, His "friend" (Isa. 41: 8; Deut. 7: 8), even in judgment God holds fast to His promises; "and even then, when they are in the land of their enemies, will I not reject them and not abhor them, so as to exterminate them and to break my covenant with them, for I am Jehovah, their God, says Jehovah" (Lev. 26: 44, 45).

IV. ISRAEL'S PRESERVATION

In three chief times of distress Israel experienced preservation by God: in the Egyptian, Assyrian-Babylonian, and Roman exiles.

(1) *The Distress in Egypt* (about 1500 B.C.) was a "reproach of

Christ" (Heb. 11: 26). What Pharoah did, was, without his knowledge,[1] a battle of the "serpent" against the "woman's seed" (Gen. 3: 15). For with the extermination of the Jews the coming of the Redeemer would have been made impossible, because, since Abraham, the promise concerning the Seed of the woman and the Treader-down of the serpent was definitely connected with this people (Gen. 12: 1–3; John 4: 22; Gal. 3: 16). Thus at the outset of the Jewish development the history of the "kingdom" stands behind all history of State and people. Israel suffered in Egypt on account of the Messiah; and through the expression "reproach of Christ" the letter to the Hebrews testifies that already then the prophet Moses had possibly some presentiment of this super-historical background (Deut. 18: 15; 34: 10).

But God, with uplifted hand and outstretched arm, led the people out of the "iron-smelting furnace" of Egypt (Deut. 4: 20; Ex. 6: 6; Ezek. 20: 5).

(2) *The Assyrian-Babylonian Distress* (722 B.C. ff., and 606–536) was the disgrace of *sin* (II Kings 17: 7). The Captivity came because the children of Israel were "adulterous" through idolatry (Hos. 1–3; Ezek. 16 and 23), had loaded themselves with "abominations" (Ezek. 8: 13), "filled the land with violence" (Ezek. 8: 17), and thus had made themselves "utterly unprofitable" (Jer. 13: 7). That it lasted for exactly seventy years corresponded with the disregarded sabbatical years in the preceding centuries (II Chron. 36: 21; comp. Lev. 26: 34, 35). Then, in Babylon itself, God called—besides Daniel—the prophet Ezekiel, "the Moses of the Exile;" and in Cyrus, the mighty warrior, the founder of the Persian empire, He granted to them the long-desired liberator (Isa. 45: 1–7; Ezra 1: 1–4).

(3) *The Roman Distress* was and is disgrace for the *sin of sins,* the rejection of the Messiah. Therefore it is the longest and the hardest (Deut. 28: 49–68). It begins with the destruction of Jerusalem, A.D. 70, and ends with the setting up of the kingdom of Messiah at the return of Christ. For, prophetically, the last of the four empires of Daniel endures to the end of the age (Dan. 2 and 7). "His blood come upon us and upon our children" (Matt. 27: 25). This word, spoken by themselves, stands as a flaming token of judgment over this history which covers millenniums.

"Israel must, indeed, be dumb if one asks them today: Tell me, pray: How can it be that the Eternal sent the fathers out of their land into captivity in Babylon for only seventy years, on account of all the abominations and idolatry by which they for centuries defiled the Holy Land:—and now Israel has been dis-

---

[1] Comp. Luther's word: "*Non agunt, sed aguntur:*" "They think to push, and are pushed."

persed among all peoples for over eighteen hundred years, and Jerusalem, the city of the great King, is trodden down by the nations until this day? What, then, is the great and terrible blood-guiltiness which perpetually prevents you from dwelling in peace in the land of your fathers?—But Israel is not willing to know!"

And yet it is precisely its sin against its Messiah that is indeed the root of Israel's misery. The hatred of the cross has made the Jewish soul the "tormenting thorn in the world." The Jewish people stands henceforth under the "curse of the flight from the cross." "Hence the restlessness and lack of peace of the eternal Jew, because he has never inwardly done with the figure of Jesus Christ. The flight from the cross has made him a homeless fugitive in the world. The rebellion against the cross has made him the leader of so very much rebellion against God on earth."

But also exactly at this point occurs a chief riddle of history, even the continuance of the Jewish people in spite of the numerous periods of judgment into which God caused unbelieving Israel again and again to fall.[1] The laws which govern the existence of many other peoples are in part explicable by the philosophy of history. But Israel's development mocks at all explanation. For, in spite of everything, Israel is Jehovah's people, and the Lord its God is a God Who hides Himself (Isa. 45: 15). Every Jew is a walking mystery.

V. ISRAEL'S HOPE

Indeed, "if, according to the testimony of the prophets (Isa. 53; Luke 24: 26, 27), the claim of Jesus to be the true Messiah must first be sealed by suffering and rejection, then Israel's title to this very Messiah can never through such rejection be annulled or cancelled." Much rather will the Lord redeem all His promises to Abraham and David; and then will "Jacob" be changed to "Israel," the "thornbush" (Exod. 3: 2) into a fruit-bearing "fig tree" (Hos. 9: 10). Comp. Isa. 55: 13. And as Israel is now a curse among the nations, so will it be at last an abundant blessing (Zech. 8: 13). "Where the sin has over-

---

[1] August A.D. 70.—Destruction of Jerusalem, 1,100,000 Jews killed. A.D. 132–135.—Defeating of Bar-Kochba, 500,000 Jews killed. May to July, 1096.—12,000 Jews killed in the Rhineland, Germany. 1 Nov. 1290.—Expulsion of all Jews (over 16,000) from England, under threat of punishment by hanging. Permission to return only after 370 years. 20 April to Autumn 1298.—100,000 Jews killed in Franconia, Bavaria, and Austria. Sept. 1306.—Expulsion of 100,000 Jews from France under threat of the death penalty. 2 Aug. 1492.—Expulsion of 300,000 Jews from Spain by the Inquisition under threat of the death penalty. Nov. 1648.—Slaughter of 12,000 Jews in Narol, Poland, by the Cossacks. 1648–1658.—Death of about 400,000 Polish Jews in the Russo-Polish-Swedish war. 1939–1945.—Murder of many hundreds of thousands of Jews during the years of the second world-war.

flowed, the grace has become still more unbounded" (Rom. 5: 20).   And as in the course of history all races have co-operated in Israel's judgment—the Hamites in Egypt, the Semites in Assyria and Babylon, and the Japhethites in the general exile; so will they one day in the kingdom of glory *all together,* along with Israel, be blessed (Isa. 2: 2–4; 19: 24, 25).   "Oh, the depth of the riches both of the wisdom and knowledge of God.   How unsearchable are his judgments, how untraceable his ways! To him be glory for ever.   Amen" (Rom. 11: 33, 36).

CHAPTER V

THE SIGNIFICANCE OF THE LAW

Wherefore now the Law? (Gal. 3: 19)

WHY did not Christ come at the time of Abraham (about 1900 B.C.)? Does not the New Testament say plainly that salvation depends on faith alone? And was not faith already present in Abraham and this indeed in very mature degree (Rom. 4), even in the knowledge of God, of the free character of grace, of justification, sacrifice, resurrection, the Messiah, the heavenly city? Is not, then, a period of law covering fifteen centuries superfluous, a needless delay, indeed, a retrogression?

There [in Abraham] a direct inward life of faith—here [under the Law] outward mediating forms; there, restful sublime simplicity—here, complexity, scarcely to be comprehended: there, the word and the promise prevailing—here, demand and symbol dominating.

But the simple is nobler than the complicated, and the word is more direct than the symbol; the promise is more creative than the command, and the inward higher than the form.

Nevertheless God gave the Law in such solemn majesty, with thunders and lightnings, accompanied by a quaking mount and trumpet blast (Exod. 19: 16-19; Heb. 12: 18, 19)! And yet He suffered mankind to languish in the shadow of death and to wait another millennium and a half for the coming of the Redeemer (Isa. 9: 1, 2; 60: 1-3; Luke 1: 78, 79). For this there must be weighty reasons. What are they?

The answer of Scripture is, that the chief meaning of the Law lies in the developing of an expectation of the Redeemer by revealing human sinfulness, so that thereby the Law should be "a tutor [schoolmaster, corrector, one who disciplines] to bring us to Christ," and to Him as the Saviour of *sinners* (Gal. 3: 19, 24; Rom. 3: 20; 7: 7ff.). So as to fulfil this its task it occupied a particular relation to the past, the future, and the present, and, as regards the last, toward the outer, the above, the beneath, and the inner. It is

as to the past — an addition,
as to the future — an insertion,
as to the present — an instruction, and this

against the outer   — a hedge,
from above   — a restraint,
against the beneath — a barrier,
of the inward   — a mirror.

i. *The Law as an addition.*

In no sense has it set aside the covenant with Abraham, or
stepped into its place, but has completed it, and is set by its side.
It was "added" (Gal. 3: 19; Rom. 5: 20); and as having come
later, by as much as 430 years, it naturally could not annul that
which had been long before in force (Gal. 3: 15–17).   Therefore
with all the significance which the Mosaic Law has, it acquires
nevertheless no fundamental significance.   For Israel's history
the promises of the covenant with Abraham are alone fundamental.   Therefore Paul in his doctrine of justification turns
back not to Moses but to Abraham (Rom. 4; Gal. 3: 9, 14), and the
epistle to the Hebrews (ch. 11) is able to name a whole series of
heroes of faith from the period of the Law.

Nevertheless this addition was necessary.   For with all
its grandeur and depth the covenant with Abraham lacked a
sufficient emphasis on sin.   Its chief imperfection lay in this
too light unfolding of man's lost condition and incapacity for
self-redemption; and yet the perception of these is really the
weightiest prerequisite for experimental acquaintance with Golgotha!   Therefore it must be supplemented, and this comes to
pass through the Law.

Henceforth the whole pre-Christian revelation of salvation
divides into two chief sections: the covenant of promise and the
covenant of law.   In the former the positive stands in the foreground, in the latter the negative.   With Abraham it is the
blessing (Gal. 3: 9, 14), with Moses the curse (Gal. 3: 13), with
Abraham life (Rom. 4: 17–25; Heb. 11: 19), with Moses death
(II Cor. 3: 6; Rom. 7: 9, 10).   The Mosaic covenant reaches its
summit in the Crucifixion (Gal. 2: 19, 20; 3: 13), the Abrahamic
covenant in the Resurrection (Heb. 11: 19; Rom. 4: 17, 19, 23–
25).

But they both belong together.   For the sinner is to be
redeemed, and to this end renewal and new birth are needful.
But the new birth has man's conversion as a presupposition, and
conversion is twofold; a turning from and a turning to, a NO to
oneself, and a YES to God, or, as the New Testament puts it,
Repentance and Faith.   Only here is revealed to us the true
meaning of the Old Testament histories:

Throughout centuries God spoke the word "Faith" into
the history of salvation—this is the meaning of the covenant
with Abraham.   Through two thousand years it was an
education in faith.

Throughout centuries God spoke the word "Repent" into the history of salvation—this is the meaning of the law of Moses.   Through one thousand five hundred years it was an education in repentance.

"Repent" and "believe the gospel" (Mark 1: 15) says Christ, and thereby conjoins both in redeeming oneness. This is the New Testament purport of the Old Testament.

ii.   *The Law as an Insertion.*

It was added "until" the Seed should come to which the promise referred (Gal. 3: 19).   This "until" indicates that the Law in its Mosaic form is something only temporary and transitory, that it stands to the Seed in a merely preparatory relationship, that it has its goal in Him and, concerning its Old Testament level, spirit and Levitical order, disappears with His arrival. This is a most important, marvellous truth in the history of salvation which, as to its actual realization, as with all principles of God's redemptive plan, is conditioned by and takes practical effect in real personal belief and thus in a surrendered, sanctified life of obedience and faith (I Cor. 9: 20, 21; Matt. 5: 17ff., comp. I Cor. 9: 8–10; 14: 34; Gal. 6: 2, 3; I Tim. 1: 8f.).   "Christ is the end of the Law *unto righteousness* to every one that believeth" (Rom. 10: 4).

Therefore even in the time of the "old" covenant Jeremiah spoke of the coming of the "new" (Jer. 31: 31–34), and David the "prophet" (Acts 2: 29, 30) foretold an eternal priesthood of the Messiah: "Thou art priest for ever after the manner of Melchidezek" (Psa. 110: 4).

But inasmuch as David already knew that this his "Lord" (Psa. 110: 1) would at the same time be his son (Matt. 22: 41–45; I Chron. 17), and consequently, as Isaiah's "branch" (Isa. 11: 1), would be also a descendant of *Judah* (I Chron. 5: 2), the Old Testament had already testified that in Him there would come a transfer of the priesthood from the tribe of Levi to the tribe of Judah and therewith a change of priesthood in general (Heb. 7: 11–17).   And further, because the priesthood is the foundation of the whole legal system, and the latter forms one continuous indivisible unity (Jas. 2: 10), therefore "with the changing of the priesthood there of necessity takes place a changing of the law" (Heb. 7: 12), and thus already, through David the psalmist and Jeremiah the prophet, the Old Testament testified that the Law is only a temporary insertion.   This is the view of the Old Testament itself.

iii.   *The Law as Instruction.*

In reference to its own particular period the Law is hedge, bridle, rule, barrier, and mirror.

In its outward aspect it is a *hedge* which separates Israel from the nations of the world (Eph. 2: 14, 15). *In its Mosaic and Levitical form* the Law was not given to all men but to Israel alone: "He made known his word to Jacob, his statutes and judgments to Israel. To no other nation has he so done" (Psa. 147: 19, 20). *As regulated by Moses* the sabbath was the token between God and Israel (Exod. 31: 13, 16, 17; Ezek. 20: 12, 20). But, *in the sense of Sinaitic statutes,* the nations have "no law" (Rom. 2: 14). This alone refutes all carrying over of the Sinaitic Law into the present gospel of grace to the nations, such as legal holiness, Judaic celebration of the sabbath, Old Testament forms of worship, special priesthood, priestly vestments, incense, etc. The Mosaic Law was never given to the nations, whether heathen or "Christian," but only to Israel. But nevertheless Israel and its Law are given to be "an object-lesson in the grandest style upon the stage of world history (I Cor. 10: 11) so that all peoples of all centuries can read it as they pass by."

From *above* the law is the bridle with which Jehovah rules His people Israel. For right conduct it is the rule.

From *beneath* it is, for sin, the barrier which should restrain its development (comp. Gal. 2: 15; I Pet. 4: 3).

From *within* it is a mirror (Jas. 1: 23, 25). "Through law comes knowledge of sin" (Rom. 3: 20). This is really its proper and chief task. Therefore the holiness of the Lord is its foundation thought. As the Holy One, the Lord is the exalted, unapproachable, jealous, perfect, and heavenly One; and in this order these five foundation qualities of His holiness come into relief in the Old Testament.

(1) God's holiness in its *majesty,* especially in the Patriarchal age.

(2), (3). God's holiness in its *unapproachableness* and *jealousy,* especially in the Mosaic age (Exod. 19: 12, 13, 20, 21; 20: 5; Josh. 24: 19).

(4) God's holiness in its *ethical (moral) perfection,* especially in the writings of the prophets (Isaiah 29 times, the "Holy One of Israel:" see 6: 3).

(5) God's holiness in its *heavenliness,* especially since the captivity in Babylon ("God of the heaven"): see Neh. 2: 20. The New Testament finally crowns this unfolding in that it reveals in Christ

(6) God's holiness as *love* (John 17: 6, 25, 26).

Thus there is indeed in the history of salvation a historical, progressive, gradual unfolding of God's holiness in ever new aspects.

But through this its inward working the Law points to things *in advance*; it awakens in the sinner the cry for redemption (Rom.

7: 24), and thereby becomes a "disciplinarian to direct us to Christ" (Gal. 3: 24).

Thus the Law is a gift from the redeeming God; and while in the matter of the sanctification of the individual grace *ex*cludes the Mosaic Law, yet in the general development of salvation it *in*cludes it in itself.

CHAPTER VI

THE WAY OF DEATH THROUGH THE LAW

The letter kills (II Cor. 3: 6)

THE Law is an organism and therefore an indivisible unity. "Even if anyone keeps the whole law and sins in any one thing, he is fully guilty" [or, is responsible to it entire] (Jas. 2: 10; Gal. 3: 10).

Therefore every distinction between a moral "law" and a ceremonial "law" is false, because thereby arises an impression that there are *two* laws, of which the one—the "ceremonial" law—could be fulfilled by the work of Christ, but the other not. It is only correct to speak of moral or ceremonial "laws" in the plural, in the sense of individual enactments, "commandments" in both spheres (comp. Jas. 2: 8).

Nevertheless the Law, like every organism, is divisible into members, and in this sense it has three associated groups of ordinances: moral appointments, those of Divine worship, and social regulations. Of these the first two have special, spiritual significance in the story of salvation.

Yet frequently the social appointments, in great part, also have significance in this history, often as prophetic typical foreshadowings of the New Testament truths of salvation; for example, the year of jubilee (Lev. 25; Luke 4: 19), the law as to redemption by a relative (Ruth), the cities of refuge (Josh. 20); etc. In such a case the social provisions stand in line with the typical ceremonial appointments.

The Law produces knowledge (Rom. 3: 20; 7: 7), namely:
i. Knowledge of sin, as missing the goal, as transgression, as rebellion.
ii. Self-knowledge by the sinner of his sinfulness, powerlessness, and lost condition.

I. KNOWLEDGE OF SIN

This advances in three stages. Sin is

(1) *Missing the Mark.* The New Testament word for "sin" (Gk. *hamartia*) meant originally "missing the mark." Thus about 100 times in Homer (900 B.C.), as when a warrior missed his foe with his spear (comp. Judges 20: 16, LXX); or in Thucidides (450 B.C.), if one missed the road. Only later, since Aristotle (350 B.C.), was it transferred to the spiritual and moral realm.

In the absolute sense, "sin" is only against God; "against

thee, thee alone, have I sinned" (Psa. 51: 4).   But the sinner is blind (Eph. 4: 18, 19); his conscience is deceitful (Acts 23: 1; comp. I Tim. 1: 13; I Cor. 4: 4); and he does not perceive the Divine ideal.   Therefore it must be made unmistakably plain to him through revelation.   This comes to pass through the Law.   *On the stage of world history it has been given as the model example, an appointed demonstration through Israel of the Divine will for the moral conduct of men.*[1]   Thus first is made manifest what "missing the mark" is.

But sin is more, even more than "ignorance" (Acts 17: 30), than "error" (Heb. 9: 7), than "defeat" (Rom. 11: 12), than "fall" (Eph. 2: 1, literally).   It must be unsparingly unmasked.   It is

(2) *Disobedience, Transgression, Lawlessness* (Rom. 5: 19; Heb. 2: 2; I John 3: 4).   Therefore the Law must not only describe the ideal, it must *pre*scribe it, must require, command, demand that man fulfil it, it must amount to "law."

But by this the character of sin becomes *aggravated*.   For where there is no boundary line one cannot speak of "trespassing" over the boundary; "where there is no law there is also no transgression" (Rom. 4: 15).   But where such line exists, in case of non-observance there is transgression.   Before Moses there were indeed from time to time, from case to case, "command and transgression" (Rom. 5: 14, 18; I Tim. 2: 14); but only since Moses has there been an institution systematic and educative in the knowledge of sin and transgression, working in unbroken continuity through the centuries, in word (especially Exod. 20) and symbol (Heb. 10: 3; 9: 7).

Thus law does not refer so much to the existence of sin but to the possibility of its being imputed: "sin is not imputed if there is no law" (Rom. 5: 13).   Law does not indeed "make" the sin; but it makes the "sin" a "transgression."   But thereby a milder condemnation of sin becomes impossible: "the Law works wrath" (Rom. 4: 15).

But the conflict becomes keener.   Sin is unmasked as

(3) *Rebellion*.   For through the mere existence of law the evil feels itself all the more provoked to display its real self. "Forbidden fruits taste sweet."   By the prohibition the desire is inflamed (Rom. 7: 8), the sin "springs to life" (Rom. 7: 9); it awakes out of "death" (Rom. 7: 8b), advances to "lust" and to "deed" (Rom. 7: 8); and sin expresses itself in sins (Rom. 7: 5). Thus the law is the "strength of sin," which forces the evil from within to without (I Cor. 15: 56); and sin itself is as the fire in iron glowing but not yet red-hot, which at first burns quietly without being noticed, but if splashed with water hisses and rebels.   Thus sins increase as a result of law.

[1] Apart from certain concessions by God on account of man's "hard-heartedness" (Matt. 19: 8).

But precisely herein sin comes, as it were, to the help of the law. For now the law has an increased opportunity to complete its work as the exposer of sin. Thus the more sin sins *against* the law, so much the more it sins in unwilling service *for* the law, against itself; and thus through the law every outbreak of evil is used in the service for good, and Satan must work against himself.

Yet sin had not willed this! *It* would have misused the Divine law as "occasion" (Rom. 7: 8, 9), a handle to thrust down mankind into so much the greater misery! Not only human weakness but more especially "the *commandment*, which was given to me unto life, the same proved to be to me unto death; for sin, taking occasion through the *commandment* deceived me and killed me *through the same*. Did then that which is good turn out to be unto me death? That be far! but sin—in that *through the good* it worked death unto me" (Rom. 7: 10–13). But this means—that the very life-gift of God changed sin into a murderous weapon, the very ruler's staff of the Most High into a dagger, the very salve by which the eye should be caused to see into poison. With that which is *holy* it would have murdered mankind! The holy itself should be made to serve sin, and God's revelation become a tool of Satan.

Yet at this very point the overruling of God shows itself in a specially victorious manner. For now the nature of sin is first properly unmasked; it is *rebellion against God, enmity against the Most High, revolution in the kingdom of the spirit*, and, in its intention, *usurper of the throne of the Divine world-sovereignty!*

But God has permitted all this that sin might be revealed as not merely "sin," but as "exceedingly sinful" (Rom. 7: 12, 13). "The Law came in besides that the transgression should overflow" (Rom. 5: 20). Thus while the evil attempted to make the good serviceable to *itself* (Rom. 7: 13), the reverse took place —the good used the evil in *its* service, and the patience of God led only to severer judgment on sin.

III.   SELF-KNOWLEDGE IN THE SINNER

But the path to the goal becomes yet darker. Because the Law reveals the guiltiness of sin, it shows at the same time the guilt of the sinner. Sin indeed is not "a" guilt but "his" guilt, and deed and doer belong together. Only through this does the message of the Law become personal. In the first place

(1) *The sinfulness* of the sinner is revealed, and with the perception of guilt unto death there vanishes the enjoyment of life. The Law has enormously increased the responsibility of the doer. Thereby it has set the sinner under the "curse" (Deut. 27: 26; Gal. 3: 10). "The law worketh wrath" (Rom. 4: 15).

Therewith life for him has ceased to be "life" at all.   "When I was still without law, then I 'lived,' but when the command-ment came sin revived; but for me came—death" (Rom. 7: 9, 10). Now there remains for the soul only a disastrous presentiment, a fearsome expectation of righteous judgment.   The Law, the "letter," has "killed" (II Cor. 3: 6), and although "holy" in its character, "righteous" in its sentence, and "wholesome" in its purpose (Rom. 7: 12), it has nevertheless proved itself to be the "servant of death and judgment" (II Cor. 3: 7, 9).   It has *effected* the death of the sinner without being the cause of it.

(2) *The Helplessness of the Sinner.*   Yet there awakens in the man the "willing," the intention, the preference for the good (Rom. 7: 18), that is, his better *ego,* the "mind" reasons (Rom. 7: 25).   It fights against the evil, "assents joyfully" to the Law (Rom. 7: 16), indeed, as regards the "inner man," is "well pleased" with God's commandment (Rom. 7: 22).

In a most tragic and dramatic manner this conflict of soul is set forth in Romans 7.   This chapter speaks neither of the experi-ence of a Christian *after* his conversion (as Augustine, Jerome, the Reformers explain), nor of Paul's experience under the Law *before* his conversion (so, e.g. Neander).   Much rather Paul speaks of himself *as he would be if he were considered as "in himself"* (ver. 25, *autos,* ego, that is "I, of myself, standing in my own strength," apart from the Holy Spirit.   In Romans 7 he is always "in himself," but in Romans 8 always "in Christ".   Thus these two chapters do not treat of two successive experiences but of two conditions, two ways of considering the matter.   Even a regenerate Christian can (abnormally indeed) sometimes (or often) be in Romans 7 as to his *experience,* while, as to his *standing,* he is always in Romans 8, and should certainly *walk* constantly in Romans 8.

In this conflict the victory seems easy.   The good "lies at hand" (Rom. 7: 18; Gk. *parakeitai*).   And yet! the outcome—perpetual defeat (Rom. 7: 15, 16).   As last the man no more understands himself: "my whole conduct is incomprehensible to me" (Rom. 7: 15).   He perceives that not he himself has the determining of his actions, but sin dwelling in him.   He is not even the lord in his own house (Rom. 7: 17, 20).   He is *inwardly* torn to pieces—for what he will he does not do, but what he does not will that he does (Rom. 7: 15, 16): he is incapable of all good (Rom. 7: 18; Acts 15: 10), "sold" under sin (Rom. 7: 14).   More-over, sin is a "law," and he, the man, is its slave.

In the fight for the fortress,[1] for the soul of man, which is

---

[1] That in Rom. 7: 21–23, there passes before Paul a picture of military life is shown by his expressions "fighting against" (*antistrateuomenon*) and "dragged away as prisoner of war" (*aichmalotizonta*).   In Rom. 7: 21–8: 3 Paul speaks of six laws (see above), to which the "law of the spirit of the life in Christ Jesus" is added as a seventh.

I

waged between the two spiritual kingdoms, the "law of God" and the "law of *sin*," "the law in the *members*"—which on the battlefield of the personality is the advance division of the host of the law of sin—always succeeds in winning the victory over the "law of the *mind*," this division of the host of the law of God. Thus the soul is always conquered for sin (Rom. 7: 23); and this comes to pass so compulsorily that this victory must itself be described again as "law" (Rom. 7: 21). The "Law of Moses" cannot help (Rom. 8: 3), but can only, like a mirror, light up the chaos. But thus there arises in the man the perception that he is

(3) *Lost.* Hoping he despairs and despairing he hopes, and, put to shame by all within, he looks without and above and cries: "O miserable man! who will deliver me from the body of this death?" (Rom. 7: 24).

But this was exactly what the Law would have: the perception of the necessity for and the holiness and divineness of his Deliverer. With His coming it can therefore itself disappear. Christ as the "goal" of the Law is at the same time its "end" (Rom. 10: 4).

Thus out of the Old Testament purpose of the Law follows the New Testament freedom (Rom. 7: Gal. 3). The fearful way of death by which the Law had led the sinner, was, in Christ, at the same time, also a "death" of the sinner *in reference* to the Law. "*I through* the Law have died *to* the Law" (Gal. 2: 19; comp. Rom. 7: 1–6; Col. 2: 20, 21). The Law had led the sinner downwards even unto despair, to feeling dead; but precisely thereby had it led him upwards to laying hold of life. It was the path of that godly sorrow which works salvation (II Cor. 7: 10). Now, after the descent into the hell of self-knowledge, there can begin the heavenly ascent of the knowledge of salvation and Christ. To testify more exactly of Him—that was the purpose of the appointments of the Divine service in temple and priesthood.

CHAPTER VII

THE WAY OF LIFE THROUGH THE LAW

The law refreshes the soul (Psa. 19: 7)

To set forth the relationship in the kingdom of God between Israel and God, and to prophesy in types of the work of Christ—this was the twofold sense of the Jewish temple service of God. The one is symbolic, the other its typical meaning.

A *symbol* is a visible cover of something invisible, a material garment of a higher truth, an impression and expression of something spiritual and super-sensual.

A *type* is a *prophetic* symbol, a person, thing, institution, or event which refers to Christ and His redeeming work, "a shadow of the good things to come" (Heb. 10: 1; 9: 11; Col. 2: 16, 17), a setting forth in advance of the "heavenly things" (Heb. 9: 23).

Thus the symbol is concerned with its own time, is confined to the Old Testament, and relates to Israel; the type speaks of Christ, points to the future, and is Messianic prophecy. The symbol remains in the Law; the type looks on to grace and is a fragment of the gospel in the old covenant, a fragment of the New Testament in the midst of the Old.

The right and duty to interpret the type follows from the nature of the Old Testament as being in itself a Divine revelation in preparation for salvation, as well as from the general organic historical unity of Holy Scripture (comp. pp. 134–140; 145–147). Furthermore it is established above all by the Lord Jesus Himself (John 3: 14; 6: 32, 33), and also especially, by Paul (I Cor. 5: 7, 8; 10: 4, 11; Rom. 5: 12–19), and in the epistle to the Hebrews (esp. chs. 5–10).

In this manner the Old Testament Divine service reveals a double feature:

A. symbolically: The Old Testament fellowship with God;
B. typically: The New Testament fellowship with God;
and as to the latter:

   (*a*) by the sacrifices—
      the New Testament ground of salvation;
   (*b*) by the Tabernacle—
      the New Testament conception of the world from
        the aspect of salvation;
      the New Testament Mediator of salvation;
      the New Testament fellowship of salvation.

Thus it carries out its task by the fulfilment of four groups of typical appointments:

(1) The place of the service of God: the All-holy, the Holy, and the forecourt. In succession, the Old Testament had *three* places of Divine service; the tabernacle, the temple of Solomon, the temple of Zerubbabel (extended by Herod).

(2) The persons in the service of God: High priest, priests, and Levites, with three categories of the last, Kohathites, Gershonites, Merarites (Num. 4).

(3) The activities in the service of God: offerings (with and without blood); precepts regarding purification (as at birth, death, and leprosy); religious practices (as circumcision, vows, fasts).

(4) The seasons of the service of God: sabbaths, seven chief festivals, sabbatical year, jubilee year.

A—The Old Testament Fellowship with God

Through this four-fold bond the Lord united Himself with His people. The moral ordinances had showed the *distance* which existed between the Holy One and the sinner; but the chief object of the ceremonial service of God was *fellowship*. In the sacrifices there was indeed an annual "remembrance of sin" (Heb. 10: 3)—and so far they stood on the same level as the moral laws; but nevertheless their chief and strict meaning was a certain *forgiveness* of sins (Lev. 4: 20; 5: 10—see p. 133) and, as a consequence of this, a corresponding intercourse with the Most High. Therefore also the priests were called "those drawing near" (Lev. 10: 3); and the place of the service of God was called the "tent of coming together," that is, the "tent in which God and Israel came together" (Exod. 33: 7; 40: 34), not merely "tent of assembly." Therefore the cover of the ark of the covenant was the centre and the most holy vessel of the whole worship. "In that spot will I *come together* with thee and will speak with thee—from the propitiatory, between the two cherubim on the ark of the testimony" (Exod. 25: 22).

Thus the foundation idea of the Mosaic sacrificial service is not only propitiation but reconciliation, not merely compensation through legal righteousness, but relative resumption of fellowship and intercourse through redeeming love. But the Mosaic sacrifice made this reconciliation possible through a "covering up" of sin. Wherever in our Bibles the word "atonement" stands, in the Hebrew the verb "kaphar" is used (the same word as "cover" [Eng. "pitch"] in Gen. 6: 14). From the same verb comes also "kapporeth," literally a "covering article" for sins, i.e. a propitiatory cover [the lid of the ark]. The system of sacrifices could not indeed take away sins, for "it is impossible

that the blood of bulls and goats should take away sins" (Heb.
10: 4, 9, 11);—the sacrifice of Christ alone could effect that (Heb.
9: 26)—but, looking forward to Golgotha, to cover those sins
which occurred through weakness, and thus as it were to permit
them to fade from the sight of the Lord, this was the office and,
because of its relation to the cross, the strength of the system of
sacrifices.

For conscious, wilful sins carried out with purpose and
reflection, "with uplifted hand"—the old covenant had only
stoning (Num. 15: 30, lit.; Lev. 24: 10–23). The Sinaitic
covenant must here be viewed in its singularity. Thus the
Mosaic sacrifice could not mediate a complete forgiveness of
sins, not even in its relation to the sacrifice of Christ. Always
it was merely an outward purifying, a setting aside of the offences
against the statutes of the Old Testament covenant committed
through weakness and "oversight" (Num. 15: 22–29), and thus
primarily a *foreshadowing* of the true forgiveness.

So, then, before Golgotha mankind as a whole possessed only
the "indulgence" of God (Rom. 3: 25, Gk. *paresis*); but Israel,
on the ground of its sacrifices, had a certain forgiveness of sins
(Gk. *aphesis*; Psa. 32: 1), and a relatively limited fellowship with
God. Therefore even in the Old Testament the prophets and
psalmists exulted (Psa. 32: 11; 33: 1; 68: 4) over the blessings
and life-giving effects of the Law. For them the Law was not
only exposure of guilt and a leading on to despair (comp. Rom.
7), but "joy of heart" (Psa. 19: 8), "delight" (Psa. 119: 47;
36: 9), "bliss" (Psa. 32: 1).

"Knowledge of sin," says Paul (Rom. 3: 20):
> Of "crowning with grace" speaks David (Psa. 103: 4).
"The letter kills," says the apostle (II Cor. 3: 6):
> "The law is refreshing" [quickening], says the
> psalmist (Psa. 19: 8).
"Miserable man!" is read in the epistle to the Romans
(Rom. 7: 24):
> "Blessed is the man," says the Psalter (Psa. 1: 1; 32: 1).
Of the "curse," the one-time Pharisee speaks (Gal. 3: 13):
> "The Lord bless thee," says the high priest (Num.
> 6: 24).

Yet both speak of the same Law! And yet both are
right! For the Law is as the needle of the magnet with its two
poles: a pointer to Christ as the only goal, lying outside of itself,
and yet at the same time in itself a unity of two opposites: in
its requirements for conduct a loving holiness, in its service of
God a holy love; in its moral laws distance, in its ceremonial
laws fellowship; in its rules for conduct it binds, in its priestly
ordinances it sets free; there authority, here redemption; there
*un*covering, here covering *up*; there the propitiation, here the

reconciliation. In brief: the moral laws are judgment hall and royal palace; the ceremonial laws are a temple.

And yet both belong together as do the poles of a magnet. All spiritual life, even in the New Covenant, is marked by polarity. For there is only one Law of Israel (Jas. 2: 10), with only one Mediator, Moses, and only one goal, Christ.

But He brings the fulfilment of both: as regards the moral laws, "grace," the forgiveness of sins; as regards the ceremonial laws, "truth," the substance instead of the shadow (Col. 2: 17; Heb. 10: 1). Thus is "the law given through Moses, but the grace and the truth is come to pass through Jesus Christ" (John 1: 17).

All this shows that it would be completely false to conceive of the Old Testament as only a surmounted first step to the New. Even the Old Testament saints had a mighty possession of faith which the Old Testament bore immediately in itself. "The Holy Spirit was the hidden soul of the Law" (see I Pet. 1: 11; Heb. 3: 7; Exod. 31: 3). Only because of this could the psalter of the Old Testament congregation become the hymn book of the original New Testament communities (I Cor. 14: 15, 26; Eph. 5: 19; Col. 3: 16). Thus the Old Testament is twofold: viewed from the goal, it is subordinate to the New, and yet, as regards itself, it is independent. The Old Testament without the New is "an edifice without a pinnacle;" the New without the Old is "a house standing in the air."

So the Old Testament retains its right and the New its privilege. The New is veiled in the Old, but already well contained there: the Old is unveiled in the New and at the same time gloriously expanded. "In the Old the New is concealed, in the New the Old is revealed" (Augustine). "The Old Testament is the bud, in which all the splendour is already present, but shut up; the New Testament is the full flower, which has burst forth, which displays its glory and allows its fragrance to be enjoyed. The Old and the New Testaments are one, and yet each is distinct."

B—New Testament Salvation in the Old Testament

The decisive fundamental assertion of the Old Testament is: "The Lord thy God is one God." In contrast to the polytheistic religions of the ancient Orient, especially Egypt and Mesopotamia, and the similar polytheistic religions of classical antiquity, especially Greece and Rome, this knowledge shone forth ever clearer in the circle of light of God's Old Testament revelation. At the same time in this realm the finiteness and sinfulness of fallen human nature was regarded with the utmost seriousness. God is the eternal and we are the temporal. He is the Holy and we are the sinners. He is the Living One and we have fallen under death. If nevertheless there is to take place a union between Him and us, then He must, entirely from Himself, create this union through introducing something from eternity in some place in the world of space and time.

This came to pass in the establishing of the Old Testament covenant. Henceforth there is a point of union at which the Deity "comes together" with mankind (Exod. 25: 22), a moral centre of world affairs, which first gives to all history living continuity and goal, a point of contact between time and eternity at which the sinner enters the presence of the Holy One. But if the sinner is not to be destroyed in that presence, this point must above all contain in itself a double element, a negation and an affirmation, a breaking down of the old and an introduction of the new, namely, clearance from sin and sanctification, forgiveness and new lordship, reconciliation and leading, or, in Old Testament language, covering and instruction, *kapporeth* and *thora,* propitiatory and tables of the Law. Therefore these two were most essentially connected with the ark of the covenant, that symbolic central vessel of Old Testament Divine service (Exod. 25: 17–22; Heb. 9: 4).

"This centre which world affairs thus acquired was a movable point, which moved onward with the progress of history. It wandered with Israel through the desert so long as they were a nomadic people. After Israel became settled, it established itself in the temple. But later, in place of the temple of stone, which was ordained to destruction, there came the 'spiritual house,' the church, which is built of 'living stones' (I Pet. 2: 5). Thus does the living centre, the moral centre of the world, pass through history. Christ remains with His church to the end of the world."

It thereby becomes clear that this entire development is one single great sequence, from beginning to end, one single all-pervading divine work of reconciliation. The revelation of Christ is the completion of that which commenced with the Abrahamic covenant. Therefore Jesus is also called "the Christ;" that means, the One of whom the Old Testament prophesied, whom Israel awaited, the God-given "Anointed" One (Psa. 2: 2; I Sam. 2: 10; Dan. 9: 25), already described under *this* name by the prophets of the Old covenant. His title of Christ expresses His indivisible oneness with the revelation of God in the Old Testament.

From this historical oneness connecting the millenniums it follows that even in the Old Testament time God was able to give a certain advance presentation of the coming salvation, certain prophecies in act and fact, in offices and institutions, in historical leadings and individual happenings, which had Christ and His redeeming work as their end. Therefore the Lord and

His apostles many times acknowledged in the Old Testament such a typical prophetic meaning which, while maintaining the reference to history of the time of the prophecy, was nevertheless, viewed from the goal, the actual, true meaning (Col. 2: 17; Heb. 10: 1). Thus the brazen serpent is a type of the cross (John 3: 14), the prophet Jonah of the resurrection (Matt. 12: 40), the manna in the desert of Christ as the bread of life (John 6: 31–35). Above all it is the sacrificial and priestly arrangements of the Old Testament which are here to be noted. In them, prior to Christ, the work of Christ was set forth in symbols. They were *likenesses* of Him as the original; they were *types* of Him as the fulfilment (Heb. 8: 5; 9: 23–25).

Yet still more. In the Old Testament sacrifices, the work of Christ was already really effective even *in their time*. They were typical acts with actual saving effect, not only advance representations, but the creation of a certain fellowship with the Holy One, not only symbol but sacrament (Lev. 4: 31).

Nevertheless in this connexion none of these priestly acts had value in itself (Heb. 10: 4). They received all their virtue only from the one sacrifice of Golgotha. They were powerless and yet effectual, poor and yet making many rich, impotent and yet dispensing blessing, as it were bills of exchange of a national bank, which in themselves are only paper, and yet—in view of the day of their redemption—even *before* their due date of payment possess value as cash. Then Jesus Christ, by His sacrificial death on the cross, has met all those Old Testament "bills of exchange" to their full value.

☆ I. THE MOSAIC SACRIFICE

The supreme act of the temple service of God in Israel is the sacrifice. Its root idea consists in four chief requirements:

(1) *The offering being without blemish* points to the holiness of the Lord Jesus: His freedom from inherited sin through His miraculous birth and His freedom from all actual sins through His holy walk (I Pet. 1: 19).

(2) The offering becoming one with the offerer through the *laying on of hands*, points to the acceptance of guilt by the Lord Jesus. In the reality, when Christ, the sinless, submitted Himself to "the baptism of repentance unto the forgiveness of sins" (Mark 1: 4) He fulfilled the typical declaration of readiness to accept the place of the sinner, to become one with him, and to bear the sins of mankind (Matt. 3: 14, 15), a typical declaration of readiness which He then carried out historically on the cross (I Pet. 2: 24).

(3) The *enduring of punishment* Christ suffered on Golgotha, and thus the killing of the sacrifice became a prophecy of the cross

(Heb. 9: 13, 14).   "Without shedding of blood no forgiveness takes place" (Heb. 9: 22).

Thus these first three requirements of the sacrifice refer to the work of Christ *on earth,* to Christ *for* us, Who in the days of His flesh completed the acquiring of salvation (Heb. 5: 1–9).

But what is acquired must be appropriated, and this comes to pass only through faith and the thereby resulting organic oneness of the debtor with the surety (John 6: 53).   Therefore must Christ *for* us be also Christ *in* us, and to His priesthood on earth His heavenly priesthood must be joined.   Now this organic oneness was foreshadowed with exactness by

(4) *The sacrificial repast.*   And so Christ said: "If you eat not the flesh of the Son of man and drink not His blood, then you have no life in you" (John 6: 53–57).   Hence the continuance of the humanity of Christ in His bodily resurrection; hence the sending of His Spirit for the purpose of this oneness with His redeemed; hence the necessity of the new birth of the individual and the organic fellowship between the "head" and the "members."

Thus the Mosaic sacrifice embraces the whole work of Christ; from birth to baptism, from baptism to the cross, and beyond the cross, on to resurrection and the sending of the Spirit, indeed to His eternal high priesthood after the manner of Melchizedek.

II.   THE TABERNACLE

Israel had in succession three chief places of Divine service: the Tabernacle of Moses in the wilderness and in Shiloh (I Sam. 1: 3; 1500–1000 B.C.); the temple of Solomon on Moriah (I Kings 6: 1; 1000–586); the temple of Zerubbabel after the return from captivity (Ezra 3: 8), completed by Herod (John 2: 20; (536) 521 B.C. to A.D. 70).   In essentials all three went back to the same plan (Exod. 25–27 and 30), and had the same meaning in the plan of salvation.   The duty of the Tabernacle was, first of all, to be

(1) *an Image of the Universe,*

and this from the point of view of the kingdom of God.

Philo of Alexandria, the Jewish contemporary of Jesus, had already interpreted the Tabernacle as being a type of the universe, and so did Josephus.

This application becomes specially clear at the entrance of the high priest into the All-holiest on the great Day of Atonement in conjunction with its New Testament fulfilment in Christ (Lev. 16; Heb. 9: 23, 24).

The vessels of the Tabernacle were copies of the things in the heavens (Heb. 9: 23).   But after Golgotha Christ did "not enter into a sanctuary set up by human hands, which is only a *copy* of the true sanctuary, but into the *heaven itself,* in order now, unto our salvation, to appear before the face of God." But this implies that the earthly sanctuary is a copy of the heavenly; and as on the Day of Atonement the Aaronic high priest, with the blood from the altar of burnt offering in the forecourt, passed through the holy place into the All-holiest (Lev. 16: 11–14), so did Christ, the priest after the order of Melchizedek, with His own blood[1] (Heb. 9: 12) from the "brazen altar" of Golgotha, pass from the earth "right through the heavens" (Heb. 4: 14), in order then in the "All-holiest" of the universe "above all heavens" (Heb. 7: 26; Eph. 4: 10), to appear before "the throne of grace" of God (Heb. 4: 16).

Thus the forecourt is the earth, where Golgotha was; the holy place is the heaven; and the All-holiest is the throne of God.

On *earth* God will do a double work: the *justifying* and *sanctifying* of the redeemed. Therefore there stood in the forecourt two vessels; the altar of burnt offering and the laver of purification (comp. Eph. 5: 25, 26).

In *heaven* is the *life* and the *light* and the *worship* of the Eternal in the midst of heavenly spirits. To these things bear witness the shewbread table (bread of life; comp. John 6: 48), and the lamp, as well as the altar of incense (comp. Psa. 141: 2; Rev. 8: 3), with the surrounding figures of the cherubim on the cover of the ark and the veil (Ex. 26: 1).

But "above all heavens" is the throne of God itself. There is the Law which rules the universe, even as the tables of the Law were present in the All-holiest (I Kings 8: 9). There is also the grace which forgives sins and which makes the throne of sovereignty of God to be a "throne of grace" (Exod. 25: 17; Heb. 4: 16)., and there, above all, is the light of the glory of God, which, like the cloud of the Shekinah, irradiates all other things (Exod. 40: 34, 35; I Tim. 6: 16).

But all His plans of love God carries out in Christ, and therefore at the same time the Tabernacle becomes a pointer to Christ, that is

(2) *a Type of the World Redeemer.*

In fact, in Christ, Who as the incarnate Word "tabernacled" among us (John 1: 14) (Gk. *eskēnosēn,* = tented, from *skēnē,* a tent), all its types are fulfilled, (so already Cocceius (Professor of Reformed Theology in Leiden, died 1669)).
Christ is

our *justification*—the altar of burnt offering (I Cor. 1: 30);
our *sanctification*—the laver of purifying (I Cor. 1: 30).
He has set us in

---

[1] i.e. by the virtue of His sacrifice of Himself, not with His own material blood. [Trans.]

"*heavenly places*" (Eph. 1: 3; 2: 6)—the holy place as a copy of the heaven (Heb. 9: 24); and there, in our heavenly position, He is

our *light*—the seven-branched lamp (John 8: 12);
our *bread*—the shewbread (John 6: 48),

and

our *supplicating High priest* after the order of Melchizedek—the golden incense altar (Heb. 7: 26; Psa. 141: 2, comp. John 17).

But finally He will conduct us into

His presence (the All-holiest), and there, as the Lamb that was slain (Rev. 5: 6–14)—as the fulfilment of the ark of the covenant with the blood besprinkled propitiatory (Rom. 3: 25)—He will receive from His own people eternal worship.

But in Him we ourselves also shall be conformed to His likeness (Rom. 8: 29; I John 3: 2), and so the Tabernacle is at the same time

(3) *a Type of the Way and Fellowship of Salvation.*

Those believing

viewed *beneath*—are justified from the darkness and power of sin:
the altar of burnt offering;
viewed *within*—are sanctified through the washing with His Word:
the laver of purification, Eph. 5: 26;
viewed *without*—are shining as light-bearers of His testimony:
the lampstand, Rev. 1: 12; 2: 5, comp. Zech. 4;
viewed *above*—they pray with the incense of worship:
the golden altar, Rev. 8: 3; Psa. 141: 2;
viewed *on all sides*—are strengthened with the bread of life:
the shewbread, John 6: 48;
looking *forward*—they hasten so as to appear before His throne:
the ark of the covenant.

By all these things the Israelitish Divine service became a sublime prophecy of the goal. It is the most prophetic element in the Old Testament law and thus far is a connecting link between law and prophecy.

(4) *The Superiority of the New Testament Order.*

But in all this the fulfilment far surpasses all types (Matt. 13: 16, 17).

(*a*) In the Old Covenant *a portion passed for the whole*:

one-twelfth for *twelve* twelfths—as with the priestly tribe of Levi (Num. 8: 16–19, in place of Exod. 19: 6);

one-tenth for *ten* tenths—by the tribute of the tithe (Lev. 27: 30);

one-seventh for *seven* sevenths—by the sanctifying of the sabbath (Exod. 20: 8–11).

But in the New Covenant the whole is found:

not one priestly tribe, but a priestly people (I Pet. 2: 5, 9);

not a tenth, but all (Col. 3: 17);

not a day, but the week (Col. 2: 16, 17; Rom. 14: 5, 7, 8);

and with the week the year, and with the year the life, and with time eternity.

(*b*) In the Old Covenant only the "shadow" was present; but in

the New the "body" is come (Col. 2: 17; Heb. 10: 1). "The grace and truth [which means the essential, the reality] came through Jesus Christ" (John 1: 17).

(*c*) In the Old Covenant there were concessions "on account of hardness of heart" (Matt. 19: 8), especially avenging of homicide (Josh. 20), polygamy (Gen. 30; Deut 21; 15; I Kings. 11: 1–3), slavery (Lev. 25: 44–46), and lawsuits (Exod. 21: 24; Matt. 5: 38–40).

In the New Covenant there stands the majestic "But I say unto you" (Matt. 5: 22, 38, 34, 39).

(5) In the Old Covenant there were many sacrifices; the official number annually no less than 1,273 (according to Num. 28 and 29), and thus together from Moses to Christ nearly two millions, apart from the unnumbered millions upon millions of private offerings (Lev. 1; 3; 4; 5).

But of Christ it is said: "by *one* offering He has perfected for ever those being sanctified" (Heb. 10: 14).

Thus does Christ fulfil and surpass all which the Law includes. The Law was hedge, bridle, rule, barrier, and mirror; but the cross of Christ is its seal, eternally valid (Dan. 9: 24). "Therefore let thy conceit and feelings depart, and regard this Scripture as the highest, noblest, All-holiest sanctuary, as the very richest mine of wealth, which can never be sufficiently fathomed, so that thou mayest find the Divine wisdom, which God here sets forth so simply that He may quench all pride. Here thou wilt find the swaddling clothes and the manger wherein Christ lies, to which the angel directed the shepherds. Poor and mean swaddling clothes they are, but precious is the treasure that lies therein, even Christ" (Luther, Pref. to the Old Testament, 1523).

D—THE TESTIMONY OF GOD BY PROPHECY

CHAPTER VIII

THE PROPHETS OF GOD (THE PROPHETIC OFFICES)

L AW and promise—these are the two chief pillars of Old Testament revelation. The one is the royal, the other the prophetic. The connecting link between the two is the temple. The priestly service is at once law and promise.

Thus these two expand to a triunity in the history of salvation, and thereby the entire history of Isràel became a leading on to the Messiah, Who, as the threefold anointed, is at once prophet, priest, and king.

Therefore also Israel had three theocratically leading classes: The princes (elders, judges, and kings) were the political leaders of the nation; the priests and prophets concerned themselves with the inward and eternal. In this connexion the priests were the permanent and, by birth, the appointed guardians of the *written deposited* Divine revelation (comp. Heb. 7: 16), while the prophets were as occasion required the bearers of the *progressive* Divine revelation, appointed not through birth but by personal vocation (I Sam. 10: 12).

Four names are the leading descriptions of the Old Testament prophets. They show us at the same time how the men must be qualified whom God will use as His witnesses.

i. Prophets are "speakers" (Heb. *nabi,* comp. Arabic *nabaa,* to speak). They are interpreters (*interpres Dei*), expounders (*hermeneus theou,* Philo), tellers forth (Gk. *pro — phētēs,* not in every case speakers in advance: comp. English "forthteller," not always *foreteller*), "mouth" of God (Jer. 15: 19). They stand to the Lord in a relation similar to that of Aaron to Moses: "thy brother Aaron shall be thy prophet" (Exod. 7: 1, 2), and "thou shalt be to him 'God'" (Exod. 4: 15, 16). The Spirit of the Lord "impelled" the prophets (II Pet. 1: 21), laid His words in their mouth (Deut. 18: 18; Jer. 1: 9), spoke through them (II Sam. 23: 2). Their tongue is "the pen of a ready writer" (Psa. 45: 2), and their messages are the "utterance of God" (I Pet. 4: 11). Therefore (according to Dr. Evans) in the Old Testament (this Bible of the Lord Jesus and His apostles) it declares about 3500 times "Thus saith the Lord."

ii. Prophets are *seers* (Heb. *roeh,* I Sam. 9: 9; I Chron. 9, 22; Isa. 30: 10). They must first have "seen" their message before they can pass it on (I Chron. 29: 29; Isa. 30: 10). Therefore this, even when it is wholly or almost unaccompanied by "visions," is nevertheless quite generally called simply "vision" (Isa. 1: 1). The modes of the prophetic view were different.

(1) Perception through the *outward* sense. The prophet remains "in the body" (comp. II Cor. 12: 2, 3): he is not "in the spirit" (comp. Rev. 1: 10, lit.).   He hears and sees with his bodily senses (Num. 12: 8).

Moses sees and hears at the flaming bush (Exod. 3);
Samuel hears, but sees nothing (I Sam. 3);
Daniel sees, but hears nothing (Dan. 5: 25);
Abraham sees and hears (Gen. 18).

(2) Perception through the *inward* sense. The prophet is "in the spirit" (Rev. 1: 10), the condition of rapture (ecstasy). To outward things his eyes are "closed", inwardly they are "open" (Num. 24: 3, 15).   Inwardly he "sees" or "hears." Through inward "sight" he receives the pictorial revelation ("vision") of which nevertheless he often needs an explanation (Amos 7: 7; 8: 2; Zech. 1: 9; 4: 4; Dan. 8: 15); through inward "hearing" he attains to the verbal revelation, which more directly imparts to him knowledge.

(3) Perception through mere enhancing of the natural activities of the human mind.   Here God intensifies *dreams* and makes them media of the divine message (as, for example, with Pharoah, Nebuchadnezzar, Joseph); or He intensifies the activity of the *understanding* and elevates its speech to inspired height, e.g., in the songs of praise of Hannah (I Sam. 2), Mary (Luke 1), Zacharias (Luke 1).   The one is the connecting link between the natural dream life and the inward *pictorial* revelation, the other the intermediate stage between the "sermon" and the inward revelation by *word*.

Thus God has spoken to the prophets by "manifold and various ways," but the basic theme was always the same: the loving holiness of the Lord and its victorious glorification in this world, through judgment and grace, right on unto perfection.

Of special significance here is the "law of prophetic perspective."   For the heavenly world there is no limitation of time.   "Before the eyes of the Eternal everything is present." By his exit from the sphere of the temporal into the sphere of the divine the prophet steps at the same time into the sphere of the *super*-temporal, and as the "speaker" of the Eternal he stands now royally above all conceptions of time.   Thus he can indeed see the future as *future* (e.g. Isa. 9: 7), but, in the same sentence, at the same time, also as *present* (ver. 6, lit.), yea, even as *past* (ver. 6, and especially Isa. 53).   "Prophecy often sets near together events remote from each other in time, and, while holding fast to the historical anchorage of the events, it frequently flies over the whole intervening period between the present and the future, though the gap may perhaps last more than thousands of years."

Thus arises prophetic "perspective." It is at once the perfection and imperfection of the prophet. Events of the near and distant future are brought close together *like the peaks of the mountains for the wanderer in high lands*. The return of Judah from Babylon and the gathering of Israel in the End time (Isa. 49: 8–12; 43: 5–7; 27: 12, 13), the coming of Christ in lowliness and His appearing in glory (Isa. 61: 1–3), are viewed together in one picture, for the former is the type of the other, and the second is the fulfilment of the first.

An especially significant example of this is Isaiah's prophecy of the coming jubilee year (Isa. 61: 1–3), at the public reading of which, in the synagogue at Nazareth, the Lord broke off in the middle of a sentence, because in that same sentence the prophecy, without interval, had passed over from the first to the second coming of Messiah, and on that occasion the Lord wished to speak only of His first coming (Luke 4: 18, 19). Another example is Mal. 3: 1–4.

That in such places at least 2,000 years lay between is nowhere intimated; indeed as the prophets "searched diligently concerning the times and points of time," their lack of understanding was made intelligible to them, even by a special "revelation" to the effect that they did not need to know this, because in their service they were acting "not for themselves" but for the generations of a coming age (I Pet. 1: 10–12).

So the prophets see the "peaks"—often three or four behind one another; they also perceive clearly that "valleys" lie between; but how "wide" these are and what each in detail hides in itself, they do not know. They understand that the "sufferings" of Messiah must precede His "glories" (I Pet. 1: 11; Luke 24: 25, 26), and that therefore an interval divides the one from the other; and therefore also they prophesy in this same sequence[1]; but how long this interval lasts, whether quite short or long, and what it more exactly signifies (the building of the church), this remains to them a "secret" (Eph. 3: 2–10; Col. 1: 26; Rom. 16: 25; Matt. 13: 17).

They prophesy of the End time, of the kingdom of Messiah, of the new heaven and the new earth (Isa. 65: 17; 66: 22), but that the Messianic kingdom consists of *two* sections, a thousand years on the old earth (Rev. 20: 2, 4–7) and eternally on the new

[1]

Sufferings.	*Glory.*
Psa. 2: 1–3	Psa. 2: 4–12.
Psa. 8: 4, 5a	Psa. 8: 6, 7; Heb. 2: 5–9.
Psa. 22: 1–21	Psa. 22: 22–32.
Isa. 52: 13–53: 9.	Isa. 53: 10–12.

earth (Rev. 21: 1; 22: 5), and that world judgment, even world
destruction and glorification, lie between (Rev. 20: 9–15), this
they do not see.   Therefore they paint the new earth with the
colours of the kingdom of glory of the old (Isa. 65: 17–25;
especially ver. 20 "death"), and the picture of the millennial
kingdom melts into one with the picture of the consummation.

Thus then the Lord Jesus said to His disciples: "of a truth,
I say unto you, many prophets and righteous men have desired
to see what you see, and have not seen, and to hear what you hear,
and have not heard.   But blessed are your eyes, that they see,
and your ears, that they hear" (Matt. 13: 17, 16).

iii.   Prophets are "watchmen" (Heb. *zophim*).   "I will
enter upon my watch, and set myself on the watch tower, and
will watch carefully so as to see what He will say to me" (Hab.
2: 1; Isa. 21: 8).

From the lofty look-out they have an eye for the *present*:
"Watchmen have I set over you, and warned you: heed the sound
of the trumpet" (Jer. 6: 17).   As men of history they speak in
historically conditioned form to men of that history.   As members of their present age they address themselves to their contemporaries, starting with their then situation.   Therefore are
they at the same time the warners of the people, the exhorters of
the nation (Isa. 3: 17), the "supervising officials" of the ruling
kings, the "conscience" of the community, and as such its
guardians and "shepherds" (Zech. 10: 2, 3; 11: 3, 16, 17; Ezek.
34: 2).

But as "watchmen" they look out into the *future* also and
see judgment (Isa. 21: 5–12) and consummation: "Hark! thy
watchmen let their voices ring out and exult all together!   For
eye to eye they see, full of joy, how the Lord returns to Zion"
(Isa. 52: 8; 62: 6, 7).   Taken together they are the counsellors,
conscience, eyes, ears, and overseers of the people.

iv.   Prophets are "*men of God*" (I Kings 13: 1).   They are
personalities *consecrated to God*, "holy men" (II Pet. 1: 21; Matt.
13: 17).   Unsanctified prophets (such as Balaam, Num. 22–24;
and Saul, I Sam. 19, 23; comp. Caiaphas, John 11: 51, and Phil. 1:
15, 18) are exceptions and are never God's permanent servants.
For God desires the heart, not only the mouth, the worker, not
only his work.   "In those who draw near to me I will be sanctified, and before the whole people I will be glorified" (Lev. 10:
3; Isa. 52: 11).

But as "men of God" they are also *individuals*; for God will
not set aside human nature but He transfigures it.   He wishes
not its elimination but its use in His service, not slaves but
friends (John 15: 15; Amos 3: 7), not media but just "men."

So we have the picture-language of the countryside from the

shepherd Amos (Amos 7: 14; 2: 13; 3: 4–6); the national prophecies from the Minister of State, Daniel (chs. 2; 4; 7; 8; 11); the summons to build the temple from the priest Zechariah; the description of the future priestly service, likewise through a priest, the prophet Ezekiel (Ezek. 1: 3, comp. chs. 40–48). And as regards the individual temperaments and characters, we have the thundering language of the choleric Amos and Isaiah, the plaintive and mourning style of the melancholic Hosea and Jeremiah, the psalm-like poetry of the poetical Habbakuk (ch. 3). Sometimes even the personal names of the prophets are like a superscription and motto for their message: Isaiah, the "evangelist" of the Old Covenant, means "Jehovah gives salvation;" Ezekiel, the Moses of the restoration, "God strengthens;" and Daniel, the prophet of world history and world judgment, "God is judge."

Also their divine message is often conditioned by contemporaneous affairs. Old Testament prophecy is no mere aerial line which does not touch the ground. Much rather, at many points, there is allusion to events and persons of the then present or the near future. From a definite situation the prophets speak to men in a definite situation. They often draw from their surroundings the shapes and colours for the presentation of their message. Everything is historically conditioned and yet at the same time interpenetrated with eternity. All is at once human and divine, temporal and super-temporal.

They speak of the Assyrian distress and at the same time of the great Immanuel (Isa. 7–12; Matt. 1: 23); they speak of the exodus from Egypt and the mourning at Ramah on the carrying away to Babylon; and at the same time they prophesy of the history of the Messiah's childhood (Hos. 11: 1; comp. Matt. 2: 15; Jer. 31: 15; comp. Matt. 2: 17, 18). They speak of the return from Babylon and simultaneously promise the gathering of Israel at the still future inauguration of the kingdom of peace (Isa. 11: 11–16). They speak of the coming kingdom of God of the End time and simultaneously depict the glory of the new earth and of the final perfecting of all things (Isa. 65: 17; 66: 22; 54: 11, 12; comp. Rev. 21: 1, 18–21).

Thus they prophesy *prophecies* in advance. In *words* they promise prophecies in the form of deeds. They foretell events which again will be in themselves prophecies, and which, when they have been fulfilled, as shadow-pictures and pledges of redemption, must then themselves be *fully* fulfilled. This all appertains to the historical anchorage of their eternal message.

In the divine inspiration the sacred writer is less like a pipe or channel, with the inflowing current flowing out again without having taken up any of the particular qualities of its channel, but he is like a wind instrument which, each according to its

K

kind—flute, horn, or trumpet—imparts its own definite peculiar tone to the same melodies of the same player; or he is like a pen, which to the writing of the very same writer and the very same text, by reason of its own thickness or fineness often gives a very different appearance.

So each prophet "bears the stamp of his time as a *man,* just as he bears the stamp of his God as a *prophet.* . . . Each, according to his kind, is a 'mouth' of the Lord; but the tones which come from these throats are now higher (as Isa. 40–65), now deeper (as Isa. 13–23). The tone and strength of the voice differ with the individual; but the choir forms a wonderful harmony, for the Composer is but One."

The history of prophecy covers seven periods:
1. Its earliest beginnings: Adam to Moses.
2. Moses to Samuel.
3. Samuel to the prophets who wrote (Acts 3: 24); schools of prophets.
4. The prophets who wrote: Joel to Malachi (about 800–400 B.C.).
5. The silence of God: Malachi to the New Testament.
6. The prophetic ministry of Christ (Heb. 1: 1, 2).
7. Prophesying in the church (I Cor. 12: 10; 14; Eph. 4: 11).
Then comes the great time of fulfilment in the Messianic kingdom and consequently the ceasing of all special prophesying: Heb. 8: 11; comp. Zech. 13: 3–6; I Cor. 13: 9, 10.

NOTE. We should distinguish between "verbal" prophesying, i.e. prophesying in *words* (e.g. Micah 5: 2; Isa. 9: 1, 2) and "typical" prophesying. A typical prophecy foretells (by words) a type (a fore-picture). It has a double fulfilment: as a verbal prophecy it is fulfilled by the appearance of the type; as a typical prophecy it is only completely fulfilled when this type also is "fulfilled," that is, in the Messianic development of salvation (e.g. Hos. 11: 1, with Matt. 2: 15).

In this sense prophecy concerning the Israelitish kingdom is frequently at the same time a prediction relating to the period of the church. Only this fact puts into our hand the key as to why the New Testament applies spiritually to the present church age certain Old Testament prophecies which, in the meaning of the Old Testament prophets, unquestionably refer to Israel and the future End times (e.g. Rom. 15: 12 with Isa. 11: 10; I Pet. 2: 10; Rom. 9: 25, 26 with Hos. 1: 10; Acts 2: 16–21 with Joel 2: 28–32; I Pet. 2: 9 with Exod. 19: 6), of course without intending to deny their future literal application (Rom. 11: 29). From God's side these prophecies meant more than the Old Testament prophets were themselves aware (I Pet. 1: 11, 12).

Mere spiritualizing is therefore indeed false, for it takes away from Israel its God-given promises; but *mere* explanation as having only literal future significance is likewise one-sided, for it does not do justice to the manner of the New Testament citations. "Spiritualizing" is to a great extent the method of the New Testament. This one should do and not leave the other undone.

Further, Old Testament prophecy, when it speaks of the coming, visible, glorious kingdom of God on the old earth, is very often a typical prophecy of the final consummation on the new earth. If this were not so we should be confronted by the utterly incomprehensible fact that the entire Old Testament promise of the kingdom refers only to a very short period of one thousand years, and says nothing at all of the actual final goal of the history of salvation.[1] No! it is at the same time "typical" prophesying of eternity, and allowing for all literal and direct references to its environment and to the coming millennial kingdom, this must be said: Its real, essential kernel is not the earthly kingdom of God on the old earth (this *first* portion of the coming kingdom of God) but the eternal kingdom (to which the former will have been only introduction and approach), this *second* and properly *chief* portion of the coming kingdom of God, the nations on the new earth and the new Jerusalem there. See Isa. 65: 17–25; 66: 22.

Thus, then, Old Testament prophecy has a fourfold interpretation in the history of salvation:
1. As contemporaneous history: with reference to the Old Testament circumstances of the prophets themselves;
2. Spiritually and typically: with reference to the church age;
3. Literally as regards the End days: with reference to Israel and the nations of the world in the coming kingdom of God on the old earth;
4. In the light of eternity: with reference to the new heaven and the new earth.

On the way to the consummation each stage in turn serves only as a porch. The Old Testament is the vestibule to the church age; the church age is the vestibule to the visible earthly kingdom of God. But even that visible earthly kingdom of God is not the final goal, but likewise only a vestibule. Only in eternity, in the new heaven and on the new earth, is the royal palace of perfection opened.

[1] But note the frequent use by the prophets of "for ever" in reference to the future of Israel, e.g. Isa. 9: 7; 51: 6, 8; 60: 21; Jer. 7: 7; 25: 5; Ezk. 37: 24, 25; 43: 7, 9; Joel 3: 20; Mic. 4: 6, 7. And Isa. 65: 17, 18. [Trans.]

CHAPTER IX

THE PROPHETIC MESSAGE

THE Spirit of Christ is the source of knowledge and of strength in all prophecy (I Pet. 1: 11; II Pet. 1: 21). Christ is not only Content and Goal of all prophecy, but also its origin and inherent energy. In the prophets Christ as "Logos" (= word, John 1: 1, 14) spoke concerning Himself. The Logos speaks of the person and work of the Messiah. The prophets spoke and acted "in the name of the coming Christ" (Luther).

In three chief spheres prophecy completes in detail the discharge of its calling.

i. Illumination of the past, especially as historical writing:

ii. Judgment of the present, especially as admonition and call to repentance:

iii. Foretelling of the future, especially as warning and comfort, namely:

    (1) judgment upon Israel;

    (2) judgment upon the nations of the world;

    (3) the conversion of Israel;

    (4) the conversion of the nations of the world;

    (5) The Messiah and His kingdom.

I. ILLUMINATION OF THE PAST

As "speakers" and "mouth" of God, plainly the prophets are not only foretellers of the future but at the same time are declarers of the Divine judgment upon past and present. Therefore the writing of history in the light of God is one of their essential and chief duties. Thus Samuel, Nathan, and Gad each wrote a chronicle of the life of David (I Chron. 29: 29). Ahijah of Shiloh and Iddo the seer continued the account (II Chron. 9: 29). Shemaiah was chronicler in the time of Rehoboam (II Chron. 12: 15) and Jehu in that of Jehoshaphet (II Chron. 20: 34). So in the Hebrew Bible the historical books do not stand as a group by themselves but rightly among the "prophets."

But the Israelitic writing of history is of a special mode. It is less theoretical *presentation* of history than practical *instruction* in history. The pictures of the past shall be mirrors for the present. "The word of *that time* speaks *today*." The prophetical writers are free from all nationalistic colouring of history. Even in the case of the greatest national heroes failings and sins are mentioned unsparingly. (Thus Luther said that a true historian must be an excellent man, with the heart of a lion to write the truth unflinchingly). They present neither ecstatic legends of saints nor worship of deified heroes. For them even the hero is only a tool in the hands of God (e.g. Cyrus, Isa. 45: 1), and the "saviours" and deliverers of the nation are "raised up" of the Lord (Judges 3: 9; II Kings 13: 5; Neh. 9: 27, lit.). They are candid enough to mention what is good in the lives of the evil (e.g. Ahab's repentance, I Kings 21: 27–29), and honest enough not to keep silent on the evil in the lives of the good (e.g. Abraham's half-lie, Moses' impatience, David's adultery, Solomon's idolatry, Elijah's despondency).

So should posterity learn from the history of its forefathers, and the narrative of yesterday shall be an appeal to the present day (e.g. II Kings 17: 7–23). In the Bible history is a living history, not merely a happening which "lies" enclosed in the past, but a Divine action that continually "comes" to us in the present; and the prophetic narrative is "less an account than an address, not an *it* but a *thou,* not a *once upon a time* but a *now.*" It is an operative word, which requires not only to be known but to be acknowledged. Only "where this comes to pass, there God's word *comes to pass,* there true history comes to pass."

II. JUDGMENT OF THE PRESENT

Far from being a product of the Jewish mind, the Old Testament fights *against* the Jewish way of life! The prophets unsparingly scourge the sins of the people (Isa. 58: 1), such as avarice, rapacity (Isa. 5: 8; Amos 6: 4–6; Mic. 2: 2), over-reaching, usury (Ezek. 22: 12, 13), exploiting the poor (Isa. 1: 17; Mic. 3: 2, 3; Amos 2: 7; 4: 1; 5: 11; 8: 4–6), oppressing widows and orphans (Isa. 10: 2; Jer. 5: 28), bribery in lawsuits (Isa. 1: 23; 59: 4), business deceit with false weights (Mic. 6: 11; Ezek. 45: 10–12), haughtiness and pride of fashion (Isa. 2: 12–17; 3: 16–24), idolatry and foreign customs (Ezek. 8; Hos. 7: 11; 5: 13; 11: 2; Isa. 2: 6), sanctimoniousness (Isa. 58: 2–5; Jer. 7: 4; Hos. 7: 14; Mic. 3: 11), self-righteousness (Mal. 1: 6; 2: 17; 3: 13), dead formality (Isa. 1: 11–17; Mal. 1: 10; Amos 5: 21–23; Hos. 6: 6).

They describe the people as "apostate" (Jer. 3: 8,11), its incense as "abomination" (Isa. 1: 13), its sacrifice as "murder" (Isa. 66: 3), its meal-offerings as "swine's blood" (Isa. 66: 3). They describe its heart as "stony" (Ezek. 36: 26), its hands as "full of blood" (Isa. 1: 15), its tongue as full of "adders' poison" (Psa. 140: 3).

Jerusalem is a "harlot" (Isa. 1: 21; Ezek. 16: 23; Hos. 1–3); the nation is "Gomorrah" (Isa. 1: 10; Ezek. 16: 46); its leaders are "seducers" (Isa. 9: 16). Its princes are "rebels and companions of thieves" (Isa. 1: 23), murderers (Isa. 1: 21; Ezek. 22: 6), and "princes of Sodom" (Isa. 1: 10).

"The best among them is as a thornbush and the most righteous worse than a thorn hedge" says Micah (7: 4; comp. Exod. 3: 2), and Isaiah proclaims to the Jewish people of his time:

"Woe to the sinful race, the guilt-laden people, the brood of evil-doers, the degenerate children" (Isa. 1: 4). And finally, after centuries of patience, Jehovah, the God of the *Old* Testament, says concerning Jerusalem: "This city hath been to me a provocation of mine anger and of my wrath from the day that they built it unto this day" (Jer. 32: 31).

Thus do the prophets stand as "iron pillars," as "brazen walls" (Jer. 1: 18), as men with foreheads of "diamond, harder than flint" (Ezek. 3: 8, 9). They sew no soft pillows (Ezek. 13: 18); they whitewash no broken walls (Ezek. 13: 10). They do not cry: "Peace, peace, when yet there is no peace" (Jer. 6: 14; Ezek. 13: 10).

And yet they had a burning love for their people and were in truth the best of patriots (comp. Rom. 9: 1–3). But just on this account they are not silent as to its sins, even when it tore their own hearts (Jer. 4: 19). Plainly they were no lying prophets and did not prophesy "for money" (Mic. 3: 11; Dan. 5: 17; Ezek. 13: 19). An inward pressure lay on them; they were "persuaded" of the Lord (Jer. 20: 7). Their service was not a profession but a *call*, not rendered of their own will but under "necessity," laid upon them from above. *They* did not have the message but the *message* had them! "Woe is unto me if I preach not" (I Cor. 9: 16).

They were not national prophets but prophets of the Divine kingdom, not prophets of the masses, but solitary mountain peaks of the Spirit. And although in reality they were true real patriots, yet the masses reckoned them as foreigners, not national, not Jewish enough, as pessimists and obscurantists (I Kings 18: 17), as foes to the fatherland (I Kings 21: 20) and traitors (Jer. 37: 13, 14).

They were hated and despised (II Chron. 36: 16), imprisoned (Jer. 38: 28), thrown into the lion's den (Daniel). They were stoned, sawn asunder, or otherwise killed. They wandered in deserts and ravines and in the caves of the earth, and yet they were men that the earth was not worthy to bear (Heb. 11: 37, 38).

Such are the prophets of Israel. It is only precipitate error which, in rejecting what is bad in Jews, is able also to repudiate the work of the prophets, the Old Testament. Not the Old Testament, but the Talmud is the product of the Jewish spirit! The Old Testament is the product of the Holy Spirit! (I Pet. 1: 11; II Pet. 1: 21; Heb. 3: 7). And between these two there exists a gulf like that between Jesus and the Pharisees. As Jehovah, the God of the *Old* Testament, says to Ezekiel: "Nettles

and thorns are with thee, and thou dwellest with scorpions . . .
for it is an obstinate house" (Ezek. 2: 6). Not *through* but *in
spite of* Israel will the Lord one day triumph. The Old Testament is not the book of Jewish national religion in accordance
with their national character, but it is the Book of God and of
His revelation in the conflict *against* this religion. Jewish-
Talmudic-Pharasaic moralizing and the Old Testament are not
one and the same. But perhaps God has chosen this people
precisely because, against the background of its stiffneckedness
and hostility to Him, He could all the more display the solemnity
of His crushing judgments and the depth of His forgiving grace.
(Acts 7: 51; Luke 4: 25–27; Matt. 8: 10; 11: 21, 23; 12: 42; Rom.
2: 24).

For Israel's course is an instructive object lesson, given on
the open stage of world history, a warning example for all
nations, a mirror for every individual (I Cor. 10: 11). "Let us
not be Pharisees! Fornicators and adulterers, cowards and liars,
perjurers and murderers have not been found in the Jewish
people alone. They have been at all times in all peoples, and
it will still be so in the future. But the Old Testament purports
to be neither the book of Jewish history only nor a collection of
pious and moral narratives, but the testimony of the Holy Spirit
to the sins of men—of *all* men—and to the grace of God which
pardons the repentant, believing sinner. For our own salvation
and blessing, it desires to tell us *how* cowards and liars, perjurers
and murderers and sinners alike came to a halt at the call of
God, and began a new life in the ways of God."

This is also the purport of the "offensive" stories in the Old
Testament: and precisely the prophetic recklessness of its narratives displays the incorruptibility and truthfulness of the whole!
On this very account the Bible is the *book* of mankind because it
is the *picture* of mankind; and this picture of mankind, because
it describes the reality, is indeed very "offensive"! (Psa. 14: 2 , 3).
Therefore, with all the differences and dissimilarities, the superiority and inferiority of the various races, there remains the
verdict, not to be quashed by any self-deification; "There is here
no difference: they are all alike sinners" (Rom. 3: 22, 23, 9),
"Where then remains boasting? It is excluded!" (Rom. 3: 27).

As regards vendettas, polygamy, slavery, and especially the
harsh warfare of Old Testament history, to which objection is
frequently taken, the fact is to be observed that the Old Testament, as an educative stage towards the New, did not reveal the
full light of New Testament moral teaching, and therefore,
according to the testimony of the Lord Himself, contained concessions "on account of the hardheartedness of men" (Matt.
19: 8) which Christ with His majestic "But I say unto you"
invalidated (Matt. 5: 22, 28, 32, 34, 39, 44).

Further: if the Canaanites were to be exterminated by the Israelites, then, *firstly,* must it not be overlooked that peoples are organisms, and, throughout generations, they carry on a uniform life corresponding to the soul of their race, and therefore also as a unit are held responsible by God.   In the *second* place it must not be overlooked that, in the case of the Canaanites, the narrative deals here with peoples *ripe for judgment* who were only destroyed when the measure of their sins was full.   Wherefore the four hundred years of respite between the promising of the land to Abraham (Gen. 15: 18–21; Gal. 3: 17) and its conquest by Moses and Joshua was explained in advance to the patriarch in the words of the Old Testament which say: "*For* the measure of the sin and guilt of the Amorites is until now not yet full" (Gen. 15: 16).   "God cannot be gracious to His friends without at the same time being righteous to His foes.   Therefore must the fulfilment of His promises often wait."   Thus Israel's acquisition of Canaan was conditioned by the judgment on the Canaanites, and the judgment on the Canaanites was conditioned by the Divine righteousness, which first allows sin to ripen fully.

III.   FORETELLING OF THE FUTURE

(1) *Judgment upon Israel.*   Without repentance no salvation! Without the individual humbling himself before God there will never be a raising of the nation to abiding welfare and real blessing.   "Woe to the sinful race, the guilt-laden people, the brood of evil doers, the degenerate children" (Isa. 1: 4).   "Blow the signal-horn at Gibeah, the trumpet at Ramah . . .   The enemy is behind thee, Benjamin" (Hos. 5: 8).   "Israel has rejected the good: let the enemy pursue him!" (Hos. 8: 3).

"Destruction" (Isa. 1: 28; Hos. 4: 6), "trampling down" (Isa. 5: 5), "wasting" (Ezek. 6: 4), "shattering" by the nations (Isa. 30: 14; comp. 5: 25; Ezek. 23: 22, 23), desolation through natural catastrophies (Joel 1: 2–12; Amos 4: 9, 10), "casting out" from the face of God (Jer. 6: 30; 7: 15; 32: 31)—this is the unhappy lot of the apostate Jews.   So do the prophets of the Old Testament declare.   The proofs could be multiplied a hundredfold.   Downfall of the State (Jer. 25; Ezek. 4), disgrace upon the individual (Jer. 29: 18), contempt and hatred from the nations (Jer. 24: 9; 25: 18; 26: 6), the wrath of God as a flaming fire (Jer. 4: 8), His anger as a water flood (Hos. 5: 10), His aspect —a terror (Isa. 2: 21), Himself—a lion (Hos. 5: 14)—and all this yet but a prelude to the actual "day of the Lord" (Joel 2).   Thus do the prophets prophesy against the Jewish people.   "To the law and to the testimony!   If they speak not according to this word, there is for them no dawn of morning!" (Isa. 8: 20).

(2) *Judgment upon the nations of the world.*   But the nations also stand under wrath.   "Violence" (Hab. 1: 9), love of plunder

(Nah. 2: 12, 13; Hab. 2: 8), bloodshedding (Nah. 3: 1), a wild beast nature (Dan. 7: 3–7), self-exaltation and deifying of their own strength (Isa. 10: 12–15; 14: 13; Jer. 50: 31, 32; Nah. 3: 8; Ezek. 27: 3; 28: 2–5; 31: 1–14; Hab. 1: 11; Ezek. 28: 9), hatred against Israel, and despising the Lord (Amos 1: 11; Obad. 11; Isa. 10: 5–7; 47: 6; Jer. 48: 27; 50: 7; Ezek. 25: 3, 6)—all these render the nations ripe for judgment.　Their religions are delusions (Isa. 44: 9–20; Jer. 50: 38), their gods are nullities (Psa. 96: 5, lit.), all their doing is interpenetrated with sin (Psa. 14: 2, 3).　And yet they daringly affirm that *their* belief is better than reverencing the Lord (Isa. 36: 18–20; 10: 10; Dan. 5: 3, 4).　So do they revolt and rebel against the Lord of the starry world (Isa. 40: 26), and yet themselves—taken all together—are only a "drop in the bucket," a "speck of dust on the balance" (Isa. 40: 15).

On this account the sentence of the Lord runs: "I begin to execute the judgment at the city that is called by my name; and shall you receive nothing?　No: I call for the sword against *all* the inhabitants of the earth" (Jer. 25: 29).　"Woe unto Assyria" (Isa. 10: 5), this "fiery dragon" (Isa. 14: 29; 27: 1).　The sword upon Egypt (Ezek. 29: 8), this monster in the Nile (Isa. 27: 1; Ezek. 29: 3).　The pit and the snare upon Moab (Jer. 48: 43), this vain boaster (Isa. 16: 6).　"Take from my hand this cup full of the wine of wrath and let *all* the peoples, to whom I send thee, drink from it" (Jer. 25: 15, 16).　Ammon shall become a pasture for camels (Ezek. 25: 5), and Tyre a "bare rock" (Ezek. 26: 4). Elam shall die (Ezek. 32: 23, 24) and Edom be a place as "silent as death" ("Dumah") (Isa. 21: 11; 63: 1–6).　And above all, Babylon, this "hammer of the Lord" (Jer. 51: 20–23), shall become for ever "as Sodom and Gomorrah" (Isa. 13: 19, 20; Jer. 50: 40).　Thus are the prophets at the same time prophets to the nations, and the Old Testament is a warning signal to the world.

Because of this the greatest prophets have lengthy connected "speeches to the nations:" Isa. 13–23; Jer. 46–51; Ezek. 25–32; Dan. 2; 4; 7; 8; 11; Amos 1; 2.

(3) *The Conversion of Israel.* "But darkness does not continue to the land that was distressed" (Isa. 9: 1).　Through judgment shall Zion be redeemed (Isa. 1: 27).　The "remnant" will "turn around" (Isa. 10: 21; Jer. 24: 7; Hos. 3: 5), and, through the appearing of the Messiah, will become a renewed people (Isa. 11: 1; 4: 3; 6: 13; Ezek. 37: 26–28).

The prophets paint this coming salvation in overflowing fulness and the most splendid vivid colours.　They speak of it in hundreds of places.　But always their prophecies of salvation refer to the *converted* and *renewed* Israel; to the unconverted, exploiting, supplanting "Jacob," whether still dwelling in the land, or scattered among the nations because of his sins, the

Old Testament gives not one single promise of lordship and blessing.

But when the Messiah appears, then will Israel, in Palestine (Jer. 16: 15), experience its great national repentance (Zech. 12: 10–14; Rev. 1: 7) and spiritual rebirth—not from its own national energies but from Jesus of Nazareth! And then will come to pass the Jewish miracle, and the people now so unclean and unholy, will be so holy, so clean, so transformed, that all things, even the smallest, will be dedicated to the Lord. "At that day will be graven on the bells of the horses 'Holy to the Lord,' and every cooking pot in Jerusalem and Judah will be holy unto the Lord of hosts" (Zech. 14: 20, 21). Thus the spiritual and national "resurrection" of Israel from the dead (Ezek. 37: 1–14) is bound up with its coming holiness, and with the holiness its blessing (Isa. 60: 18; 61: 10), and with the blessing the glory of God (Isa. 40: 5; 46: 13). "The zeal of the Lord of hosts will perform this" (Isa. 9: 7).

(4) *The Conversion of the Nations.* But the nations also are to be blessed. For God is not the God of the Jews only, but also of the nations (see Rom. 3: 29). Israelitish prophecy sees the nations as *one* family, and all nations partake together of the Messianic salvation. Therefore will the Lord one day "destroy the veil which veils all the peoples, and the covering which covers all nations" (Isa. 25: 7). Then will the peoples *as peoples* be converted (Jer. 3: 17; Zech. 8: 20–22; Isa. 2: 3; Mic. 4: 2; Isa. 42: 4), and for the first time in history there will be Christian nations and races in the sense of Holy Scripture. The present age (from Pentecost to the return of Christ) has not the christianizing of races as its goal, but the calling out of *individuals* "*out of* all peoples," and thereby the formation of the church out of Jews and Gentiles (Acts 15: 14).

"On that day there will stand an altar to Jehovah in the midst of the land of Egypt, and near to its border a pillar to Jehovah, and the Egyptians will serve Jehovah in union with the Assyrians. And Jehovah of hosts will bless them and say: 'Blessed art thou, Egypt, *my* people, and thou, Assyria, the work of *my* hands; and thou, Israel, *my* inheritance'" (Isa. 19: 19, 23, 25).

In fact, Israelitish prophecy here offers its utmost; for it is not incorporation of the converted heathen into Israel, the renewed people of God, which is here the hope, but "a brotherly alliance between Israel and the nations on the basis of the same Divine redemption."

And in Malachi God says: "From the rising of the sun until its going down shall my name be glorious among the Gentiles, and *in all places* shall incense and a pure offering be offered; for my name shall be glorious among the nations" (Mal. 1: 11).

By this the Old Testament prophet—only with Old Testament colours—foretells the New Testament truth which Jesus spake to the Samaritan woman: that the Father should receive worship, in spirit and truth, not in this or that city, but *in all places on earth* (John 4: 21–24). Thus, therefore, will Israel in its land and the nations in their lands experience a spiritual, divine rebirth (Psa. 87: 4–6), and the Lord will reign as the Divine King over all the earth (Zech. 14: 9), and righteousness and peace will rule all humanity.

(5) *The Messiah and His Kingdom.* The conversion of Israel and of the nations will be effected through the appearing of the Messiah. He is the crown and the shining star of all prophecy. "The prophets are the stars and the moon, but Christ is the sun" (Luther). Of Him "testify all the prophets, that through his name all who believe on him shall receive forgiveness of sins" (Acts 10: 43). *Christ is the theme of the Old Testament.* He said so Himself (John 5: 39; Luke 24: 25–27, 46). So His greatest apostle testified (I Cor. 15: 3, 4; Acts 26: 22, 23). It is only from the King of Scripture that the testimony of His preceding heralds can be understood; it is only from the New Testament that the question as to the Old Testament solves itself.

CHAPTER X

THE MESSIANIC PROPHECIES

THROUGHOUT the Old Testament Christ[1] is regarded as the coming One. In the Old covenant the gospel is coming into being. "The Old Testament is the dusk and dawn of morning. The dawn belongs to the sun. Thus the Old Testament belongs to Christ." "The Old Testament tells *what* Christ is, the New Testament tells *who* He is, and in such a way that it becomes manifest that he alone knows 'Jesus' who recognizes Him as the 'Christ,' and he alone knows who the 'Christ' is who knows that He is 'Jesus.' So do the two Testaments correspond to the two chief names of the Redeemer; the Old to the name of His vocation, Christ, the New to His personal name, Jesus; but both are inspired by one Spirit and explain each other."

Therefore the portrait of the Messiah in Old Testament prophecy is all-embracing. It depicts:

    i The Person of the Messiah:
        His humanity as to family, place, and time.
        His divinity (this in veiled form—see p. 19).
    ii. The Work of the Messiah:
        His coming in lowliness.
        His coming in glory.

I. THE PERSON OF THE MESSIAH

Before He became man Christ is already the centre of the history of salvation.

His anticipatory presentation in the Old Testament is at the same time a *self*-presentation, for the "Spirit of Christ" was in the prophets (I Pet. 1: 11). The pre-Christian history of revelation is a "history of Christ" before He came.

(1) *His humanity.* Conscious of the goal, advancing in the course of centuries, Old Testament prophecy described the humanity of the Redeemer in ever narrowing and concentrating circles of light, like a pyramid tapering upwards. First of all

(*a*) The family. The world's Redeemer descends from *mankind,* is "the woman's seed" (Gen. 3: 15)—

        thus was it spoken at the time of Adam and Eve: about 4300 B.C.;

---

[1] Exactly the same verbal form *Christos* was used in the third century before Christ's birth in the Bible of the exiled Jews in Egypt, the Septuagint, the Greek translation of the Old Testament prepared by the Jews. It is found in such passages as Psa. 2: 2; I Sam. 2: 10; Dan. 9: 25.

from all the races of mankind, out of *Shem's* family (Gen. 9: 26)—
      thus Noah prophesied: about 2300 B.C.;
from among all Shemites, out of the *seed of Abraham* (Gen. 12:
1–3)—
      thus said God Himself: about 1900 B.C.;
from among all the nations descended from Abraham, out of
Israel—
      as is proved by the transmission of the covenant to Isaac
         and Jacob: about 1850 B.C., see Gen. 26: 3, 4; 28: 13, 14;
from among all Israelites, out of the royal tribe of *Judah*—
      as was said about 1800 B.C.: Gen. 49: 10, comp. I Chron.
      5: 2; Heb. 7: 14.

Actually Reuben had the right of the firstborn. Nevertheless the Messiah is not "Lion out of the tribe of Reuben."
For, on account of sin (as recorded in Gen. 35: 22), Reuben was
deprived of his firstborn rights and the right concerning the
Messiah (I Chron. 5: 1; Gen. 49: 3, 4). The next following
brothers, Simeon and Levi, were also excluded (Gen. 49: 5–7)
on account of their bloody deed at Shechem (Gen. 34: 25).

Thereupon Reuben's rights as the firstborn were divided as
follows:

The double share of the material inheritance (Deut. 21: 15–17)
went to Joseph (in Ephraim and Manasseh; I Chron. 5: 1, 2);

The priestly dignity (see Exod. 13: 2, 15), having regard to.
Exod. 32: 26–28, went to Levi (Num. 3: 12, 45; 8: 17, 18); and

The ruler's dignity (see Gen. 43: 33; 48: 14, 18, 19) went to
Judah, Jacob's fourth son (I Chron. 5: 2). Therefore is the
Messiah the "Lion out of the tribe of Judah" (Rev. 5: 5; Gen.
49: 9, 10).

After this the particularizing of the promise stopped for some
centuries. Moses, indeed, about 1500 B.C., writes his fivefold
work, and prophesies of the coming of a *Prophet* like to himself
(Deut. 18: 15; Acts 3: 22; 7: 37); and, above all, the Tabernacle
and the sacrifices are types of Christ as the *Priest* (esp. Exod. 25–31;
Lev. 1–7; 16; John 5: 46); but he carried the promise no further
towards its summit.

The heathen seer, Balaam, Moses' contemporary, likewise
confined his prophecy of the coming *King* entirely within the
general framework of Israel: "I see him, but not just now; I
behold him, but not near at hand: there rises a star out of Jacob,
and a sceptre out of Israel exalts itself" (Num. 24: 17).

It is not before Nathan, the prophet of David's time (about
1050 and thus 700 years later) that the specializing of the prophecy
is resumed. In the meantime the kingdom of Israel had arisen
(with Saul, 1100); and this, from the point of view of God's
kingly rule (Exod. 19: 5, 6; Deut. 33: 5), was a retrograde step
(I Sam. 8: 7), a concession to the hard-heartedness of mankind

(see Matt. 19: 8).   But the plan of God cannot be frustrated by
the counter-workings of men.

The divine-human Messiah king was to come out of Israel.
Some one Israelite must therefore be His ancestor.   But that this
ancestor must be a king was in no wise necessary.   To the kingship of Messiah no earthly royal dynasty was essential, nor even
desired according to the plan of God.   Any private person out of
the tribe of Judah could be chosen as the forbear of the Messiah.

But after the kingdom had come and, if not at first willed by
God, yet in fact instituted by Himself, the overruling by God of
men's shortcomings consisted in this, that God now chose for
the ancestor of the Messiah not a private individual but rather a
believing wearer of the crown.

This is the meaning in the plan of salvation of the mission
of Nathan (I Chron. 17: 3–14).   Through the prophecy of
Nathan to David, the Messianic promises within the royal tribe
of Judah were conferred on him, the crowned son of Jesse
(see Isa. 11: 1).   From now onwards the Messiah is the "Son
of David" (see Rev. 5: 5).[1]

The further specializing of the promise then continues right
through David's royal family.   Out of David's numerous sons
(II Sam. 5: 13, 14) two especially became transmitters of the
Messianic blessing, Solomon and Nathan, both sons of Bath-
sheba (I Chron. 3: 5).   From Solomon was descended Joseph,
the *legal* "father" of the Lord Jesus (Matt. 1: 6, 16); from Nathan,
the virgin Mary, His *actual* mother (Luke 3: 23, 31).   Taken
strictly Christ thus descends not from the chief royal line of
Solomon, but from the *non*-reigning collateral line of Nathan.
The one is the legal, the other the organic; the organic has more
significance than the legal.

Matthew gives the ancestral tree of Joseph, Luke that of
Mary, or, to be more accurate, of her father Eli (Luke 3: 23), the
father-in-law of Joseph (hence ver. 23; comp. Neh. 7: 63).   The
Talmud also calls Mary a daughter of Eli.   Thus explain Luther,
Bengel, Lange, Delitzsch, and many others.

Thus, by gradual diffusion of the light, prophecy had advanced from the general to the particular, from the office to the
office-bearer, from the material to the personal, as it were from
"Christ" to "Jesus."   The Old Testament had been a "drawing
by the Father to the Son," even as the New Testament is a
"drawing by the Son to the Father" (I Cor. 15: 28).

Later, the earthly kingdom went to ruin.   With Zedekiah
the family of David lost its crown (II Chron. 36: 11–20).   But
nevertheless the kingdom and the power and the glory continued

[1] The name "David" occurs about 980 times in the Old Testament and about
50 times in the New Testament, that is over 1,000 times in all.   The name "Jesus"
occurs almost 1,000 times.

with David (Isa. 55: 3), and in the End time Christ, even as "David", will shepherd His people and the nations (Ezek. 37: 24, 25; Hos. 3: 5; Isa. 11: 1–10; Jer. 23: 5). "My servant David shall be their prince for ever" (Ezek. 37: 25, comp. Rev. 22: 16). Thus man attained what *he* had desired (the earthly kingdom): but nevertheless at last God maintained *His* right (the heavenly kingdom).

(*b*) *The Place.* With the prophecy of Nathan to David the question as to the family of the Messiah had been conclusively answered (about 1050 B.C.). But the question as to the place and time was not yet clarified. Therefore two further leading prophecies were added, these being, after 300 years (about 725), Micah's prophecy as to the place (5: 2; comp. 1: 1), and after 500 years (about 536), Daniel's prophecy as to the time (Dan. 9: 24–27; comp. 1).

Although founded by a descendant of the heroic Caleb (I Chron. 2: 50, 51), and in the times of the Judges for seven years the seat of Ibzan the judge (Judges 12: 8–10), in the centuries before David Bethlehem–Ephratah (House of Bread, the fruitful) enters the history of Israel only with a very *in*glorious reputation, connected indeed with death and mourning (Gen. 35: 19, 20) idolatry (Judges 17: 7ff.), immorality, fratricidal strife (Judges 19–21 and famine (Ruth 1: 1)[1]. But it was from this very city that God, who always condescends to the lowly, chose for Himself the ancestor of the Messiah; and thus Bethlehem Ephratah, as David's city, became the place in which "Christ the Lord" should be born (Mic. 5: 2; Luke 2: 11).

But the prophecy became yet more precise. Nearly two hundred years after Micah had foretold the place (about 725) Daniel (about 536) announced

(*c*) *The Time.* This took place in the prophecy of the "seventy year-weeks," or, more exactly, the sixty-nine year-weeks before the advent of the seventieth. With this the prophecy reached its culminating point and at the same time its conclusion.

"Therefore know now and mark: From the time that there goes out a command that Jerusalem shall again be built unto the anointed one, the prince, are seven weeks and sixty-two weeks; so will the streets and walls be built again, though in a troubled time; and after the sixty two weeks the Anointed One will be rooted out and be no more" (Dan. 9: 25, 26).[2]

---

[1] Though the connexion is only indirect, the Levite Jonathan, the household priest of the idolatrous Micah, had come to him from Bethlehem (Judges 17: 7–10, 1–5; 18: 30).

[2] That by this "anointed one" Christ is meant (and not perhaps Cyrus, or, according to II Macc. 4: 34, the high priest Onías, murdered in B.C. 172) was the interpretation of the ancient church and of such later expositors as Hengstenberg, Auberlen, and Keil.

The seventy weeks (sevens) are each seven years. An Israelite like Daniel would grasp this very easily, since under the Mosaic law every seventh year was reckoned a sabbath year (Lev. 25: 4). Thus the $7 \times 62 = 69$ year-weeks "unto the anointed one (the Messiah) the prince" embrace 483 years.

Their beginning is the issue of the command to rebuild Jerusalem (ver. 25). This cannot mean the decree of Cyrus (536 B.C.); for it was concerned chiefly with the rebuilding of the temple (II Chron. 36: 23; Ezra 1: 1–4; 5: 13–15; 6: 3–5), a task which was carried out by the prince Zerubbabel, the high priest Joshua, and the prophets Haggai and Zechariah by the year 516 (Ezra 5: 1; 6: 14, 15). The actual rebuilding of the city was first carried out some decades later by the priest Ezra, the governor Nehemiah, and the prophet Malachi.

Their activity set in with the decree of the Persian king, Artaxerxes I Longimanus (Arthasastha), in the seventh year of his reign (465–424), regarding the political reorganization of Palestine, and therefore in the year 457 B.C. (Ezra 7: 25, 7). *The beginning of Ezra's activity is thus the beginning of the seventy year-weeks.* That it was only some years later (445) that Nehemiah could commence the building of the wall was because serious difficulties had at first stood in the way of laying the foundation. But nevertheless that first decree remains the beginning and "going out" of the command to rebuild the city.

If we add to this year 457 the foretold sixty-nine year-weeks, that is 483 years, we come to the year 26/27 A.D., that is, to the exact year in which, according to Luke 3: 1, 2, shortly after John the Baptist, Christ began to proclaim the message of the heavenly kingdom. For when the Lord appeared in public He was about thirty years of age (Luke 3: 23), and since Herod the Great was living at the time of His birth (Matt. 2), yet had died in the year 749 of the city of Rome, that is in the year 4 B.C., the Lord must have been born some four or five years before the beginning of the Christian reckoning of time, and thus at the commencement of His public ministry, in the year 26/27, was literally "about thirty years old."

It is well known that Victorinus of Aquitania (died A.D. 465) and the Roman Abbot Dionisius Exiguus (died about 556) erred by four to six years in fixing the Christian era. Year "1" of the Christian era ought not to correspond to the year "753" of the city of Rome, but at least to 749, if not to one or two years earlier. The year 26 is also the "fifteenth year of Tiberius" (Luke 3: 1), for Luke does not there reckon the years of reign from the *sole* rule of Tiberius (that is, from the death of Augustus, 19th August, A.D. 14), but from his elevation to the *joint* sovereignty (shortly before the 16th January, A.D. 12).

Thus here also the fulfilment has confirmed the prophecy in

a most surprising manner, and because Old Testament Messianic prophecy has accurately determined the humanity of the Redeemer as to family, place, and time, it has at the same time proved itself to be a perfect Divine picture.

(2) *The Prophetic Anticipation of the Deity of the Messiah.*

But the Deity of the Messiah is also indicated in the Old Testament, even if only in veiled form and in pictures and riddles. First in the comparatively clear fashion in Nathan's prophecy: "I will be his father, and he shall be my son" (I Chron. 17: 13). Based on this David calls his son his "Lord" (Psa. 110: 1; Matt. 22: 44, 45); and the typical David, as if stepping down from his throne, lays his crown at the feet of Him Who, sitting at the right hand of Jehovah, is the real, true David (Hos. 3: 5; Ezek. 37: 24, 25). Furthermore the same Psalmist says: "Kiss the son, lest he be angry" and "Jehovah has said to me, Thou art my son, this day have I begotten thee" (Psa. 2: 12, 7), an expression which the New Testament applies to the resurrection of Jesus (Acts 13: 33; comp. Rom. 1: 4), which was promotion from life in the form of a servant to life in exaltation and thus His "begetting" into the royal estate.

Isaiah also further shows pictorially the deity of the Messiah in that he describes the "root-branch out of Jesse" (Isa. 11: 1) as "*zemach* (shoot) of the Lord" (Isa. 4: 2), and as "Wonderful Counsellor, Mighty Hero, Eternal Father, Prince of Peace" (Isa. 9: 6). For *Micah* He is "Jehovah, whose going out has been from eternity unto eternity" (Mic. 5: 2); for *Jeremiah* "Jehovah our righteousness" (Jer. 23: 5, 6); and for *Malachi* "Jehovah whom ye seek" and "the Angel of the Covenant whom ye desire" (Mal. 3: 1).

To this appertains also the self-testimony of the eternal "Wisdom" in Prov. 8: 22–31, comp. John 1: 1–3. The above sequence is in historical order. Nathan and David about 1050 B.C., Isaiah and Micah about 720, Jeremiah about 586, Malachi about 430.

II. THE WORK OF THE MESSIAH

As the person of the Messiah was viewed by the prophets under harmonious contrast, so also His work. There it was the contrast between deity and humanity; here between humiliation and exaltation. The "sufferings which should come unto Christ" and "the glories thereafter"—this is the twofold content of all their prophesying (I Pet. 1: 11).

(1) *Christ's Coming in Lowliness.* In a positively sublime miniature they portrayed His first coming, the dark background to His radiant Kingly glory.

L

His birth in Bethlehem: Mic. 5: 2; Matt. 2: 1.
His public appearance in Galilee: Isa. 9: 1, 2; 6; Matt. 4: 12–16.
His gentleness and tenderness: Isa. 42: 2, 3; Matt. 12: 17–21.
His consuming zeal: Psa. 69: 9; John 2: 17; Matt. 21: 12.
His miracles and healings: Isa. 53: 4; Matt. 8: 16, 17.
His entry into Jerusalem: Zech. 9: 9; Matt. 21: 4, 5.
The rage of His enemies: Psa. 2: 1–3; Acts 4: 25–28.
His desertion by His friends: Zech. 13: 7; Matt. 26: 31.
His betrayal for thirty pieces of silver: Zech. 11: 12; Matt. 26: 15.
His piercing on the cross: Psa. 22: 16; John 20: 25–27.
None of His bones broken: Exod. 12: 46; Psa. 34: 20; John 19: 31–37.
The casting of lots for His garments: Psa. 22: 18; Matt. 27: 35.
Vinegar given Him to drink: Psa. 69: 21; Matt. 27: 34.
His cry of pain in distress: Psa. 22: 1; Matt. 27: 46.
His cry of victory: "It is finished:" Psa. 22: 31; John 19: 30.
The spear-thrust of the soldier: Zech. 12: 10; John 19: 34, 37.
His resurrection on the third day: Psa. 16: 10; Acts 2: 25–31; Hos. 6: 2.
His ascent to heaven: Psa. 110: 1; Acts 2: 34, 35.

Through all this He is the suffering and victorious "Servant of God" Who, as the substitute for the sinner, completes redemption, and thus fulfils Isaiah 53, that most wonderful prophecy of the Old Testament (Acts 8: 32–35).

(2) *Christ's Coming in Glory.* The *second* coming of the Lord is also portrayed in the most living and splendid colours. In this the prophets, according to the law of "prophetic perspective," often view the first and second comings of Christ together in one picture (Isa. 61: 1, 2; Luke 4: 18–20).

Crowned with the golden-silver double crown (Zech. 6: 11–13) of the kingship and priesthood of Melchizedek (Psa. 110: 4), the Messiah rules over His kingdom in righteousness and sevenfold fulness of the Spirit (Isa. 11: 2–4).

These are some of the glories of this golden age:
Conversion and union of Israel: Hos. 3: 5; 2: 17–19; Isa. 11: 9; Zeph. 3: 13; Ezek. 37: 15–22.
Renewal of the nations: Zeph. 3: 9.
Peace among the peoples: Mic. 4: 3, 4.
Blessings upon Nature: Isa. 11: 6–8; Hos. 2: 21, 22.
Enhanced brightness of sun and moon: Isa. 30: 26.

Thus the Old Testament is like a star-spangled heaven at night even as the New is a bright sunny day, "and there is no word in the New Testament which does not look back to the Old, wherein it is announced in advance . . . for the New Testament is nothing else than a revelation of the Old: just as if one had first a closed letter and thereafter broke it open" (Luther, *Kirchen-postille* of 1522). It is to the last Messianic prophecy of the Old Covenant (Mal. 3: 1) that the first announcement of the birth of the New Covenant is attached (Gabriel to Zacharias, Luke 1: 5–17). For Christ is the *Omega* of the Old and the *Alpha* of the New Testament.

III. THE SILENCE OF GOD

The prophets had spoken. For almost 4000 years God had revealed Himself, first to mankind in general, then to Israel in particular. Especially since Moses had there been an unbroken chain of prophetic messages.

Then suddenly with Malachi prophecy became dumb. God withdrew to His high heaven and was silent; silent for 400 years —silent and waiting.

And mankind here below, in this vale of tears, had to wait for the promised Redeemer for almost half a millennium! Yet *everything was already said* which had to be said before the appearing of the Saviour of the world! The Old Testament revelation of God was completed and closed 400 years before the birth of Christ.

To what end then for the believing in Israel was this discipline of longing, this extended interval between Malachi and John the Baptist? Why did not Christ come in the time of Malachi?

The answer lies in this, that preparations for the gospel had to be made not only by way of revelation, but also in the world and in civilization. And this is exactly what came to pass in the interval between the Old and the New Testaments, and especially through Alexander the Great, Hellenism, and the Roman empire. Thereby the kingdoms of the world come into the view-point of the preparation for salvation, and the God who as regards revelation had become silent was at the same time in action as regards *world* events. It is especially the book of Daniel that illuminates the night of these 500 years.

The record of salvation in the Bible knows two long periods without revelation: the time between Malachi and John the Baptist and the time between Christ and the coming of the kingdom of God. The first lasted 400 years; the second has lasted already almost 2,000 years. Both belong to the "times of the nations" (Luke 21: 24).

The lamp of the first is the prophet of the nations, Daniel; the guiding star of the last is the *Revelation* of John. The book of *Daniel* was given to the saints of the Old Covenant on entering the night between the first destruction of Jerusalem (586 B.C.)

and the first appearing of the Lord.   The *Revelation* of John was given to the saints of the New Covenant on entering the night between the second destruction of Jerusalem (A.D. 70) and the second appearing of the Lord.   Thus they both belong together: the one is the counterpart of the other and the second is the completion of the first.

E—THE PREPARATION OF THE NATIONS FOR SALVATION

CHAPTER XI

THE "TIMES OF THE NATIONS"
(*The four world empires of Daniel*)

The peoples are as the roaring sea, as breaking billows,
which rage tumultuously (Comp. Isa. 17: 13)

WITH Nebuchadnezzar (586 B.C.) began the "times of the nations" (Luke 21: 24), that is, the times during which Israel is given into the hands of the world powers. They will end only with the setting up of the visible kingdom of God.

Nebuchadnezzar and Daniel were privileged to view the entire unfolding of world powers in a prophecy which covers world history in general, but each from a different standpoint, corresponding to his place in the plan of salvation.

Nebuchadnezzar, the heathen ruler, saw the *outer* side of world history, its *human* countenance, its "humanity," its organic connexion (*one* figure), the sublime, heroic, imposing in it; the colossal human statue "of extraordinary brightness" (Dan. 2: 31); *to him* the kingdom of God appeared to be only a "stone" from the mountain (Dan. 2: 34, 44, 45).

Daniel, the Minister of State, but at the same time a holy seer, saw the *inner* side of history, its *sub*-human, its wild beast nature (Dan. 7: 4–7), its "brutality," its discordant, dismembered state in the conflict of the peoples with one another (Dan. 8: 4, 6, 7; 11: 2, 4, 11), the crushing (Dan. 7: 7, 19), "the blaspheming" (Dan. 7: 8, 25) elements in it; and *to him* the kingdom of God is the kingdom of the "Son of man" (Dan. 7: 13, 14, 27), that is, a kingdom in which, for the first time, there will be set up on earth a rule of true humanity in the sense of the Holy Scriptures.

The first kingdom was a *unit* (Babylonia, *one* head), the second a *duality* (Medo-Persia, breast and two arms), the third *four*fold (the four Grecian States that succeeded Alexander, the leopard with four horns), the fourth will be a *ten*fold unity (the fourth world kingdom of the End time; ten toes, ten horns, but which through Antichrist will be bound together in a single unit). But finally, when Christ appears, this will all become a *multiplicity* of ruins (Dan. 2: 35; Rev. 16: 19; 19: 11–18; Matt. 21: 44), and then the Lord, as the proper Monarch of men, will bring all peoples and races into a true unity, under one head, Himself (Eph. 1: 10; Zech. 14: 9).

Going from east to west the development and direction of history may be compared to the course of the sun—closing with night. Downwards, away from God, move sin and the world. From gold it passes to silver (Dan. 2: 39), from silver to copper, copper to iron (compare Ovid's four ages of the world), and on feet of clay stands Nebuchadnezzar's colossus (Dan. 2: 33). The parts of the body also descend in rank:

first the head, the seat of the intellect;
then the breast, the seat of the vital organs;
then the belly, the seat of the digestion;
finally the feet, which walk in the dust.

Therefore the end is a "breaking to pieces." The giant statue is "crushed" (Dan. 2: 35, 45) and the sovereignty of the beasts is taken away (Dan. 7: 12). Then, suddenly, in the midst of the deepest night, the sun arises. The Son of man, coming from heaven (Dan. 7: 13; Matt. 26: 64), establishes the true kingdom of humanity. The "stone" increases to a "mountain" and "fills the whole earth" (Dan. 2: 35), and "the kingdom and the sovereignty and the greatness of the kingdom under the whole heaven will be given to the people of the saints of the Most High" (Dan. 7: 27).

From the eighth to the sixth century before Christ it was "spring-time" with the peoples of the world. No other epoch in the history of the pre-Christian world was of such basic significance in the formation of the intellectual life of mankind. A wave of inspiration passed right over the whole civilized world. In Eastern Asia lived Confucius and Lao-tse, the greatest of Chinamen; in Southern Asia Buddha, the most influential Indian; in Persia Zoroaster, the prophet of the religion of Cyrus. In Western Asia was the full flower of Israel's prophecy under Isaiah, Jeremiah, Ezekiel and Daniel; and in Greece the first germinating of philosophy (Tales, Heraclitus, Pythagoras, and Socrates) and the flowering of classical poetry (Sophocles, Euripides and Aeschylus).

But politically there raged the spring *storms*, In 650 B.C. Nineveh was still standing, and the great king of Assyria was the lord of the Middle East. Yet in 612 Nineveh fell, and thenceforward events followed one another like waves in a fast flowing stream. After a few decades Nebuchadnezzar's empire was overthrown by Cyrus (538). The empire of Cyrus was overthrown by Alexander the Great (333). After Alexander's death his kingdom fell into four States (301), and then Rome took over the whole inheritance. Only with the Roman empire came for some centuries quietness from storms.

I. THE NEW BABYLONIAN WORLD EMPIRE (612–538 B.C.)

"Thou art the head of gold:" thus did Daniel explain the statue to Nebuchadnezzar.[1]   The first of the four beasts which Daniel himself saw corresponded to this kingdom.   The new Babylonian empire was the *lion with eagle's wings* (Dan. 7: 4), for what gold is among metals and the head among members, so the lion is among the beasts of the earth and the eagle among the creatures of the air, and the new Babylonian empire combined a lion-like royal might with eagle-like swiftness and rapacity.

It was founded by Nabopolassar (625 B.C.), consolidated by Nebuchadnezzar (604–562), and destroyed by Cyrus the Persian (538).   It lasted almost exactly seventy years and the period of its existence was almost the same period as the Babylonian captivity of the Jews (606–536).   With its destruction was fulfilled the prophecy of Jeremiah: "The Lord has stirred up the fury of the kings of the Medes; because his device is against Babylon to destroy it; for it is the vengeance of the Lord, the vengeance for his temple" (Jer, 51: 11, 24; Isa. 13: 17).   But at the same time with the fall of Babylon the whole world-rule of the Semitic race collapsed permanently (538 B.C.).

II. THE MEDO-PERSIAN WORLD EMPIRE (538–332 B.C.)

Cyrus is uniquely saluted in the Old Testament.   In the history of the nations he is the only warrior who a century or more before his birth is mentioned by name in Israelitish prophecy, that is, by Isaiah (44: 28; 45: 1) about 200 years before Cyrus himself.   The Lord, for the sake of His servant Israel, had taken him by the right hand to subdue peoples before him (45: 1, 4).   He calls him His "shepherd" (44: 28), His "anointed," who will carry out all His will (45: 1), and He says to him: "I will go before thee and make the impassable places level; I will break the brazen gates and break to pieces the iron bars.   I will give over to thee the treasure hidden in darkness, and the well-concealed precious things, so that thou shalt know that I, Jehovah, it is, the God of Israel, Who has called thee by thy name" (Isa. 45: 3, 4).   Thus did the Old Testament salute the founder of Aryan (Japhetic) world-rule.

The Medo-Persian empire was the *silver breast,* with the two arms (Dan. 2: 32), the *bear* which raised itself up on one side (Dan. 7: 5), the *ram* with the two unequal horns, of which the higher grew up last (Dan. 8: 3, 20).

The Medes and Persians were brother peoples, yet at first the Persians were under the overlordship of the Medes.   But in 559 B.C. the Persian prince Kurush (Kuras, Cyrus, Kores) of Ansan completely overthrew the Median king Astyages, and

---

[1] Even before this, the old Babylon of the time of Hammurabi (1900 B.C.) had been the "brains" of the Middle East and the intellectual "head" of civilization.

thenceforth the Median kingdom became Persian. The bear had, as it were, "raised itself up" on the one side, i.e., the Persian side, while the other, the Median, lay beneath; of the two horns of the ram the one that had grown later had surpassed the other.

With powerful thrusts the Persian kingdom stormed forward, especially after the fall of Babylon (538 B.C.). "I saw how the ram pushed westward, northward, and southward" (Dan. 8: 4). It is significant that the east is not mentioned; for as a matter of fact the Persian kings undertook no conquests towards India. But in the other directions this insatiable empire "devoured" land after land in succession: "Stand up; devour much flesh" (Dan. 7: 5). In the "mouth" of the bear there were three particular "ribs," the Lydian (from 546 B.C.), the Babylonian (from 538), and the Egyptian kingdom (from 525), and with its 127 provinces it embraced almost the whole of the then civilized world (Esther 1: 1). Only against Greece were its attempts futile, and it was there that the germ of its later fall reposed (Dan. 11: 2).

III. THE GRECO-MACEDONIAN WORLD EMPIRE
333 B.C. and subsequently

The collapse of the Persian empire, after a duration of 206 years (538–332), was effected by Alexander of Macedonia, the son of king Philip. His empire is *the copper belly and the loins* of Nebuchadnezzar's statue, the *panther* with the four wings and four heads of Daniel's dream-vision (Dan. 7: 6), and he himself is the "great horn" of the "*goat*" which, coming "from the west" in "furious" assault, brought about the overthrow of the Persian "ram" (Dan. 8: 5–7, 21).

"Ram" and "horn" were in themselves obvious pictures for a military leader and royal power (Jer. 50: 8; Zech. 10: 3). They were particularly suitable for Persia, especially in distinction from Alexander's empire, the goat. For as the ram is more peaceable than the goat, which is agile and able to defend itself, and more tractable than the latter in its wildness and waywardness; and as in its thick woolly coat it can present a fitting picture of comfort and prosperity—so it was with the Persian empire at the time of Alexander. Moreover the Persian kings, when they appeared at the head of their army, did literally often wear a ram's head instead of the diadem, and likewise there were ram's heads on the pillars of their chief city, Persepolis.

On the "goat" as the symbol of Alexander the Great, Hävernick remarks:

> The city of Edessa in Macedonia received from king Caranus the name of Aega (comp. Gr. *aix, aigos*, the goat), and from this the Macedonians themselves had the name Aegeades, which according to the classical writers was given

them expressly because of the goats which enabled the king to capture that city (Justin). That city, under that name, long remained the residence of the early Macedonian rulers (Diod. Sic.). The son of Alexander the Great by Roxane was called Alexander Aegus. One finds several of the Macedonian kings portrayed on their coins with the horns of a he-goat, and goats served as a device on the banners and standards of the Macedonian army (Justin).

The victorious march of Alexander is the mightiest spectacle of antiquity. With furious speed, as if the swift-footed goat, flying, did not touch the ground (Dan. 8: 5), like a four-winged leopard (Dan. 7: 6), Alexander rushed impetuously against the less active ram, the plump, massive Persian bear. In incomparable victories at the Granicus in western Asia Minor (334 B.C.), at Issus in Cilicia, not far from Tarsus (333), and at Gaugamela, near Nineveh (331), the youthful warrior destroyed the gigantic hosts of the weak Darius Codomannus. At Gaugamela Alexander's army was twenty times weaker in number than the Persian army. "In the ram there was no strength to stand before him, and he threw him to the ground and trampled upon him, and no one saved the ram out of his hand" (Dan. 8: 7). After scarcely *three* years of war the young man of five and twenty years was lord of the *two thousand* years old Orient. To the leopard "lordship was given" (Dan. 7: 6); the goat "became great above measure" (Dan. 8: 8).

But then tragedy entered the mighty spectacle. At the height of his power, in the flower of his age, in the world centre of Babylon, Alexander died after a carousal, of a high fever. It was June 13th, 323 B.C., in his thirty-second year. It was a sudden death, and he left no heir to his throne. The "horn" was "broken" (Dan. 8: 8, 22). "A hero king will arise and rule over a great kingdom, and will carry out all that he wishes. Yet scarcely will he have arisen when his kingdom will collapse and will be divided to the four quarters of the heaven, but will neither be handed on to his descendants, nor will the power remain with which he has ruled" (Dan. 11: 3, 4).

After twenty years of conflict by his generals over the inheritance of Alexander there emerged substantially four chief kingdoms:

1. The Syro-Babylonian kingdom of Seleucus (the "king of the north:" Dan. 11: 6, 7, 11);
2. The Egyptian kingdom of Ptolemy Lagos: (the "king of the south:" Dan. 11: 5, 9, 11);
3. The Macedonian-Greek kingdom of Cassander; and
4. The Thracian-Bithynian kingdom of Lysimachus.

Thus, through the battle of Ipsus (Phrygia) in the year 301 B.C. there was a literal fulfilment of the prophecy by Daniel in the

sixth century B.C. (Dan. 7: 1, 6; 8: 1): "The he-goat waxed exceed-
ing great; but when it was at its strongest, the great horn broke
off and four other notable horns grew up in its place toward
the four quarters of the heavens" (Dan. 8: 8). Therefore also
the panther had not only four wings but also four heads (Dan.
7: 6).

Out of these four successor States, those of chief account for
the history of salvation are the two greatest, the Egyptian "king
of the south" and the Syrian "king of the north," and of these
again principally the latter. And so to them a specially detailed
prophecy is devoted (Dan. 11). From 301 to 198 B.C. Israel
was under the rule of Egypt, then, after the battle of Panea, it
belonged to Syria.

Here, after only a few decades, there came that mighty
conflict between world civilization and revelation embodied in
the names of Antiochus Epiphanes and Judas Maccabeus.

Out of one of the four horns of the he-goat, which grew up
in the place of the broken off Alexander-horn, there emerged a
particular "little horn which became exceedingly great toward
the south and east and toward (Palestine) the glorious land of
the earth. And it waxed great even to the host of heaven, and
cast down some of the host and of the stars of heaven to the
earth and trampled upon them" (Dan. 8: 9, 10). "A king will
appear insolent of face and a master of intrigues. His power
will be notable, and he shall cause extraordinary misery. He will
be mighty, and also will ruin the people of the saints" (Dan. 8:
24).

Antiochus IV, Epiphanes, is meant, the eighth king of the
north (175–164 B.C.). Because of his many follies his contemporaries called him "Epimanes," the mad, instead of "Epiphanes," the brilliant. Nevertheless, in spite of his crazy ideas
and ferocity, we may not depict him as only a raw barbarian,
but as an enthusiastic partisan of Greek culture. After the
conquest of his father Antiochus III by the Romans (190 B.C.) he
dwelt for thirteen years at Rome as a hostage, and was so saturated
with Roman-Greek ideas that the German historian Mommsen
calls him "the Roman ape by profession." Especially after
168 B.C., when the Romans forbade him to conquer Egypt
(Dan. 11: 30), he purposed the inner strengthening of his power
by means of a religious-political amalgamation of all parts of his
kingdom. In this he encountered opposition only in Palestine.
Solely to break this down and to carry through the slogan,
one king, *one* state, *one* civilization, he persecuted those Jews
who worshipped Jehovah. His real object in this was the introduction of Greek civilization into Jewry, united with the worship
of the Olympian Zeus, Jupiter.

He therefore prohibited circumcision and the temple services

(Dan. 8: 11; 11: 31–36), forbade the observance of the sabbaths and feasts, caused the sacred writings to be seized, torn up, and burned, and killed those with whom such were found (Dan. 11: 33). Therefore he robbed the temple of the gold-plated altar of incense, the golden lampstand and table of shewbread, and the veil between the Holy place and the All-holiest (169 B.C.). Therefore also he compelled the people to eat the flesh of swine, and, indeed, on the 25th Kisleu (about December) 168, on the annual festival of the Olympian Zeus, he caused a small altar consecrated to that god, to be placed on the altar of burnt offering at Jerusalem (I Macc. 1: 20–24, 41–64)—the "abomination of desolation" in the Holy Place to which the Lord Jesus, in His discourse on Olivet referred as a typical prophecy of the future (Matt. 24: 15; comp. Dan. 11: 31; 9: 27; 12: 11). By all this he became a type of him whom the apostle John terms the "Antichrist." Therefore he also was represented in the prophecy as the "little horn" of the *third* world empire (Dan. 8: 9, 23), even as the Antichrist is the "little horn" of the *fourth* world empire (Dan. 7: 8, 20, 24, 25).

Against this violating by civilization of the revealed faith the heroes of freedom, the Maccabees, raised their revolt (168–141 B.C.). "The people that know their God will show themselves strong and will act accordingly" (Dan. 11: 32). After heroic conflict they won back freedom of religion (165 B.C.), and finally even political independence (141). Yet at that very time the history of their opponent showed that, in the interval, a new era for the peoples of the world had dawned. For in the background in the life of Antiochus, limiting and restricting him (Dan. 11: 30), there stood a new power, hitherto unknown to the Orient—Rome.

IV. THE ROMAN WORLD EMPIRE
201 (133) B.C. and subsequently.

The rise of a western world power, and the collapse of the Semitic-Assyrian Orient, had long since been foretold by Balaam, the contemporary of Moses in the middle of the second millennium before the birth of Christ. "Woe! Who will remain alive when God allows this to take place? For ships come from the Kittim (that is, Cyprus; see Gen. 10: 4; Isa. 23: 1, 12; Ezek. 27: 6; Dan. 11: 30), they humble Asshur and humble Eber (Gen. 10: 21); but he also will go to ruin" (Num. 24: 23, 24). After 1,200 years this was fulfilled in the Roman empire.

In its beginning small as a corn of wheat—in full flower the mistress of the peoples from the rising of the sun to its setting: this is the development of Rome. At the time of the foundation of the Persian empire but a tiny town in mid-Italy, which the

Greek historian Herodotus does not even mention, in the days of the Lord Jesus Rome was "the common centre," "the meeting place of the world."

The impulse to its development Rome derived from Greece. The Romans themselves would probably never have been in a position to call into existence a civilization of their own, lofty, artistic, and philosophical. Their strength lay principally in militarism, government, and law. In discipline and devotion to the State they were incomparable; but even in the periods of their highest power they remained inwardly half barbarian. This is shown by the rough amphitheatre, that horrible place of amusement of Roman brutality. The Roman empire was indeed iron (Dan. 2: 40). It corresponded to the legs in the royal statue of Nebuchadnezzar (Dan. 2: 33), and was the first stage and phase in the development of the fourth empire, the fourth "beast" in the night vision of Daniel, "terrible and fearful and extraordinarily strong; it had great iron teeth, it devoured and crushed, and what was left it trod down with its feet" (Dan. 7: 7).

The interpretation of the royal image of Nebuchadnezzar (Dan. 2: 31–43) and of the four corresponding beast figures of the night vision of Daniel (ch. 7) as the Babylonian, Persian, Grecian, and Roman world empires is found as early as Irenaeus (died A.D. 202) and in Josephus and the Jewish Rabbis. Luther says: "Upon this interpretation and meaning all the world is harmonious, and fact and history strongly prove it." And all difficulties vanish when one reflects that the all-knowing God can as easily make known to His servants the most distant future as the nearest. Comp. Isa. 42: 9; 44: 7.

Originally (1) a small State of *husbandmen*, land-hunger, caused by a growing population, drove Rome almost of necessity to conquest. After victorious wars against similar neighbours (especially the Samnites 343–290), by 300 B.C. Rome was (2) *the great power of Italy*. Entrance into world politics was the unavoidable consequence, and it followed of itself that there came at the same time rivalry with Carthage, the neighbour opposite to Italy in the Mediterranean. By the overthrow of this most dangerous opponent (201 B.C., especially in the victory of Publius Cornelius Scipio over Hannibal at Zama, 202), Rome became (3) *the undisputed leading power of the western Mediterranean*, and equally compulsorily—even without direct intention to become a world power—an intervention of Rome in the Orient became unavoidable.

But now it became "as smashing iron" (Dan. 2: 40), blow upon blow. After four years *Macedonia* was broken (197 B.C., by the victory at Magnesia, north-east of Smyrna). In 168 B.C. Macedonia was *destroyed*, consequent upon the victory at Pydna in that land. In 146 *North Africa* became a "province," by the destruction of Carthage, and *Greece* also, in the same year, when Corinth was conquered. In 133 *Spain* was subdued, by the conquest of Numantia, and by inheriting the kingdom of Pergamum (133), *Asia Minor* was incorporated in 129.

Thus, chiefly in the second century B.C., the prophecy of Daniel was fulfilled: "It will devour and tread down and crush the whole world (Dan. 7: 23), as "iron crushes and breaks to pieces" (Dan. 2: 40). Zama, Kynoskephala, Magnesia, Pydna, Numantia—these are the five chief steps by which Rome rose to world power. To speak broadly, Rome had taken over the inheritance of Alexander the Great, and since 146 B.C. (or 133), she was generally acknowledged to have become (4) *the dominant military republic of the eastern and western Mediterranean* areas. "It was as if the god of war with iron feet had stalked over the earth and caused streams of blood to flow at every step."

But now came the time of fermentation. The ascent had been too violent. A period of (5) *revolution* had to follow (133–31). "May it please heaven that I am a liar; but I see Rome, proud Rome, falling as a sacrifice to its prosperity" (Propertius, first century B.C.).

With the expansion of Roman rule Rome had become the centre of the world. All the treasures of the nations flowed together to the ruling classes. The result was senseless luxury, most riotous prodigality, debauchery, and corruption. As early as 190 B.C., while the young Antiochus Epiphanes sojourned in Rome, a prosecution was going on of not less than ten thousand persons, the majority of whom were condemned to the death penalty. With the conquest of the world republican Rome dug its own grave. Originally Rome had been a peasant State, but, especially from the second century B.C. and onwards, after it had become the world power of the entire Mediterranean, everything changed. In order to hold the giant empire together they were compelled to maintain a large standing army of citizens. But because in the long period of military service the house and homestead of the small farmer decayed, he sold them to the richer landowners. Thus there arose the great landlord with his vast estate, which he cultivated through slaves. The middle class was ruined. The peasant population was driven from the countryside to the great cities. The "flight from the land" set in. The great antithesis between capitalism and the proletariat arose. Then, because of the emptying of the country districts, the former military levy system was no longer possible, and the mercenary system was adopted.

The mercenaries were blindly devoted to the general who enlisted them. The decisive factor with them was who would lead them to most robbery and booty and would promise them the highest pay. The personality of the individual *demagogue* would turn the scale.   The appearance of various ambitious leaders, especially Marius and Sulla, Caesar and Pompey, Antony and Octavius (Augustus), was followed by *civil wars* which agitated the Roman State for over a century (133–31 B.C.); and out of the civil wars there came finally the sole sovereignty of the Caesars of the time of Christ.   Thus Rome had entered upon its sixth stage; it had become (6) *a world military monarchy* (from 31 B.C. and onward).   The seventh and last stage is the collapse already foretold by Balaam (Num. 24: 24), and particularly the fall of the western Roman empire in A.D. 476, and the eastern in 1453.

This development is unique and without any parallel in world history.   The fourth beast "was different from all other beasts" (Dan. 7: 7, 19).   With it one thing followed out of the other by strict compulsion.   The will of the Divine World Ruler governed Rome's history with, as it were, the power of fate.   *On account of Christ* Rome *had to* become that which it became.   It is true that the Romans were "the robbers of the world," but without their knowledge their robberies played a part in the annals of salvation.   Rome had to create a reservoir for human civilization in preparation for the spread of the gospel of mankind.   Thus it was her task "to gather, or shall we say quite plainly, to gather for Christ."

CHAPTER XII

THE FULNESS OF THE TIME

But when the time had been fulfilled God sent his Son
(Gal. 4: 4)

W E stand in the year 323 B.C. As a flying "leopard"
(Dan. 7: 6) Alexander has overrun the Persian empire,
the "bear" (Dan. 7: 5) and "ram" (Dan. 8: 7) now
become strengthless. In the spring of 334, with only 35,000
men, he had undertaken his victorious march; in the autumn of
331 the Persian empire lay in ruins. Alexander had already
directed his gaze toward the west. But death suddenly snatched
him away in the garden palace of Nebuchadnezzar at Babylon
(Dan. 11: 3, 4). The "great horn" was "broken" (Dan. 8: 8).
His empire also fell to pieces (Dan. 8: 8, 22).

Nevertheless Alexander is of abiding significance in world
history and in the history of God's plan of salvation. For not
content to have conquered both east and west in a political and
military sense only, his plan consisted rather to weld them *culturally* and to unite them into a single nation.

He drilled 30,000 Persians according to Greco-Macedonian
military rules. He introduced Greek as the language of world
intercourse. Greek theatres, schools, and sports grounds were
established over almost all the old Orient, and with them the
Grecian spirit and mentality spread more and more in the east.

Conversely, Alexander transferred Persian customs into the
Grecian world. At the royal court there were introduced oriental
costumes and Persian ceremonial, especially veneration of the
king. Alexander himself married the Bactrian princess Roxana,
the "pearl of the Orient." Eighty of his generals, as well as
ten thousand of his Macedonian soldiers, followed his example,
in connexion with which they celebrated for five days a brilliant
marriage feast, rich in wedding presents, held in the Persian
Susa, the former residence of Queen Esther (Esther 1: 2).

There arose thus a cultural union between East and West,
the so-called Hellenism; and in this respect also Alexander's
empire was like the leopard of Daniel's vision; for the magnificent
variegated skin of the leopard now corresponded to the rich and
mixed colouring of European and Oriental civilization.

Hellenism is thus the product of a deliberate policy. It is
the civilization created by Alexander personally. Precisely in
this stands his incomparable significance for all times. The

general consciousness of the people has, half unwillingly, indicated this, in that on Alexander, as the foremost of all mortals, it has bestowed the surname "the Great."

Alexander's empire fell to pieces directly after his death, but Alexander's real life-work remained in existence.   Later, especially from the second century B.C., the Romans entered on his inheritance.   But the peculiar thing is that they never, as must have been expected, set the policy of Romanizing in the foreground of their civilizing activity, but everywhere continued the *Hellenizing* of the world.   Thus the Roman empire became a relatively uniform reservoir of Hellenistic cultures.   It extended itself from the rising to the setting of the sun, from the waters of the Nile to the banks of the Tyne near the frontier of Scotland, from the straits of Gibraltar to the highlands of Iran.   And yet! Although the Romans were the military and political masters of the world, *culturally* they were conquered by the Greeks, so much their superiors mentally and philosophically.

Thus there arose the world that cradled early Christianity, the "fulness of the time."   It is characterized by the following six basic features:

i.   World centralization,
ii.   World cultural unity,
iii.   World trade and intercourse,
iv.   World peace,
v.   World demoralization,
vi.   World mingling of religions.

I.   WORLD CENTRALIZATION

The Roman knew nothing higher than the State.   His ideal of manliness consisted in devotion to it.   To be a servant of "Rome the eternal" was the summit of his ambition.   Hence the disappearance of the man in the citizen.

This conception of the State was embodied in its head, the Caesar.   He was the unifying summit of the whole, the "first citizen of the State."   From the Caesar in Rome issued mandates to all quarters.   One will ruled the whole Mediterranean world. Even the Son of the heavenly King became, in His incarnation, a Roman subject (Matt. 22: 21).

Hence also the high significance of Emperor worship.   It was the religious expression of the unity of the State which was seen in the empire, especially since Caligula (A.D. 37–41) and Domitian (81–96).   Its chief meaning lay in the realm of politics. It was the religious recognition of the outer and inner unity of the world empire, the real State religion, and therefore the solitary religious compulsion in matters of belief by the otherwise so very tolerant Roman empire.   The Emperor ranked as "God and sovereign Saviour of human life" (so already Julius Caesar), "God's son" (Augustus), "Lord and God" (Domitian), "High Priest," "Saviour of the World" (Augustus, Claudius, Nero), "King of Kings." His decrees were called "gospels" [good news], his letters "sacred writings." His arrival was termed a "parousia" (advent), his visit an "epiphany." Through all this a clash with early Christianity was unavoidable; it was the chief ground of the persecution of Christians; and at the same time the empire of the first century became a type of Antichrist's empire of the End time (the "beast", with the "names of blasphemy" on his heads adorned with diadems, Rev. 13: 1).

And yet even this imperial will was subject to the will of the Most High. From the centre of the Mediterranean world there issues a purely political order, affecting nations, the census decree of Caesar Augustus (Luke 2: 1); but in the last analysis it is only a means in the hand of the Lord of all lords to bring about the fulfilment of an old prophetic word concerning a very small city in the land of Judah, the small city of Bethlehem Ephratah, the city of David (Mic. 5: 2; Luke 2: 1–7). Here verily the great and the small touch, and *in* the small the Greatest of all!

II. WORLD CULTURAL ONENESS

There have been empires more widely spread than the Roman, empires with greater population; but never before or since in history has there been an empire that has united in itself all the civilized peoples of its time as did the Roman. It was a mighty confluence of the civilizations, a grand equalizing and blending process, which came into being through the Hellenizing and Romanizing of the Orient and the Orientalizing of the Occident.

(1) *The Three Chief Streams.* Essentially the Hellenism of the Roman empire was a conjunction of three chief currents: the *Greek,* with its art, science, and philosophy; the *Roman*, with its military, political, and juristic life; and the *Orient*, with its religious and mystic cults. Yet there was still no living, organic universalism created; this was frustrated because antiquity, apart from the Stoic philosophy, lacked in general the conception of "humanity;" yet the general consciousness was very much widened towards *world*-consciousness, and the world was prepared for the universalism of Christ's message of salvation.

(2) *Greek as the Language of the Early Christian Mission to the World*. Of yet greater significance was the single language of international intercourse. For in spite of the continuance of national languages and local dialects (Acts 14: 11; 21: 40), yet Greek was so understood in the whole world that one simply called it "the common" speech (Gk. *Koinē*). Thereby, for the first Christian evangelistic work, soon to commence, there

M

dropped out one of the chief difficulties, namely, the learning of languages, and the victorious march of the gospel was able to advance with more than double the speed that would otherwise have been possible.   This was true especially of the large cities, and among them of the coast cities in particular.   Now Paul was an evangelist to great cities and principally to harbour towns. And so, in the providence of God, through this whole development in the period of the Emperors, the Greek used in all the world was prepared in advance to become the "language of the early Christian world mission."

III.   World Trade and World Intercourse

(1) *World Communications*.   In the market place of every city there stood a milestone giving the distance from Rome.   In the market of "Rome the eternal" there stood a golden milestone, erected by Augustus, which described the capital city as the heart of this giant, pulsating organism of peoples.   Between Alexandria and Asia Minor there was a daily shipping connexion (Ramsay, *Letters to the Seven Churches*, 18, 435).   According to Pliny one travelled from Spain to Ostia, the port of Rome, in four days, and in two days from Africa.   The tomb inscription is known of a Phrygian merchant who not less than seventy-two times made the journey from Hierapolis, near Colosse in Asia Minor, to Rome, over 1,250 miles.

Without this notable world traffic the swift advance of early Christianity would have been inconceivable.   Sea traffic was specially important to them, for early Christian gospel work was in great measure a labour in harbour cities, and especially so with Paul.   "In the main the world of the apostle is to be sought where the sea wind blows."   One need only think of Paul's sojourns in the ports of Caesarea, Troas, Ephesus, Athens, Corinth, and Rome.

Yet the land connexions also were of the utmost importance. Even the most remote and isolated lands were opened up through roads and bridges.   Already at that time a tolerably complete network of well-built highways, protected by walls and fortresses, spread itself over the whole empire.   "All roads lead to Rome."   On these imperial and main roads the messengers of the gospel later travelled, bringing to the world the joyful news of the Redeemer who had appeared.   Paul alone journeyed by land and water a total of more than 15,000 miles.

(2) *The Jewish Dispersion*.   Naturally the Jews also took part in world trade.   Many of this people, in the fourth century B.C. still almost wholly unknown in the West, settled outside of Palestine.   Thus arose the Diaspora (Dispersion).   Alexander the Great had moved 10,000 Jews to the city he built, Alexandria;

king Ptolemy Lagos and his successors settled there a colony of more than 100,000 Jews. In the time of the apostles about 50,000 Jews dwelt in Rome. They were most strongly represented in Babylon and eastern Syria. In Egypt they formed an eighth of the entire population; in Alexandria, the capital, almost the half. Of the five sections of the city two were wholly occupied by Jews, and, in addition, numerous Jews dwelt likewise in the other three. Nearly the whole of the corn trade there lay in their hands (Acts 2: 9, 10).

(3) *The Proselytes.* Through the dispersed Jews Israel began to be known by the nations of the world. The Gentiles met its religion also. Many felt themselves attracted by the simple, lofty faith in the one God; indeed, the Jews themselves carried on direct mission work among them, including even the Pharisees, the "separated", the most zealous representatives of their nationalism (Matt. 23: 15). Those who had been won were called "the added" (Gk. *proselytes*: Acts 2: 11; 8: 26–40; 10: 1, 2). A full proselyte was received into Judaism by circumcision and baptism by immersion.

Paul everywhere associated himself with the Jewish Diaspora (Acts 13: 5, 14; 14: 1; 17: 1, 10; 18: 4; 19: 8; *et al.*), Without the simple synagogue or the Jewish place of prayer (*proseuche,* Acts 16: 13), the evangelistic activity of the apostle is scarcely conceivable. Thus since the time of Alexander the Great world intercourse had created the basis for one of the most important methods of the early Christian gospel work.

(4) *Paul's Starting Point in World Evangelistic Journeys.* But still more. Paul had indirectly to thank the Diaspora Jewry, created through world intercourse, even for his evangelistic centre in the eastern Mediterranean. It was through the service of converted Jews of the Diaspora, from Cyprus and Cyrene, that the Christian church in Antioch arose (Acts 11: 20), while the Palestinian Jews, from lack of living contact with and understanding of the Gentile world, carried the gospel to Jews and full proselytes only (Acts 15: 1–6). In the Antioch of Paul, a centre of luxury and sin in the ancient world, "the city of carousers," as a later Emperor once expressed it—in this very place were the disciples of Jesus first called "Christians" (Acts 11: 26). The Antioch of Antiochus, the "little horn," the "Antichrist" of the third world-empire (Dan. 8: 9–14; 11: 21–45)—here surprisingly enough was the starting point of the world mission of Christianity. What an irony of the Divine government of the world! (Psa. 2: 4). Truly, "the Light shineth in the darkness" (John 1: 5).

(2) *The Bible of the World Mission.* But this train of ideas attained its culmination in the Septuagint. The Jews who lived outside Palestine soon forgot the Hebrew-Aramaic language,

because they lived in areas of Hellenistic speech. After some generations therefore the necessity for a Greek translation of the Jewish Bible for use in the synagogue services made itself felt. In the course of several decades such a translation became a reality.

It was called the "Septuagint" (in Latin = 70) because, according to the Jewish tradition, it had been produced, in the days of the Egyptian king Ptolemy II Philadelphus (284–246 B.C.) by 72 (70) Palestinian scribes in 72 (70) days in 72 (70) cells. In reality, as the work of many translators, it came into existence gradually in Egypt (Alexandria) between 250 and 100 B.C. It appears that the last part to be translated was the book of Ecclesiastes (probably not till the first century B.C.).

This Septuagint (LXX) became now a powerful means in the hand of God to prepare and to further the work of the early Christian proclamation of the gospel. Through it the Gentile world was made acquainted with the revealed faith of Judaism. Paul and the other early Christian preachers continually used it on their journeys; indeed, the writers of the New Testament made almost all their quotations of the Old Testament from it. So this originally Jewish translation became the universal missionary Bible of early Christianity, on which account it was later, in the second century after Christ, no longer used by the Jews, out of opposition to Christianity, and even became an object of hatred.

IV. WORLD PEACE

This was an especial fruit of the rule of the Emperors. Since the Romans were the lords of the whole earth, the passions of the people became ever more allayed. There set in the much lauded "Roman Peace," *Pax Romana*. Although the period of Augustus was not entirely free from war, yet nevertheless at last the temple of Janus at Rome, the temple of the god of war, after over 200 years of uninterrupted fighting (since 236), could at length be shut, in the year 29 B.C. Every narrative of gospel effort testifies to what war or peace among the nations means for evangelistic activity in the world. Thus here also was the way paved for the gospel.

V. WORLD DEGENERATION

But morally this whole civilized world carried within itself the germ of death. The streams of gold which, especially since the victory over Hannibal (202 B.C.), flowed into the world's capital led to such luxury that filth and vulgarity soon lifted their heads in the most insolent manner. Aristocracy and proletariat were the most depraved. According to the descriptions of Tacitus, Suetonius, and Juvenal, we cannot portray with adequate blackness the low moral state to which the aristocracy and highest State officials had sunk. Debauchery and gluttony, subornation and poisoning, vulgarity and immorality, unchastity and licentiousness were the order of the day, especially in the middle of the first century. The lowest classes had sunken equally low. In the large Hellenistic cities, especially of Italy, lack of work ruined the masses. "*Panem et circenses*"—"Bread and Games"— this was their demand to the rulers. By day they loitered idly around; in the evening they went to the amphitheatre, the disgusting pleasure resort of Roman brutality. So vast were the crowds that pressed to the wild beast hunts, the gladiatorial contests, and the mimic sea battles, that the Emperors Vespasian and Titus caused to be built in Rome the vast Flavian amphitheatre[1], which had 54,000 seats, and at the dedication of which, in spectacles lasting 120 days, not less than 12,000 beasts and 10,000 gladiators lost their lives.

It was otherwise with the middle class. Here the papyri witness that there were still much decorum and morality, private family life, and strong religious feeling. Faith in the gods of Greece and the Italian deities was indeed gone, on which account the mass of the people turned to the oriental deities from the remote East, which, in large numbers, were gaining ground at that time.

VI. Mingling of World Religions

This is therefore the last chief distinguishing feature of the period of the Roman empire. Out of Egypt, Persia, Babylon, and Asia Minor there pressed forward oriental religious communities and formed secret associations, the so-called "Mysteries." Seldom was a time so religious as the "fulness of the time." From Egypt came the venerating of Isis and Osiris (Serapis); from Persia pressed in the cult of Mithras, especially in the army. At its side stood the cult of Cybēlē from Asia Minor, with the service of Attis. From the Orient had come also the venerating of the Emperor.

And now there came a migration of gods and idols from the Orient, a mixing and fusing of religions and cults, which, in its "Babylonian" confusion of deities, stands quite unique in human history. State gods, Greek gods, gods from the Orient, with mixed religion and mysteries, blended ever more into a single many-coloured, mighty main river. Religiously the East conquered the West. Rome became a venerator of all deities, often horribly grotesque, senselessly confused, ill-formed sickly phantasies. The entire Mediterranean world resembled a gigantic cauldron of mixture. A Western-Eastern religious

---

[1] The name now used, the Colosseum, arose first in the Middle Ages, no doubt in consequence of the colossal statue of Nero (*Colossus Neronis*) standing nearby.

chaos, without parallel, had arisen. The ancient religions went spiritually bankrupt. But in this very feature they revealed the overruling of the Redeemer God preparing beforehand His salvation.

(1) *Equations of Deities.* Through world intercourse and the mingling of the peoples since Alexander the Great the peoples learned to know one another, and also to become acquainted with each others' faiths and worship. Naturally the question now arose: Who of them was right? The Persians said that Ahura-Muzda was the chief god; the Greeks, Zeus; the Romans, Jupiter; the Babylonians, Marduk; the Egyptians, Ammon of Thebes. But what if they were all equally right? What if all these were only different names given by the various nations for one and the same Deity; What if Ahura-Muzda = Zeus = Jupiter = Marduk = Ammon, and likewise with the other deities? And so it came now to numberless and very often extended international equations of deities; and with the commingling and fusing of the conceptions of the gods there set in gradually a conformity in their ceremonial.

With this there arose the first tendency to a harmony of the peoples in religious questions, and the pattern till now prevailing in each land—that one god stood at the head of all other gods— began to become a similarly constructed universal scheme. More and more men thought of a common chief deity at the summit of the whole, of whom all other gods were only forms of revelation and individual manifestations. And so over the whole Gentile world of the time of the Emperors there began to hover a more or less distinctly perceptible belief in *one* God. It was indeed still nebulous and vague, theoretic and pantheistic: but it was belief in one God, which with all its indistinctness, became nevertheless a presentiment of the one true "unknown" God of heaven and earth Whom shortly the messengers of the gospel were to proclaim to the world (Acts 17: 23).

(2) *Oriental Secret Religions.* Yet more important than these equalizings of deities was the missionary activity of the Eastern religions which just now set in. That these religions came from the East was itself highly significant. For Christianity also came from the East. Thus for the people of the world at that time this origin had in it nothing strange. They were accustomed to see Oriental religious teachers coming to the West and to grant a hearing to their message.

Moreover, most of these Oriental religions had *the common root idea of faith in a Nature god who died and came again to life,* at which they had arrived by deifying the fading and reviving of the vegetable world or the rising and setting of the sun, moon, and stars. Thus in Asia Minor, in the spring (March 22–25), there was celebrated the festival of the re-animation of the

Nature god Attis, on the chief day of which, the third, the high priest announced to the people that "Attis has returned! Rejoice at his parousia!" With the fading of spring, in the burning heat of summer, they celebrated in Syria the mourning for the death of Tammuz-Adonis (Ezek. 8: 14, 15). From November 13–16, when the Nile fell and the corn was sown, as it were to die, there took place in Egypt the mourning for the death of the Nile god Osiris. And December 25, the approximate date of the winter solstice, was in Persia the "birthday," that is the revival day of the sun god Mithras, of Baal in Syria, and the like. Similar divinities were Dionysos, Orpheus, and Hyacinthos in Greece; also Melkhart of Tyre and Sandan of Tarsus.[1]

Now although this belief was built upon a totally different foundation from Christianity, namely, on the deification of Nature and in particular upon the interpretation put upon its appearing and disappearing in heaven and on earth, but not, as with the gospel, upon the *actual* revelation of God and upon the *historical* facts of the *literal* death and resurrection of the Redeemer (I Cor. 15: 13–19), yet nevertheless all those Nature religions helped to prepare the Gentiles to understand the message concerning Jesus' death on the cross and His resurrection.

But the chief matter was that all of those religions were *redemption* religions, and on this account met the mood of mourning, and of yearning for something beyond, which pervaded the period of the Roman Emperors, as of every decayed and effete civilization. In the Mithras mysteries this flight from the world advanced to even suicidal acts of repentance.

(3) *Yearning for Redemption.* But that such a sense of need for redemption awoke just then had its cause in the effective revolutionizing of the whole practical outlook on life of the ancient world effected just then by world conquest, world intercourse, and world demoralization. It is here that we most deeply perceive that the Gentile world had been prepared for the message of the gospel, that "the fulness of the time" had come.

The ancient world was centred on *this side* of the universe. The visible world was *the* reality, the other side was only shadowy; and in this respect the bent of men's minds was not toward the inward but the outward. "Hence the taste for architecture and sculpture, the decorative, the drama, the spectacular of all kinds, processions and triumphal marches. Hence also the disappearance of the man as an individual, a free personality, and his being absorbed in the mere citizen."

But now everything was changed. The great transformation which was now developing lay in the turning from *the*

[1] See Hislop's *The Two Babylons*, and Pember's *The Church, The Churches, and The Mysteries*, and *Mystery Babylon the Great* and *The Mysteries and Catholicism*.

outward to the inward, from this side to the other side. Above all it was the conquest of the Mediterranean world by Rome, the wasting by the conquerors of the treasures won, accompanied by unrighteousness, oppression of the provinces, materialism and immorality in the upper and lower classes, together with world commerce and world intercourse, which naturally could not but finally call forth a reaction against all this outward glitter and trifling, and a feeling of disappointment and emptiness in the hearts of at least all those who were not yet wholly dulled to the noble and true.

But if happiness is not to be found on *this side,* then the gaze, quite of itself, is directed with so much the greater longing to the *other side;* and this becomes no longer that gloomy, joyless shadowy world of the past, but the reverse; the life on earth is shadows, and yonder is the real, true existence. Now one continually reads of the body as the *"prison"* of the soul, and death is praised as release, as the "birthday of eternity," as was said by Seneca, the Stoic philosopher, the tutor of Nero, the brother of Gallio (Acts 18: 12).

And with this turning from the present to the hereafter, there is joined the turning from the outer to the inner. This side was indeed the visible and it had failed. Therefore the gaze at the other side was at the same time directed at the invisible, and with the invisible on the inward, and with the inward at one's own heart; and that which had been always present there in hiding —the inward discord of the soul of man, the conflict between good and evil, was now scrutinized more closely, and quite often became an object of sad self-observation. The consciousness of sin grew. Especially in the second and third centuries after Christ, after the orgies of the time of the first Emperors, there came as it were a sort of penitential attitude over the Mediterranean world.

But with the turning toward the invisible and inward there is conjoined a drawing to the transcendental, mysterious, and mystical; and the feeling of disappointment with all former experience must give to this mystical the character of sadness and melancholy, and in certain circumstances both may ascend to dread of the world and flight from it, to penance and mortification, even to self-torment and voluntary mutilation. And all this only to win peace of soul!

Hence the turning away of tens of thousands of men to the gods of the East, for these promised to men the desired deliverance.

Repression of life, and death itself, were to be conquered in the existence of the individual, and these the Oriental religions appeared to bring; for the Eastern gods were not merely deification of death and disappearance as seen in Nature, but also of the victorious conquest of death and of the new life arising out of death! And man [so it was argued] is a member of this same Nature complex, disappearing and always rising again. Therefore his deliverance must consist *in his association with universal law*; but this meant—in the sense of the Gentile deification of Nature—in mystical union with the dying and reviving Nature god.

The old must "die"—hence the penances, mortifications, and self-tortures; and the new must "rise to life"—hence the holy repasts, the mystical degrees, the immersions,[1] the secret initiations.

The conquest of death, re-birth, immortality, eternal happiness—these are the saving blessings which were the goal of the Oriental mystery religions. "*In æternum renatus*"—"born again for ever"—thus run dedicatory inscriptions and gravestones of the devotees of the Persian god Mithras. "Be comforted, ye pious: for as the god has been saved, so will you also be saved out of all distresses," so says a formula of the religion of Attis in Asia Minor.

(4) *The Expectation of the Peoples.* But thereby in wide circles was spread the presentiment that shortly *full* deliverance would dawn, and in this connexion also the gaze was directed to the East. Thence should the help come. The presentiments often clothed themselves in a *heathen* garb. The circle of the seasons, so it was said, is completed. Out of the golden age comes the silvern, and the iron follows this. But now this also is running its course. Then will the circle begin again. Saturn will once more take over the rule and the Golden Age will return.

But at times the presentiments even took a Jewish colour, and one distinctly recognizes their origin in the prophecies of Israel. Both Suetonius and Tacitus make mention of a widespread rumour that the Orient would become powerful and that a mighty movement would go forth from the Jews. Writing about A.D. 120, both historians report that it stands in the ancient priestly books that descendants of Jewry would seize world authority. (See Tacitus *Hist.* V, 13, and Suetonius, *Vesp.* 4).

Extremely noteworthy is the ring of these presentiments in the fourth Shepherd song of the Roman poet Virgil, in the century before Christ. There the poet sings of a child who will bring back the Golden Age. The child descends from heaven. Then peace rules on the earth. The land dispenses its gifts without toil. The oxen no more fear the lion. The yoke is

---

[1] For example, the horrible baptism of blood in the "Taurobolium" of the Mysteries of Cybēlē in Asia Minor. The initiate stood in a pit which was covered over with boards. Above the boards a bull was slaughtered, the blood of which streamed downwards through the crevices of the boards on to the person standing beneath.

removed from the beast that ploughs, the vintager works no more in the sweat of his brow.

But this is nothing else than Isaiah's prophecy of the coming kingdom of peace (9: 6; 11: 6, 7); and among the peoples of the outside world there sounds, plainly perceptible, the echo of Messianic prophecy.

Until at last, coming from the East, from the rising of the sun, from the mouth of simple witnesses, becoming ever stronger and stronger, there rings the world-conquering proclamation:

CHRIST—

THE ATONER FOR MANKIND,

THE SAVIOUR OF ALL SINNERS,

THE ONE CONSCIOUSLY EXPECTED BY ISRAEL,

THE ONE UNCONSCIOUSLY DESIRED BY THE PEOPLES OF THE WORLD:

CHRIST HAS APPEARED!

Thus the whole pre-Christian history of salvation is a guiding of mankind to the Redeemer of the world. The people of Israel were prepared in advance by historical revelation; the peoples of the world by the happenings of politics and civilization.

The Old Testament is promise and expectation, the New is fulfilment and completion. The Old is the marshalling of the hosts to the battle of God, the New is the Triumph of the Crucified One. The Old is the twilight and dawn of morning, the New is the rising sun and the height of eternal day.

APPENDICES

I. THE NAMES OF GOD

THE whole history of salvation is a self-revelation of God, glorifying Himself in creation and redemption. But the inner nature of a person or object is expressed in the name. "The name of a thing is the imprint of its nature and the expression of the impression its nature makes."

Therefore that history, as the self-revelation of the Godhead, must be also the manifestation of essential names of God, and the self-descriptions of God become a pointer to His self-revelation in the history. But because here the principal matters are two, creation and redemption—for the third, the glorifying, arises of itself as the ultimate purpose of these two through their completion—so must there be in this whole matter a revelation of two principal names of God, one name of His sovereignty, rule, and power, as Creator, and one name of His covenant, and of His redeeming love.

This is actually the case. Two divine self-descriptions govern the whole: "Elohim," the name of the Creator and Universal Ruler, and "Jehovah," the name of the redeeming and covenant God.

That these two names are in fact the chief names is proved by their occurrence in the Holy Scripture. While "Adonai" (Lord) occurs 450 times, "Zebaoth" and "El" (Mighty God) each 230 times, "Eloah" and "El Shaddai" (Almighty) each some 50 times, and "El Elyon" (The Most High God) no more than 32 times, "Elohim" is found 2,570 times and "Jehovah" almost 6,000 times. Thus altogether the names of God occur in the Old Testament about 10,000 times. This shows their vast and exalted significance in the Biblical revelation.

"Elohim," from *alah* (Arabic *aliha*) "to be in fear of," is the Almighty God who is to be regarded with reverence. The name is strengthened by the plural ending "im" (comp. cherub*im*, seraph*im*), the plural of Divine fulness, with which nevertheless the verb always stands in the singular, so that the Divine unity and plurality is plainly expressed. Out of the fulness of His divine power and essence God speaks of Himself in the plural. But the mystery of the *trinity* in the unity is first made manifest in the New Testament.

"Jehovah" (see note at end), from *hawa* "to be, exist," is "the Existing, Abiding, Eternal;" therefore also the "Steadfast, Permanent," and the "Dependable, True," "Who is and will ever be," or, as the exalted Lord Himself declares, "He who is and He who was and He who comes" (Rev. 1: 4, 8; 4: 8).

i. *The Name Jehovah.* In the most manifold way the glory of the name Jehovah irradiates the history of salvation.

The Foundation is

Jehovah-Jireh, the Lord Who provides, Who sees to the sacrifice which achieves atonement (Gen. 22: 14);

The Goal is

Jehovah-Shammah, the Lord is there, the Tabernacle of God with men (Ezek. 48: 35). And also

The Way to the Goal is Jehovah alone. He is

Jehovah-Rohi, the Lord my Shepherd (Psa. 23: 1);
Jehovah-Ropheka, the Lord the Physician (Exod. 15: 26);
Jehovah-Zidkenu, the Lord our righteousness (Jer. 23: 6);
Jehovah-Shalom, the Lord Who is peace (salvation, Judges 6: 24).

And, in the battle against all powers that would rob us of these blessings, He is

Jehovah-Nissi, the Lord my banner (Exod. 17: 15); yea
Jehovah-Zebaoth, the Lord of Hosts.[1]

As such He is the Leader of the hosts of the stars and sun systems (Isa. 40: 26; 45: 12; Judges 5: 20; Job 38: 7), the chief Marshal of the angelic world (I Kings 22: 19; II Kings 6: 17; Josh. 5: 13–15; Neh. 9: 6; Psa. 103: 21; 148: 2) and the Commander of His warriors here below on earth (I Sam. 17: 45; Num. 10: 36). As Jehovah-Zebaoth He commands all His hosts, so as to lead His people to triumph and His kingdom to its perfection.

This is also the reason why in the period *after* the Babylonian captivity the name "Lord of Hosts" became the chief Divine name. It is used by Jeremiah 80 times, by Haggai 14 times, by Zechariah 50 times, and by Malachi 24 times. For to the small and feeble remnant, born in deep distress, who had returned from captivity, the acknowledgment of God as " Jehovah-Zebaoth" was a comfort affording assurance that the Lord, the invisible Commander of the powers of heaven, would bring His cause to victory and His people to the goal. Therefore also in the New Testament the Greek translation of this name of God (*pantokratōr*, All-ruler), occurs in the *Revelation* (nine times, 1: 8; 4: 8; 11: 17; 15: 3; 16: 7, 14; 19: 6, 15; 21: 22), the very book in which is described the greatest distress of the people of God in the conflict with the power of the world, but also the decisive blow against the anti-Christian host and the brilliant victory of the redeemed people of God.

Therefore "Lord of Hosts" is His mightiest name, the most

[1] "Zebaoth" is the feminine plural of *Zaba* (host, army), e.g. Exod. 6: 26; 12: 17, 51; I Sam. 17: 45.

comprehensive expression of His world-wide power and the most exalted royal name of the Highest. "Open wide the gateway, and make high the doors of the world, that the King of glory may enter. Who is this King of glory? He is the Lord Zebaoth! He is the King of glory!" (Psa. 24: 9, 10).

ii. *The Double Name, "Jehovah-Elohim."* Elohim is the exalted God, the *supra*-mundane, above the limits of the created: Jehovah is the *intra*-mundane God, Who *enters* therein and testifies of Himself.

Elohim is the Creator, and thereby the Origin and the Goal: Jehovah is the Redeemer, the God of history.

Elohim is principally the "God of the beginning and the end;" Jehovah is above all the "God of the middle [period]," Who in the end glorifies Himself.

The kingdom of *power* shall become the kingdom of glory; in between lies the kingdom of *grace,* the essential content of which is the redemption; and Jehovah is the God Who in the course of this history mediates the beginning and the end and Who imbues the Elohim greatness of God for ever with the glory of Jehovah. So then the history of salvation becomes "a pathway of the creation, of Elohim, especially of man, under the guidance of 'Jehovah,' back to 'Jehovah-Elohim,' and the double name 'Jehovah-Elohim' becomes the motto of the entire history of the universe, even as 'Jesus Christ' is the motto of the New Testament age."

Note on Jahwe.

The correct pronunciation of the Hebrew "Tetragrammaton" (four-letter-name) JHWH is apparently Jahwe. The pronunciation "Jehovah" was first introduced by Christian scholars four centuries ago; and the first time that can be traced is by the Italian Franciscan monk Peter Galatinus, a baptized Israelite, in his book, "*The Mysteries of Catholic Truth,*" (*De Arcanis Catholicae Veritatis,* 1518), and so a year after the nailing up of Luther's *Theses* in Wittenberg.

On the other hand, there is the tradition of the church father Theodoret (390–457) that the Samaritans said "Jabe." This pronunciation is confirmed by Epiphanius (died A.D. 403), and A. Deissmann has pointed out the Divine names "Jaoue" and "Jabe" in Jewish-Greek papyri of the second and third centuries.

The correct pronunciation is lost, because the Jews, appealing to Lev. 24: 16, feared to pronounce the name of God at all, and therefore, in place of JHWH, always said "Lord" (Adonai), and because the original Hebrew manuscripts wrote only the consonants. But when later the Massorites (transmitters of the text) supplied the whole text with vowels, the vowels of

"Adonai" were placed under JHWH, which one read out "Adonai." So the correct pronunciation was more and more forgotten and the false pronunciation "Jehovah" arose.

II. THE TRUSTWORTHINESS OF ANCIENT BIBLE HISTORY

Christ and the New Testament guarantee the historicity and literality of the early chapters of the Bible. The Lord and His apostles everywhere treat them as narratives of actual events, and even draw from them instructive deductions. Matt. 19: 4–9; Rom. 5: 12–21; I Cor. 15: 21, 22; I Tim. 2: 13, 14; Jas. 3: 9; I John 3: 12; Rev. 20: 2. "If therefore the New Testament is truth, then so is Gen. 1–3 history."

It is impossible to maintain an unbroken faith in Christ and at the same time to put away this evident fact, perhaps with the help of certain speculations concerning the self-humiliation (*kenosis*) of Christ, or by denying the freedom from error of the incarnate Son of God, or even by believing that, against His better knowledge (!), for educative purposes, Christ accommodated Himself to the errors of His contemporaries. That the Lord accommodated Himself to the *language* of His time is evident. But that He accommodated Himself to the *errors* of His time is utterly irreconcilable with His perfect truthfulness.

The attempt to explain the narratives of ancient history as "allegorical language," on the ground that the early history and the final history belong together and the final history, especially the *Revelation*, is obviously foretold in allegorical language, cannot be maintained.

The same applies to the assertion, frequently made today, that the Old Testament can still be "God's Word" even if the events therein stated (e.g. the early histories) did not literally happen; that it matters less what were the happenings of the past than what is the message for the present; that we are not spectators, but those addressed.

For whatever truth there may be in the last statement, the first is unintelligible and illogical; for the Old Testament does not give these narratives in visions or apocalyptic symbols, as does the *Revelation* of John, nor in the form of manifest myths, pictures, and parables, but as *actual history* (e.g. Gen. 1–3), or, as regards the prophecies of Daniel, as *actual predictions*. Therefore these narratives, in the meaning of their writers, must be esteemed as actual history, without modifying the conception of "history." For God's (!) Spirit can never promote divine truth by error and pious falsification. Therefore only as historical events that *came to pass* does the "sacred history" still "*come to pass*" in us today.

The right of textual research as well as of literary and

historical inquiry, as also for comparative studies of cultural and religious facts, is not thereby denied.   Even so in exegesis, the underlying spiritual principles and typical meanings, which are contained in those past events, must at the same time be most forcibly emphasized.

It would exceed the space of our book to discuss in further detail the tension between the Biblical view of the world and that of modern natural philosophy which arises from the above matters of fact.   Our task is not apologetic, nor defence of the faith, but only a history of salvation, and this only in outline. The Bible pictures quite simply the historical connexions in God's plan, and forgoes all detailed, philosophical, apologetic dis- cussions.   Elsewhere these are doubtless of great significance and to be heartily endorsed.   Nevertheless, in the compass of an historical survey, before all else the reference to the authority of the Lord Jesus must suffice.

III.   THE GEOLOGICAL FORMATIONS

(A Summary Table)

Geology divides the history of the development of the earth into four periods, each of which, with the exception of the earliest [D] is divided into several sub-sections.

A.   *Neozoic* or New Era (Kenozoic Period).
1.   Quartiary — Erratic block
Alluvial
Diluvial
2.   Tertiary — Pleiozoic (Upper Tertiary)
Meiozoic (Middle Tertiary)
Eozoic (Lower Tertiary)

B.   *Mesozoic* or Middle Era.
1.   Chalk
2.   Jura
3.   Trias

C.   *Palaeozoic* or Ancient Era.
1.   Permian (Dyas)
2.   Carbon
3.   Devonian
4.   Silurian
5.   Cambrian

D.   *Azoic* or Original Era (Antiquity, without fossils).
1.   Stratified stone (product of water) with organic influx.
2.   The original and primitive rocks (granite, etc.).
3.   Unstratified stone (product of fire) without organic influx.

IV. The Graduated Character of the Plan of Salvation

God is the eternal, the Creator of the world. He is the supra-temporal cause of all temporal existence. "Lord God, thou art our refuge for ever and ever. Before the mountains were, and the earth and the world were created, art thou God, from eternity to eternity" (Psa. 90: 1, 2).

This "God of Eternity" has called the Ages into existence (Heb. 1: 2). From Him issues, as the "mystery of his will" (Eph. 1: 9), the decree of creation and redemption. He "Who accomplishes all things according to the decree of his own free will" (Eph. 1: 11), has "in Himself" determined this design (Eph. 1: 9; lit.), and is therefore not only the Creator of the universe but also "the King of the world periods (ages)" (I Tim. 1: 17; lit.). He is the beginning. He is the *alpha*; for "from him and through him are all things" (Rom. 11: 36). And if then the end returns again to Him "so that *God* may be all things in all" (I Cor. 15: 28), this comes to pass just because the end lies in the beginning, the *omega* in the *alpha*. "To him are all things. To him be the glory in eternity! Amen" (Rom. 11: 36).

But this His final goal—to bring together all things under one Head (Eph. 1: 10)—God did not reveal at once and to its full extent. On the contrary His wisdom was originally a thing "hidden" (I Cor. 2: 7), and the "mystery" of His decree was "kept silent throughout eternal times" (Rom. 16: 25; Eph. 3: 5, 9; John 16: 12, 13). Only by a *gradual* leading on has God made known His plans in the history of salvation. Happy therefore are our eyes that they see, and our ears that they hear, what holy men of old, in spite of searching and striving, were not permitted to perceive (Matt. 13: 16, 17; I Pet. 1: 10, 11).

Nor did this leading on take the form of a uniform progressive advance—comparable to an ascending straight line; but in the form of sections of time with fixed boundaries, like steps of a staircase leading upward. For one period God allowed men to go a certain course; then He intervened and began a new connected course of events. At first He revealed Himself to mankind *as a whole*, and dealt with it as a unit for 2,300 years. But then suddenly He left them to themselves, chose for Himself one *individual* (Abraham) and opened with him a completely new line of history. Four hundred and thirty years later He added a prescribed *law*, and for fifteen hundred years the nation of Israel had to conform thereto. But then, at the expiration of this period, God declared this law to be no longer binding, and even what had been most strictly enjoined (e.g. circumcision) was now most sharply forbidden; the former people of God were set aside and a new people formed out of all nations. But finally, in spite of all, that first people will be again taken up, and after having been displaced for long centuries will be reinstated; the second people of God will be given heavenly glory, and the whole of mankind will be visibly blessed.

Thus it passes out of the old world over into the new, and as the final goal there comes, after the judgment of fire, the consummation.

The course of salvation thus shows itself as a *richly coloured chain of periods*, a stairway leading upwards, divided into the most manifold articulated parts of a historic organism.   Indeed this character of graduation so rules the whole plan of salvation that it must be described as its chief external visible feature, as the principle of the entire structure of the history of revelation.

Bible study of the development of salvation is therefore the description of these stages in the particular character of each period, the uncovering of the steps in the advance of the whole course of salvation, the investigating of its periods, so far as they are revealed in the Bible.   The Holy Scripture is plainly not a spiritual-divine-uniform "block," but a wonderful articulated historic-prophetic spiritual *organism*.   "It must be read organically, age-wise, according to the Divine ages."

It is of slender importance whether one calls these gradations "periods of salvation," "ages" (aeons), or "dispensations" (economies, Gk. *oikonomiai*, see Eph. 1: 10; 3: 2; Col. 1: 25; I Tim. 1: 4).   Neither for any one nor for any other of these does the Scripture give a fixed definition.   Hence also the difference between individual expositors with regard to the dividing and classifying of the various ages (*eons*) or dispensations.   It matters less what term or expression is used than to see the thing in itself.   The decisive importance lies in the perception of the stages themselves and in the insight into their differences and inner connexions.

In the history of salvation an epoch, or a special time-section, is a historical period which is marked by definite special principles of God.   It has always a quite special duty and a quite special context in God's whole counsel of salvation.   Each period of salvation "brings to view the Son in a new greatness and beauty; for in the Son all ages revolve" (comp. Heb. 1: 2).

In this connexion many individual principles of such a period sometimes belong also to other epochs.   Thus circumcision was valid in the age of the Patriarchs and continued in the next following age of the law, being only then discontinued.   It thus lasted through *two* special epochs.   The principle of the dispersal of mankind by the judgment at Babel endures from the building of the tower to the setting up of Messiah's kingdom, and so through the dispensations of the Patriarchs, the law, and the church.

N

But their particular composition as a complex of principles occurs only once in that particular epoch to which this composition belongs. So epoch is distinguished from epoch, and each is in itself an inclusive whole. Thus a new period always begins only when *from the side of God* a change is introduced in the composition of the principles valid up to that time; that is, when from the side of God three things concur:

1. A continuance of certain ordinances valid until then;
2. An annulment of other regulations until then valid;
3. A fresh introduction of new principles not before valid.

Thus with the introduction of the present period of salvation there *remain* the general moral principles ruling the realm of the earlier period (Rom. 8: 4; 13: 8–10), even though in a completely new spirit; for the Law is an unity (Jas. 2: 10), and *as such* is *wholly* abolished.

Newly introduced are the principles of free grace (e.g. the free admission of the Gentiles), the building of the church, the heavenly standing of the redeemed.

Abolished are the Mosaic ordinances as to the worship of God. Circumcision—existing in the inspired history since Abraham (Gen. 17: 10)—most stringently commanded by the Mosaic law (Exod. 4: 24, 25), is, as a means of justification and salvation, most sharply forbidden for the New Testament age: "else Christ profits you nothing" (Gal. 5: 2). Whilst in the Old Covenant there were outward sacrifices, a special priesthood, incense, altars, and priestly vestments, today the principle of an *universal* priesthood of believers is in force (I Pet. 2: 9).

All those regulations had been indeed ordinances *of God*, but *dispensational* principles, which should have validity for an appointed period only, "until the seed should come to whom the promise applied" (Gal. 3: 19). But now they are "fulfilled" in Christ and have been abolished through higher spiritual laws (Heb. 13: 10; I Cor. 5: 7, 8; etc.). Here we see the immense practical bearing of this so absolutely necessary distinguishing of dispensations in God's plan of salvation. Without it the unavoidable result is legal self-sanctification, mixture, and confusion.

Many chief principles of Catholicism are the inevitable consequences of not observing this distinction, for so far as one regards the principles of the Mosaic dispensation, given to Israel (!), as valid ordinances for the peoples of the world (!) today—in spite of the testimony of the New Testament—it is of course only logical to justify as being "biblical" the existence of a special priesthood, the burning of incense, and many other things. We see that: *The distinguishing of special dispensations in the plan of salvation is at once something extraordinarily practical, and of deep import for history, doctrine, and the worship of the church.*

It can be objected: "If the Old Testament, or at least great parts of it, and even individual statements in the gospels (e.g. Matt. 10: 5, 6), are explained as not applying directly to us, is this not a contradiction of the fact that the *whole* Scripture has been given to us? (II Tim. 3: 15–17).   We reply that, of course, the *whole* of Holy Scripture belongs to us, and also that the Old Testament, from beginning to end, is God's Holy Word (II Pet. 1: 20, 21); but although all is written *for* us, not all is written *of* or *concerning* us!   For example, it would be essentially false simply to "spiritualize" the kingdom promises which God has given to His earthly covenant people Israel and transfer them to the church.   The Holy Spirit caused Rom. 9–11 to be written for the very purpose of opposing such misleading opinions!

With the Old Testament, and in part occasionally with the Gospels (e.g. Matt. 21: 45), there is to be maintained a distinction between

1. Direct *interpretation,* which does *not* always directly apply to us immediately, and
2. Indirect practical moral *application,* which *always* holds good for us (II Tim. 3: 15–17).

This distinction is the necessary parallel and the indispensable counterpart to the distinguishing of periods of salvation and gradual revelation in the Divine plan of redemption.

The Holy Scripture shows us this entire plan of redemption of God in a "perspective", seen from the Cross; that is: the farther removed—either forwards or backwards—an epoch lies from the Cross, so much the more briefly is it described in the Holy Scriptures; while the nearer it lies to the cross so much the larger it stands forth, and therefore the largest are the periods of the law and the church.   According to the remoteness is the brevity, according to the nearness is the detail multiplied.   The conclusion is exactly as the commencement, one point: "so that God may be all things in all" (I Cor. 15: 28).   But what this includes in detail is for the present still concealed.   "The secret is of the Lord" (Deut. 29: 29).

But this one thing we know already: The Bible does not reveal *all* the ages.   There were ages *before* the historical beginning of the world (Eph. 3: 9; I Cor. 2: 7, lit.), and there will be "ages of ages" in the *new* world (Rev. 22: 5, lit.).   What the Bible contains is only a limited part out of their fulness, only the way of our salvation, "only the insight and outlook which we need so as to attain to the goal of salvation."   But God will then cause to come forth out of His infinite fulness even further new ages, and in these "coming world periods will show the boundless riches of his grace in goodness toward is in Christ Jesus" (Eph. 2: 7).

V. CHRONOLOGICAL TABLE OF THE OLD TESTAMENT HISTORY

Preliminary Remarks.

The Holy Scripture does not offer a dated chronology giving the exact year and day for all historical persons and events; and this is true in spite of numerous extremely valuable genealogies and other thoroughly reliable chronological details accompanied by historical data, especially in the Old Testament, and here particularly in the time of the kings of Israel. Also the extra-Biblical historical reckonings of ancient world history cannot always be stated with absolute certainty as to the exact date or year, at least for the third, second, and the earlier half of the first, milleniums before Christ. As regards Roman history, for example, the dates precisely laid down by the old Roman historians are in truth "until the time of Pyrrhus very feebly attested" (i.e. until about 280 B.C.). This is still more true of the dates of ancient Egyptian and Assyrian history. Therefore in dealing with a time-table relating to these periods of history it is solely a question of establishing *approximate* dates, at least for the periods prior to 500 B.C. Nevertheless even these are in a position to offer us a picture, sufficient for our purposes, of the sequence and approximate intervals of the events.

1. TO THE FOUNDING OF THE KINGDOM OF ISRAEL

Palestine and Israel.	*Egypt, Babylonia.*
Before 2100 B.C. Pre-Canaanite original inhabitants in Palestine.	Before 2200 B.C. The "Old kingdom" (Egyptian. Dynasties 1–10).
Before 2000 Hamitic Canaanites in Palestine.	Approximately 2100 till about 1800. The "Middle kingdom" (Dynasties 11–17, especially the 12th).
About 2000 Elamite overlordship in Palestine.	
About 1900 Babylonian overlordship in Palestine.	
About 1900 Abraham.	About 1900 Hammurabi, King of Babel.
	Approximately 1800–1600 The Hyksos in Egypt.
	Approximately 1750–1300 Cassite rule in Babylonia.
	Approximately 1750–612 The Assyrians.
	Approximately 1600–1100 The "New" Egyptian kingdom (Dynasties 18–20).
About 1500 Moses	

Palestine and Israel.	Egypt, Babylonia.
About 1500–1400 Egyptian over-lordship in Palestine.	About 1400 The Tel-el-Amarna period Amenophis IV. Chu-enaten.
About 1400 the Hittite kingdom broke the Egyptian lordship in Palestine.	The Kabiri.
	About 1250 (? 1300) Rameses II of Egypt.
	About 1225 (1250) Mernepta of Egypt.
About 1100 Samuel.	

2. From the Beginning of the Kingdom of Israel to the Destruction of Jerusalem (about 1050–586 B.C.)

Palestine and Israel.	Assyria, Babylonia, Egypt.
(i) *The United Kingdom.* (approximately 1050 to approximately 950).	
About 1050 Saul	
About 1000 David.	
About 975 Solomon	
About 950 Division of kingdom (? 975 or 932).	
(ii) *The Dual Kingdom* Judah-Israel (950–722).	
Approximately 950–722 Ten-tribed kingdom of Israel.	10–9th century. Beginning of Rome.
Approximately 950–586 Two-tribed kingdom of Judah.	
About 860 Elijah.	
About 790 Jonah.	
About 760 Amos	753 Beginning of Roman chronology ("Founding" of Rome).
About 750 Hosea.	745–727 Tiglath-pileser (Pul) of Asshur. The actual foundation of Assyrian world rule.
About 740–690 Isaiah.	732 The kingdom of Damascus destroyed by Tiglath-pileser.
725 Micah.	727–722 Shalmaneser V of Assyria
722 Destruction of Samaria by Sargon.	722–705 Sargon of Assyria.
(iii) *The Surviving kingdom of Judah* (722–586).	705–681 Sanherib (Sennacherib) of Assyria.
About 660 (? 620) Nahum.	681–669 Esarhaddon of Assyria. Egypt conquered. Assyria at the summit of its power.

Palestine and Israel.	*Assyria, Babylonia, Egypt.*
	669–625 Assurbanipal. Decline of Assyria.
	About 650 Egypt becomes independent under Psammeticus I.
	About 650 Media an independent kingdom.
About 630 Zephaniah.	625–605 Nabopolassar of Babylon.
	625 Babylon independent of Assyria.
	612 Destruction of Nineveh by Nabopolassar of Babylon and Cyaxares (?) of Media.
	610–594 Pharaoh Necho of Egypt.
	605 Nebuchadnezzar king of Babylon.
587/6 Destruction of Jerusalem by Nebuchadnezzar.	

3. From the Destruction of Jerusalem to the Close of Old Testament History.   586 B.C. to approximately 430

Palestine and Judea.	*Babylonia, Persia, Egypt.*
626–580 Jeremiah.	
606–536 Captivity in Babylon.	605–562 Nebuchadnezzar of Babylon.
586–516 The Temple lies waste.	588–564 Pharaoh Hophra of Egypt.
592–570 Ezekial.	
606 to approximately 536 Daniel.	555–539 Nabunaid, last king of Babylon.
	558–529 Kores (Cyrus) of Persia.
	550 (approximately) Cyrus subdued Media.
	546 Cyrus conquers Croesus of Lydia.
	538 Babylon captured.
536 Cyrus permits the return from Babylon. Zerubbabel and Joshua.	
	529–522 Cambyses of Persia.
	525 Egypt a Persian province (till 332).
520–516 Temple rebuilt. Haggai, Zechariah.	521–485 Darius I Hystaspis of Persia.
	492–490 First and second Persian wars against Greece.
	485–465 Xerxes I of Persia (Ahasuerus).

Palestine and Judea.	Babylonia, Persia, Egypt.
	480–479 Third Persian war against Greece.
About 450 (?) Malachi.	465–424 Artaxerxes (Longimanus) of Persia (Arthasastha).
458/7 Ezra in Jerusalem. The 70 weeks begin.	
445 Nehemiah in Jerusalem. Wall built.	

4. THE INTERVAL BETWEEN THE OLD TESTAMENT AND AND THE NEW TESTAMENT.   APPROXIMATELY 430 ff.

Palestine.	The Empire of Alexander; his successor States; Rome.
	(343) 326–290 The Samnite wars of Rome.
	336–323 Alexander the Great.
	334–331 Decline of the Persian empire (Darius III, Codomannus).
	334 Battle of the Granicus.
	333 Battle of Issus.
332 Alexander the Great in Jerusalem. Palestine under Macedonian rule.	331 Battle of Gaugamela (Arbela).
	323–301 The Wars of Succession.
301–198 Palestine under Egyptian rule.	323 (304)–285 Ptolemy I (Lagos) of Egypt (Ptolemys till 30 B.C.).
	312–281 Seleucus I (Nicator) of Syria (Seleucidae till 64 B.C.).
Approximately 250–100 Formation of the Septuagint.	284–246 Ptolemy II (Philadelphus) of Egypt.
	264–241 First Punic war.
	218–201 Second Punic war (Hannibal).
	218 Battles of Ticinus and Trebes.
	217 Battle of Lake Trasimenus.
	216 Battle of Cannae.
	202 Battle of Zama.
198 Battle of Panion. Palestine comes under continual Syrian rule.	197 Battle of Kynoskephalae— Macedonia conquered by the Romans.
	190 Battle of Magnesia. Syria conquered by the Romans.
	175–164 Antiochus IV (Epiphanes) of Syria.

Palestine.

168 Antiochus plunders the temple in Jerusalem. Jewish worship of God prohibited.

168 (December) Erection of altar of Zeus on the altar of burnt-offering in Jerusalem.

167 Commencement of Maccabean rising (the priest Mattathias and his five sons).

166–160 Judas Maccabeus.

165 (December) Re-dedication of the temple.

164 Conclusion of peace. Religious freedom.

142 Independence of Judea recognized.

141–63 Dynasty of the Maccabees (Hasmonean).

63 Pompey in Jerusalem. Palestine under Roman rule.

47 Caesar in Palestine.

37–B.C.4 Herod the Great.

20 New Temple begun.

The Empire of Alexander; his successor States; Rome.

168 Battle of Pydna. Macedonia destroyed.

146 Corinth conquered. Macedonia a Roman province.

146 Carthage conquered. Africa a Roman province.

133 Numantia destroyed. Spain conquered.

133 Attalus III of Pergamum dies. Pergamum inherited.

129 Province of "Asia" incorporated.

133–31 The Roman civil wars.

44 Caesar murdered.

31 Octavius defeats Antony at Actium.

30 Octavius (Augustus) sole ruler.

5.   THE NEW TESTAMENT ERA

Palestine.

About 6–4 before the present Christian reckoning. Birth of Christ (not in the year 753 of Rome, but approximately 747. Herod dies in the year 749 of Rome.)

The Roman Empire.

30 B.C. to A.D. 14 (19th August) Caesar Augustus.

12 A.D. (shortly before January 16th). Tiberius elevated to be joint regent.

14–37 Emperor Tiberius.

Palestine.	*The Roman Empire.*
26–36 Pontius Pilate Procurator of Judea.	
26/27 Public appearance of John the Baptist and of Christ.	
30 Death and Resurrection of Christ.	
36 Pilate and Caiaphas deposed.	
	37–41 Gaius Caligula.
	41–54 Claudius.
	54–68 Nero.
	64 Burning of Rome.
66–72 Jewish-Roman war.	69–79 Vespasian.
70 (August) Jerusalem destroyed by Titus.	79–81 Titus.
	81–96 Domitian.
	96–98 Nerva
	98–117 Trajan.
132–135 Jewish revolt under Bar-Kochba. Jerusalem conquered Jews forbidden to be in Judea.	117–138 Hadrian.
	395 The Empire divided by Theodosius. Western Roman Empire (Honorius). Eastern Roman Empire (Arcadius).
	476 Collapse of the Western Roman Empire.
	1453 Collapse of the Eastern Roman empire.

6. THE KINGS OF ISRAEL

(a) *The United Kingdom :* approximately 1050 to approximately 950 B.C.
Saul
David
Solomon

(b) *The Dual Kingdom Israel-Judah.* approximately 950–722.

Judah.	*Israel.*
Rehoboam	Jeroboam.
Abijah.	
Asa	Nadab.
	Baasha.
	Elah.
	Zimri.
	Omri.
Jehoshaphat.	Ahab.
	Ahaziah.
	Joram.
Joram.	

Judah.	*Israel.*
Ahaziah.	
Athaliah.	Jehu.
Joash.	
	Jehoahaz.
Amaziah.	Jehoash.
Uzziah (Azariah).	Jeroboam II.
	Zechariah.
	Shallum.
	Menahem.
Jotham.	Pekahiah.
	Pekah.
Ahaz.	Hoshea.

(*c*) *The Surviving Kingdom of Judah*: 722–586.

Hezekiah.
Manasseh.
Amon.
Josiah.
Jehoahaz.
Jeoiakim.
Jehoiachin.
Zedekiah.

INDEX

ABEL, 64, 89

Abraham, his faith, 89, 96 f.; descendants, 89, 105; father of all believers, 89 f.; accounted righteous, 96 f.; covenant sacrifice, 98; tests of faith, 100 f.; expected resurrection, 99, 101; stages in development, 105; relation to Christ, 102 f.; relation to Law of Moses, 121 ff.

A.D. reckoning, 160

Adam, the first, head of race, 55 f.; his faith, 62

Adam, the last, 48

ages, the, 50, 192 f.

Alexander the Great, 168 f., 175 f., 178; successors to, 169

altar, 73

amphitheatre, the 172, 181

Angel of the Lord, 103

angels, world of, its existence, 28; service of, 29; organization, 28 f., 32 f., 84 f.

animism, 83

Antichrist, 51, 88, 171, 179

Antioch, 179

Antiochus Epiphanes, 170 f., 179

Apollo, 84

Arians, world rule of, 76 ff.

ark of Noah, 67

atonement in O.T., 132; great day of, 137 f.

authority, 72, 93

BABEL, the name, 81

Babylon, the city, 77, 81, 88, 93; the empire, 171 ff.; Israel's captivity there, 114, 118; judgment, 81

battles, decisive, 79 f.

Bethlehem, 159

Bible, the, key to world affairs, 16; its organic history of salvation, 11 f., 193; reliability, 11, 38, 190; world mission of, 179 f.

bloodshedding, 72

body, the human, 40; the spiritual, 43

burnt offerings, 72 f.

CAESAR, worship of, 176

Cain, his sacrifice and religion, 64 f.; way of, 64 f.; city, 65; civilization, 66; wife and descendants, 68

Canaan, Hamitic origin, 79; name, 80; geographical position, 111; history, 111

Canaanites, extermination of, 152

Carthage, 79 f.

Church, the, foreknown, 21; a temple, 135; fulfilment of O.T. types, 146 f.; chosen, 154; order in, 193 f.

Christ, His testimony to O.T., 11, 38, 190; centre of God's revelation, 15, 19, 48; foreknown as Mediator, 19; original Goal of creation, 43; last Adam and Son of man, 48; His resurrection, 99; relation to Abraham, 102; Angel of the Lord, 103; an Israelite, 109 f.; rejected by Israel 114 f.; reproach of, 117; priest, 123; heavenly High Priest, 137, 162; lamb for sacrifice, 136, 140; O.T. Messiah, 135; Head of church, 137; fulfilment of O.T. types, 138 f.; theme of O.T., 139; origin of title "Christ," 156; year of birth, 160

circumcision, 96 f., 170, 193

Colosseum, 181

colours, symbolic, 30, 74

conscience, 63, 93

covenants, old and new, 97; transmission of, 105 f.

Creation, history of, a double trinity, 24 f.; longing of, 58

culture, Bible approval of, 65

Cyrus, 77, 93, 118, 167

DANIEL, book of, 12, 163

Days, work of the six, 35–7

death, wages of sin, 56; remedy for, 61

demonism, 84 f.

Development, principles of, 44 f., 54

Devil, the, see Satan.

Diaspora, Jewish, 113, 178

Dispensations, principles of, 193

dreams, prophetic, 142

EARTH, redemption of, connected with mankind, 47 f.; vastness, 25 f.; centre of the universe in history of salvation, 27; filled with life, 28

Egypt, 77, 117

Elohim (God), 76, 187 ff.

Enoch, a Sethite, 68, 89; the son of Cain, 67; city of, 65

Eternity, before creation, 17, 19 ff.

Europe, 79

Eve, 62

Ezra, 160.